CONSTRUCTION PROJECT MANAGEMENT:

PLANNING AND SCHEDULING

CONSTRUCTION PROJECT MANAGEMENT:

PLANNING AND SCHEDULING

Henry F.W. Naylor, M.Sc., P.Eng.

Delmar Publishers™

I(T)P® An International Thomson Publishing Company

New York • London • Bonn • Boston • Detroit • Madrid • Melbourne • Mexico City
Paris • Singapore • Tokyo • Toronto • Washington • Albany NY • Belmont CA • Cincinnati OH

NOTICE TO THE READER

Cover Design: Barry Littman

Delmar Staff

Associate Editor: Kimberly Davies
Developmental Editor: Jeanne Mesick
Editorial Assistant: Donna Leto

Project Editor: Patricia Konczeski
Production Coordinator: Dianne Jensis
Art/Design Coordinator: Cheri Plasse

COPYRIGHT © 1995
By Delmar Publishers
A division of International Thomson Publishing Inc.

The ITP logo is a trademark under license

Printed in the United States of America

For more information, contact:

Delmar Publishers
3 Columbia Circle, Box 15015
Albany, New York 12212-5015

International Thomson Publishing Europe
Berkshire House 168-173
High Holborn
London, WC1V 7AA
England

Thomas Nelson Australia
102 Dodds Street
South Melbourne, 3205
Victoria, Australia

Nelson Canada
1120 Birchmont Road
Scarborough, Ontario
Canada M1K 5G4

International Thomson Editores
Campos Eliseos 385, Piso 7
Col Polanco
11560 Mexico DF Mexico

International Thomson Publishing GmbH
Königswinterer Strasse 418
53227 Bonn
Germany

International Thomson Publishing Asia
221 Henderson Road
#05-10 Henderson Building
Singapore 0315

International Thomson Publishing Japan
Hirakawacho Kyowa Building, 3F
2-2-1 Hirakawacho
Chiyoda-ku, Tokyo 102
Japan

10 9 8 7 6 5 4 3 2 1 XX 99 98 97 96 95

Library of Congress Cataloging-in-Publication Data
Naylor, Henry F. W.
    Construction project management : planning and scheduling / by Henry F.W. Naylor.
      p.   cm.
    Includes index.
    ISBN 0-8273-5733-8
    1. Construction industry—Management. 2. Scheduling (Management) 3. Planning.
I. Title.
TH438.4.N38 1995
690'.068—dc20   94–13155
                                                                                  CIP

CONTENTS

PREFACE

Students with a variety of goals will find this text useful: tradesmen starting their own businesses, engineering students in the first two years of their program, construction technicians in a self-study program in estimating and engineering economics, and "Night School" students intent on personal upgrading.

This text evolved from a one-semester course given to two-year Construction Management students. Half the students had worked in the construction industry and the rest came directly from secondary school or trades training. The course material started at an introductory level because most students had no background in planning or operational thinking. The teaching materials evolved each year (over a twenty-five-year period) as the result of student comments and other feedback, culminating in this text. Moreover, an advisory committee of construction managers reviewed the material over this long period.

The book is about the basic scheduling of projects. It does not consider the connections to budgeting, cost control, or the many other disciplines that require a schedule as a base because there are many good texts that deal with these subjects. The examples have a construction focus but the techniques apply to any kind of project from theatrical productions to military maneuvers. There are over 150 illustrations that expand on the written descriptions in this text. Because computer programs are nearly completely pictorial, the book subliminally introduces the visual approach to scheduling.

There are four general sections in the book: Project Definition, Basic Building Blocks for Scheduling, Refining a Schedule, and a final segment on Computer Assistance and Communications. The content develops organically, following the natural evolution of a schedule from defining the project's objectives through to a schedule for ordering materials. The techniques described in one chapter become the basic input data for applying the techniques of the ensuing chapter.

The techniques covered in the text are of the pencil-and-paper variety. I believe that the principles of scheduling must be "learned by doing" before one can graduate to the sophisticated world of computer software. The computer is a tool to ease the drudgery of mind-destroying repetitive calculations, as I learned during 15 years in the aircraft industry. Confidence in computer-produced answers derives from understanding the problem and knowing the details of how the software is resolving the problem. In the commonest case, most students believe their answer must be correct because their calculator displays 8 or 10 digits. This text presents manual methods but also includes a chapter showing how a computer can be a tremendous help in performing certain functions.

A novel technique is introduced for recording the precedence "logic" among the tasks of a project. It helps identify redundant precedence relationships and find loops in the network of tasks, and it can mark in advance where dummy tasks must be inserted in Arrow networks. The latter has been a challenge to students for some time. Also, it can clearly identify groups of tasks as candidates for sub-projects well before the network is drawn.

I must acknowledge several friends and colleagues who helped me in this labor: Keith Collier, an author, who suggested I write this book and who introduced me to Delmar Publishers; then Jeanne Mesick of Delmar who was trail boss, forcing me to keep up with the other wagons; Stewart Graham, an old friend, who finished his first book at 81 and jollied me along during the long winter; Evan Stregger, a construction consultant who provided solid advice and good construction example projects; Marsh Price of Douglas College's helpful staff, who provided computing support and timely advice; the several hundred students who criticized and questioned me over several good years; and lastly, on a very personal level, my long-suffering wife of forty years who respected this writing commitment as my first priority and seldom hinted that other things might be more important. Thank you, Jean.

H.F.W. Naylor
Vancouver, Canada
May 1994

ACKNOWLEDGMENTS

The author and Delmar Publishers would like to thank the following reviewers for the comments and suggestions they offered during the development of this project. Our gratitude is extended to:

Bruce Dallman
Indiana State University

George R. Hutchinson
Monroe, Louisiana

Harold Grimes
Hutchinson Community College

Gregory W. Mills
Western Kentucky University

Stuart Wood, Jr.
Central Piedmont Community College

1

INTRODUCTION TO THE PLANNING OF PROJECTS

LEARNING OBJECTIVES

After completing this chapter, you should be able to:

- Discuss the meaning and purposes of planning.
- Differentiate between plans and planning.
- List the different kinds of communications produced by planners.

PREPARATION FOR THIS CHAPTER

This book describes a series of techniques for preparing a time-based schedule for a project. Even though the material is fundamental in nature, it assumes that you know the terms and general aspects of the industry whose projects you want to study. If you have worked in that industry in almost any capacity, you should be able to start at the beginning of this book and add to your knowledge and skills to help you gain entry into more responsible positions.

Typical job descriptions focus on the role and responsibility associated with a particular job, but many descriptions also include the attitudes and aptitudes required of a successful applicant. This applies also to the job of learning: as you begin this book, your immediate "job" is to learn about scheduling, but the learning process should also help you to appreciate those attitudes and aptitudes that enhance your ability to learn.

Positive attitudes and an optimistic nature are conducive to efficient learning.

Keep your mind open to new ideas and methods and initially accept them at face value. After all the arguments and discussion have been presented, then you can fairly judge their worth.

Aptitude, on the other hand, is a natural or acquired ability; if you have it, you are suited to the task at hand. Your curiosity should force you look for acceptable processes in the things you do; you should be capable of visualizing the bigger picture from its many details; simple mathematical formulas should not frighten you; listening and conversational skills should be natural to you as you use them to obtain information, and clear writing that displays an adequate vocabulary will always be one of your strong assets.

INTRODUCTION

This opening chapter introduces you to the subject of **planning**, that is, the making of plans. We will study the meaning of those words that have been borrowed from common usage and given special meaning by the construction industry. We must broaden our interpretation of these words to gain more from the ideas presented here. However, we must first set the stage before we can act out the detailed concepts in each chapter.

WHAT PLANNING IS ABOUT

Planning is concerned with only the future. It is obvious that the past becomes history with the relentless passage of time. By tomorrow, today's activities will become the past and their history will be the written record of someone's opinion of what happened. Many of us study a particular author's view of history and realize that the picture he presents is seldom perfect. The future, on the other hand, intrigues us all and we often have a desire to affect how it should unfold. We first hear of the world's surprises because of the steady stream of reports from the news media. Most of these events are out of our control, but if by chance we already had prior knowledge about them, we are not surprised and do not consider them "news." We make plans to try to prevent any surprises in our own work that could turn our failings into news. "The Town Center Roof Collapses on Opening Day" is not a headline we want to read if we had a part in building it.

When we construct traditional buildings, we optimistically expect the project to be successful, with perhaps only one or two challenging surprises. But this is wishful thinking. We should try not to be pessimistic, but we should also be wary and be ready to confront deviations from our original plan with a Plan "B."

You might say, "Why should we make all these plans, when we have done something like this before?" Think about the old saying that helps us to improve the way we work: *"Experience comes from Good Judgement, but Good Judgement comes from Bad Experiences."*

To rely solely on the good experiences of the past does nothing to prevent surprises that give us **bad** experiences in the future. The pre-thinking we do for our project familiarizes us with all its inner workings and susceptibility to problems.

Before your project starts, you will often be criticized for over-planning. "Why not just get on with the job," the critics will say. Most planners will think otherwise because they are driven partly by a sense of responsibility and an appre-hension of danger that makes them want to minimize **risk** (there might also be a fear of failure). In more positive terms, they might be motivated by what could be called "the drive for personal success."

There are many positive reasons for accepting responsibility. Most challenges in life require a positive drive to resolve them, but the fear of failure is always lurking beneath the surface of our plans: failure to complete the project, failure to make a profit, fear of wasting valuable time, fear of personal embarrassment and lost credibility, and failure to miss valuable opportunities. We must do sufficient planning to reduce the risk of these surprises happening and to submerge the fears so they do not affect our behavior. The risks can never be completely eliminated, but they can be reduced to levels we can defend when challenged by the impatient onlookers.

This book then is about how to make practical plans for construction that anticipate many traditional problems, thereby reducing the risk inherent in

- organizing groups of strangers,
- expediting distant suppliers of resources,
- constructing buildings under changeable conditions.

WHY PLANS ARE MADE

"PLANS" does not mean only the set of drawings and specifications; it means THE PLAN that describes **how** we will bring together those many people and things that will make real the dreams illustrated in the drawings. These plans include data and information in memos, pamphlets, reports, computer disks, and printed computer output sheets.

A complete pre-thinking of a project produces its schedule, which is the most concise description of the project. It distills all of this thought into a highly con-densed model that can be displayed on only a few pages. Alternatively, a poorly-thought-out plan based only on gut feelings will not anticipate many problems and can turn you into a crisis manager who moves from one crisis to the next with the growing likelihood that you will not meet crucial objectives.

Was the Project Successful?

Other than the risk aspect, there is a more fundamental reason for planning, because without a plan how will you know whether your project turned out to be a "good one" or a "bad one"? There are several subjective measures for making this determination:

- Did it cost more than your client thought it should?
- Did it take too long to complete?

These and other possible accusations are impossible to counter without solid data derived from your plan, particularly when the plan was accepted by the client. Your future business depends to a great extent on your history of good performance—"bad press" can destroy your professional image and your business.

Too Much Planning?

From an economic viewpoint most projects can be over-planned. The law of diminishing returns applies if your extra planning is shown to cost twice as much as the potential saving or fails to reduce the risk. Management must consider the trade-off of spending planning dollars in the hope of saving more construction dollars.

Most companies have only a limited time to develop a bid on a project because only one bid in ten may win. Estimates and bids for straightforward projects can be quickly and confidently prepared when it is kept in mind that a detailed, low-risk plan can be developed after the contract is won. Alternatively, complex projects or projects new to you or your company must be thought out carefully in advance to lower the risks and improve the chances of success.

WHO NEEDS A PLAN?

Planning is not an aimless, part-time activity; nor is it an end in itself. Its goal is success and its product is written information. The drawings and reports that are produced are aimed at a variety of workers who are all working toward the same goal: to construct an economical, safe, useful, and efficient structure for the owner and its occupants. Planning reports can range from simple one-page memos or tables of data to several volumes, each aimed at specific users. Thus, the effective planner must know enough about the needs of the targeted users to be able to communicate clearly with them.

As the planning evolves, more and more people of differing responsibilities have a need-to-know about specific aspects of the project. For each proposed project, senior management and company directors must know the expected impact of the following aspects of the project on their firm:

- its profitability
- degree of commitment of the firm's financial and material resources
- the project's consistency with the firm's aspirations and mission

When the initial planning supports the development of a potential project, senior management authorizes more detailed planning. The results of deeper and deeper levels of planning will be distributed to more and more people. Some examples:

- Designers will require continual feedback.
- Government agencies need confirmation of compliance with bylaws.
- Trade journals will want status reports so that they can alert the business community to the size and timing of new projects.
- Prospective on-site superintendents will need to become familiar with the project to provide construction know-how to the designers.
- Senior management needs progress reports to ensure that progress is consistent with the original mandate from the Board of Directors.

Almost all planning must be documented and, as planner, you will be expected to write a wide variety of reports because of the varying level of detail required by those with a need-to-know. Some reports will be very detailed whereas others can be quite general. Without knowledge of the readers' needs, effective reports are difficult if not impossible to write.

EXAMPLE PROJECTS

These introductory remarks set the stage for presenting more detail and definitions of the terms that you must appreciate in the context of planning for construction. We will need examples of projects to do this, such as the two that follow:

1. *Planning a trip* across the continent will introduce new terms in a familiar subject area.
2. A *construction project* of a modest industrial warehouse.

The goal is to provide relatively simple examples that explain the techniques without getting bogged down in large amounts of data. A persistent dream is to find the universal example that is useful for beginners as well as experienced planners. Diverted by such a dream, it would be easy to miss the goal of the book, which is to explain the processes simply.

Planning a Trip Across the Continent

A highway route breaks down into natural segments (town-to-town, and so forth), which readily transforms into a network of shorter trips. It is a good model for introducing the special terms of scheduling. The map is a network of routes linking stopping points which can be redrawn as a network suited for analysis as a schedule. The real-life meanings of the graphical symbols used in the drawings should become immediately recognizable. The route is shown in Figure 1–1.

Planning the Construction of a Small Warehouse

I studied several real plans for real projects before deciding on this uncomplicated warehouse for light industry. However, even this simple project becomes a bit unwieldy at a later stage when material resources are considered in Chapter 8.

The project for many of the examples is the construction of a Multi-Tenant

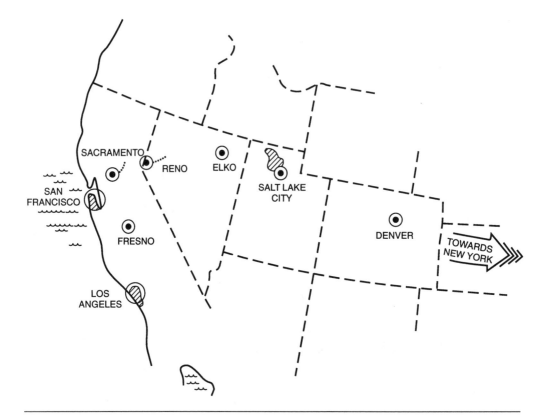

Figure 1–1   Map of the Transcontinental Trip.

Light Industrial Warehouse. Information sufficient for our application appears as needed in each chapter, but drawings and a short description appear here to assist us in getting started. The student will find it absolutely necessary to become very familiar with all details of this project by studying these drawings and by independently working through all the examples as they are presented.

This project can be expanded to satisfy the more adventurous planner by including the interior space layouts, extending the length of the building, or repeating the single building to produce an industrial park. The basic form and data allow for this. A general view of the building is given in Figure 1–2.

The warehouse was planned to be built on a small parcel of land near a deep-sea terminal where there is a market for small warehousing space for trans-shipment of goods. The site had been extensively filled sometime in the past when this coastal area was initially developed.

The building was to be built in two phases: first the shell and later the custom

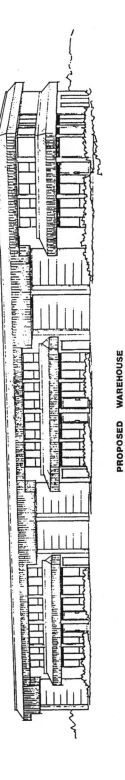

PROPOSED WAREHOUSE

Figure 1–2 Perspective of the Warehouse. (Courtesy of Costex Management Inc.)

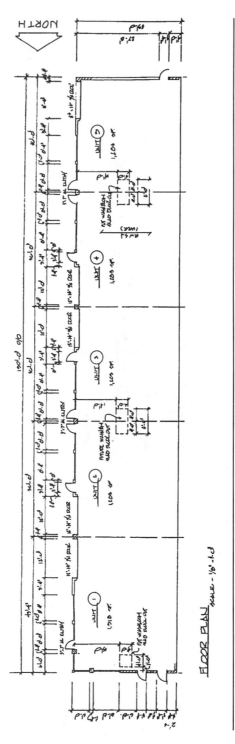

FLOOR PLAN SCALE - 1/8" = 1'-0"

Figure 1-3 Floor Layout of the Warehouse. (Courtesy of Costex Management Inc.)

interior partitions. The single story (except for interior office space) covers 6650 square feet. The structure is quite conventional. Figure 1–3 shows the floor plan. More detail is given in Appendix A.

SUMMARY

As scheduling relies heavily on graphical representations of data, one of our first tasks will be to adopt a graphical "language" to express our ideas. Chapter 2 explains a specific method of describing projects in pictorial form. The graphical presentation may remind you of a drawing of a company's organizational structure.

Chapter 3 develops symbols for the basic building blocks of scheduling diagrams. The next nine chapters show how to develop and refine a schedule to anticipate the many time constraints and delivery demands common to most projects.

Chapter 12 illustrates how several of the manual methods covered in the earlier chapters can be made easier by using a computer; the last chapter is an overview and guide for writing and compiling the reports that are the real fruits of planning. After all, what use is a plan if no one knows anything about it or cannot understand the information distributed by a planner?

This book is not intended for the experienced scheduler or computer whiz. It has been designed for the student who is familiar with the general working of his industry but who needs to be introduced to the ideas and techniques of scheduling from the very start. This book attempts to help the planner who is a beginner develop a rational system for planning a project and help him or her explain the schedule to others.

EXERCISES AND PROBLEMS

1. Make a list of the skills, attitudes, and aptitudes that will help you learn and appreciate the subject of scheduling and then objectively rate yourself in each category. Be fair to yourself and determine which items on your list require upgrading to increase your chances of success in mastering these basic techniques.
2. Consider plans you have made in the past for a project that did not satisfy you. How would you change the way you went about making those plans if you were making them now?

2

THE WORK BREAKDOWN STRUCTURE

LEARNING OBJECTIVES

After completing this chapter, you should be able to:

- Identify and write goal and objective statements.
- Demonstrate familiarity with the Warehouse Project.
- Illustrate several applications of a WBS.
- Demonstrate decision-making techniques.
- Develop a WBS for a familiar project.

PREPARATION FOR THIS CHAPTER

This material introduces new terms and discusses their meaning in terms of construction-related situations. You will be helped by your knowledge of construction projects and your skill in interpreting drawings and charts. You will be required to have good pencil skills for making neat and clear drawings and charts.

INTRODUCTION

In this chapter, we will look at the way a project can be divided into its basic construction elements and then how to concisely display the whole project in what is known as a Work Breakdown Structure (WBS). (The abbreviation appears throughout this book.) As a project's planner you must be aware of all components of the construction project to ensure that all parts of the work are accounted for and that their relationships to all the others can be determined. When you have a concise and neat WBS available, you can view the whole project at once to plan contracts, visualize the scope of managerial responsibilities, and more effectively explain aspects of the project to others.

Toward a Schedule

A Work Breakdown Structure is the first step toward constructing a schedule. You begin by precisely writing a goal statement for the project and then successively subdividing that goal into smaller and smaller portions until you have identified all the basic construction objectives.

A large building project can readily be subdivided into several hundred components; one might be "a 35-foot length of wall between pillars H12 and H13 (on floor #3)." The estimator would use the drawings and other data to accurately calculate the amount (and cost) of all the materials in this wall and then estimate how long it will take to build it. When all the elements in the building have been similarly analyzed and the construction methods are known, the first draft of a schedule can be produced. The WBS starts this process by identifying all the components and then all the activities needed to construct the building. There will be more activities than components because a component such as a "gas pipeline" requires at least the four activities of ditching, laying, connecting, and backfilling in its construction.

WHAT DO WE MEAN BY THE WORD "PROJECT"?

This may seem like a trivial question, especially since we are raising it after we have used the word so freely already, but a closer inspection should suggest several alternative meanings that will sharpen your thinking and enhance your understanding as we look deeper into the first stages of planning.

A dictionary defines **project** as "anything proposed or mapped out in the mind, such as a course of action; i.e., a plan."

Construction Terminology

In construction, we extend this dictionary wording of "in the mind" to include all the documents needed to manage the construction project. Such documents are needed before, during, and maybe even after the project's completion. The project ends when the company has fulfilled all its responsibilities. When resources are no longer being spent, the project is technically over for the company. Consider the following example.

Most of us have dreamed about owning a famous sports car, but the dream becomes a project only when we decide to spend resources and take action to get one. When we have acquired and paid for one, the project "To Own a Sports Car" is over and full ownership responsibilities begin. With a construction project, the materials and effort of the construction process consume resources and money until the job is completely finished.

Precise Wording Is Required

A project must be given a name so that we can talk and write about it. But to define it precisely for the needs of planning, we must express it in the proper terminology of **a goal statement**. If we had given our goal the title "Sports Car," the meaning would not be clear; it should more properly be phrased "I Want to Buy a Famous Sports Car." The phrasing of this goal statement must minimize ambiguity by explicitly stating the **action** ("to buy") that will be performed on the particular **object** ("sports car"). It should be short and sweet rather than long and cumbersome. The required amount of detail will be added in further subdivisions in the WBS.

Objectives

In parallel with goal statements, each item in the WBS must be properly phrased as an **objective**: it too must unambiguously define what is to be done. For example, as a component of the Excavation work package, "ditching" is an unsatisfactory way to phrase an objective. The term has several quite different meanings, among them "digging a ditch," "abruptly leaving someone," and "crashing an airplane into the sea."

Even in the context of construction the single word "ditching" can be misinterpreted. A correct and unmistakable use of the word is to put it in a phrase such as "*To excavate a ditch* for underground services."

All objectives must be worded in such a way that **an action (a verb) is taken on something (a noun)**. For the ditching example, the action word (verb) is "To excavate" and the object is "a ditch." Imprecise phrasing can confuse other people, even though its meaning may have been perfectly clear to you when you wrote it; it may not even be clear to you when you study your own work later. A true objective should also include a time element, such as "To Dig the Ditch **by Thursday**," but until we incorporate durations, make a mental note that time is part of an objective.

WHAT CAN INITIATE A PROJECT?

A Community Need

It is useful to think about where the idea for a construction project comes from. Consider the scenario shown in Figure 2–1. Here, a community need could be raised and publicized by the local media; that publicity stirs the city administration to develop a plan; your company then sees an opportunity that results from the

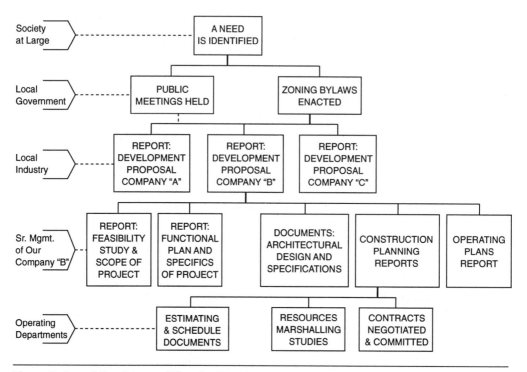

Figure 2–1   A Breakdown of Planning Documents.

change in zoning and develops a plan to build a specific project. The sequence concludes with a building that would respond to the original need of society. Often this sequence is rearranged by a company that requests zoning changes so that it can build to satisfy a client. There is an accepted sequence that is followed in these public processes.

This chart is NOT a WBS because the items name the results of **completed** activities recorded in the form of memos, reports, drawings, minutes of meetings, newspaper articles, and so forth. To convert this chart into a WBS, each name must be rephrased as an activity to be done: for example, "ESTIMATING AND SCHEDULING DOCUMENTS" would be rephrased to "TO ESTIMATE AND SCHEDULE THE PROJECT."

A true WBS for the city's activities starts with the city's planning goal at the first level and proceeds to a satisfactory level of detail needed to govern the development work within the city's area of responsibility. In this example, further breakdown into a fourth level of objectives has been reserved for the specialists in city hall to plan their own individual work. (See Figure 2–2.)

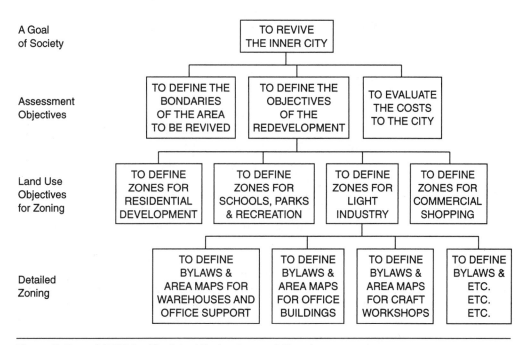

Figure 2–2   A WBS for Municipal Redevelopment Planning.

Project Initiation by a Company

In responding to one of the city's objectives, your company president might envisage an opportunity for a project as the result of the city's general objective "To Define Areas for Light Industry." He would then identify the concept of a suitable project and work through the traditional topics of development and down through succeeding levels to the individual work areas of construction. Ideas for company-initiated projects can be triggered by objectives in other jurisdictions.

Needs Versus Wants

A company's goal may be driven by a specific need (or goal) of society, but the company's goal is not necessarily driven only by "needs"; companies can also respond to "wants." The upwardly-mobile baby-boomers do not necessarily **need** a better house, but they **want** one to satisfy their desire for a higher social status. The construction company may not really care whether these are needs or wants because a "want" establishes a market just as firmly as a "need." The company sees the market demand as an opportunity to build and make a profit, thus fulfilling its fundamental business goal.

ACHIEVING GOALS AND OBJECTIVES

By their nature, goal statements are worded in general terms, such as "To Redevelop the Inner Core," and who is to say when that has been completed. To do this we must turn to the objectives in the WBS that provide the details of the goal, such as: To Build a Community Center, To Build Human Scale Accommodation, To Develop Attractive Open Space and Parks, and so forth.

Objectives can be measured and evaluated only when they are properly defined. Thus, when all the component objectives have been monitored, evaluated, and deemed complete by the project manager, his goal can then be said to have been reached. The media and other observers may not agree with the project manager's opinion because often new objectives get publicized during the long construction life of a public project. Directly relevant goals and objectives are clearly stated in contracts before work begins; new objectives are recognized only through amendments to the contract.

For a project to end with complete success, all of the participants' differing goals should be entirely satisfied, assuming that the goals of the company, the client, the city management, and social agencies are similar but not identical. Seldom is this idyllic situation ever achieved. Hopefully, the most important goals will have been reached. The main problem is for a company to determine which goals are most important and then decide when these have been satisfied, in a legal or political sense.

DIVIDING THE PROJECT INTO COMPONENTS

Most of us have worked on a project of some kind or other, usually as a member of a team. Our contribution perhaps made it a success and even though we recognized the project was much larger than our part in it, we likely considered our small bit to be THE project. The mechanical contractor considers his project to be the supply and installation of heating systems, but the prime contractor for the building considers the mechanical sub-contract to be a sub-project within the building project. Conceivably, the building itself could be a sub-project in the overall (mega)-project for redevelopment of a deteriorating inner city.

If you are responsible for a piece of work, you consider that work to be *your* project; the Mayor considers the redevelopment plan for the city to be *her* project; and the carpenter considers *his* project to be the installation of the millwork. The company responsible for the entire project is called the Prime Contractor and it lets contracts for some or all of the work to sub-contractors.

A Construction Example

Construction projects are legally defined by the contract, particularly under the section, "Scope of the Work." For purposes of this book, "project" will mean the complete list of the objectives comprising the project. One of our projects could be an assembly of other projects (a mega-project), such as "To Redevelop the Inner Core of the City," or it could be a small part of a sub-sub-project, such as "Construct the Roof." Irrespective of its size, a project will be a well-defined package of objectives that define a specific goal. Other definitions of "project" can be found in construction management books with a focus different from this book.

As an example, a contract awarded to your construction company for an Industrial Complex might consist of several sub-projects, each described by a sub-contract. A simple breakdown of a project into sub-contracts appears in Figure 2–3.

DEVELOPING A WBS

Knowledge and Experience

Developing a WBS forces you, as a planner, to compartmentalize your thinking as you develop the detailed definition of a specific project based on the series of objectives for reaching the goal. The "deeper" you go into the lower levels of the WBS, the more detailed knowledge you need to know. In the example illustrated in Figure 2–3, further breakdown of "Foundation" into its useful components will require that you understand such things as

- the design
- characteristics of the soils
- locations of the site

For example, planning to build in a remote swampy area is radically different from planning to build on a rocky city lot. The detailed design should recognize the soil conditions, but it is also important to realize that access, deliveries, and availability of equipment will affect the construction processes. Adding more detail to the WBS requires increased knowledge of the specific tasks. Experienced specialists should be consulted to fill you in on these details when your own knowledge is incomplete.

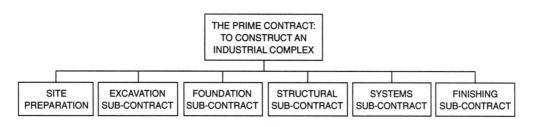

Figure 2–3   Subdivision of a Project into Sub-contracts.

Size of a WBS

When you have identified tasks in such a detailed manner that one specific crew can be named to do the work, you need not subdivide that task any further. Alternatively, if you have identified a complex task that requires the efforts of several trades, this complex task should probably be broken down into simpler components that can be more accurately estimated. The estimated duration of a simple task that can be handled by a single trade is the fundamental building block of a working schedule.

Note that the number of topics at deeper levels increases dramatically from the number at higher levels—from one at the first level, to a few at the second level, to several hundreds or even thousands at the lowest level. We can illustrate this progression by supposing that each work area of a project can be subdivided into five parts in the next level down. If that is the case, a WBS requiring six levels would have 3125 tasks in its lowest level ($1 \times 5 \times 5 \times 5 \times 5 \times 5$)! Figure 2–4, using only three subdivisions per level, illustrates the magnitude of this kind of exponential growth.

You must be careful not to overly refine your project into more details than necessary, because the number of elements can quickly become unwieldy for manual scheduling calculations. Even computer programs have their limits. An overly detailed first schedule can become a cumbersome burden, especially after you incorporate refinements dictated by the realities of construction: delays, sub-

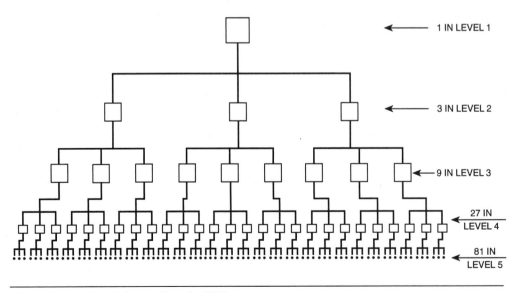

Figure 2–4   Growth in the Size of a WBS.

divided tasks, material ordering, and so forth. A compromise needs to be made between a large number of simple tasks and a smaller number of more complex ones. In some cases a sequence of tasks can be grouped together into one super-task without loss of accuracy.

The upper two or three levels of the WBS can often be developed with only a general knowledge of the project, but the lower levels will be dependent on the details of the quantity take off, contractual requirements, and methods of construction.

Deciding on the Best Option

Most people feel better when the future has been simply and neatly laid out and will often rush into work without considering alternative ways of doing the job. A good plan results from considering other routes that lead to the same objective but that may be "better"—that is, less risky, cheaper, faster—than the one that first came to mind. There is an old saying that *"The first idea is not always the best idea."*

Poorly-thought-out plans are recipes for disaster when the real physical work begins if the plan was based on insufficient thought. Therefore, we must consider alternatives and make rational decisions to enhance the value of our plans. We must make a conscious effort to find alternative ways of achieving each objective. Remember that the WBS contains only firm statements of *How We Have AL-READY Decided* to perform the work; it does not list the options we had to consider before making the decision.

Experience

When you decide to sub-divide an objective into its set of sub-objectives, you must be familiar with the design and method for doing the work. To sub-divide a work area called "Perform All Excavations," you must decide whether it includes excavating the perimeter drainage ditches or whether this segment should be assigned to the Site Preparation segment. Decisions like this may depend on the sequencing of the work and the grouping of other related jobs. For example, if a planner has to plan for the task "To Excavate a Ditch for Underground Services," he or she must decide **how** to make the excavation. Among the alternative methods are

- digging with pick and shovel
- digging with back-hoe
- drilling
- pushing a conduit through the soil

Each time we subdivide a work area into its group of tasks, we must have already considered how to do the work after having chosen the **best option** from among several competing alternatives. "Deciding" literally means "cutting off," and making a decision therefore means removing all the other alternatives from consideration. The wording of the objectives in the WBS records our decisions. A common but often ignored method for making the "Best" decision is explained in Appendix C.

We emphasize that constructive imagination is required for developing a solid, viable, low-risk plan. Many aggressive people desire to "get it all done with" by prematurely leapfrogging into a plan that may be fraught with pitfalls. This impulse needs to be suppressed. It is both good sense and good economics to spend an extra $10,000 on a better plan that saves $100,000 in construction and other costs.

Technology Transfer

You may find it comforting and safe to "do it the way we did it last time," but creating novel alternatives can save money and time for you and your project. Some good ideas can be transferred from other areas of technology. A famous transfer was PERT, a scheduling and monitoring tool for complex projects (presented in Chapter 11). It was used in managing the POLARIS submarine and missile system in the early 1960s. Certain aspects of PERT are now routinely applied in construction management computer software. You should continually search for ideas in other disciplines and industries and transfer them to your applications because they can increase productivity, lower costs, and make your company more competitive.

APPLICATIONS FOR THE WBS

Schedules

Prior to construction, planners produce a series of forecasts and estimates that describe the project in more detail as the planning advances. One of the first estimates is based on historical data from similar projects to show how the proposed project would fit into the company's operations. In Figure 2–5 we use a bar chart to compare two schedules, one based on the Level I task (the goal) and a second one based on Level II tasks for the same project. The length of the bar represents the duration of a task and subsequent task-bars are drawn to the right of earlier ones. Time increases as we move to the right.

The first single bar (from Level I) denotes the estimated duration of the total project based on experience with durations of other similar projects; the second sequence shows an improved time line with each component scheduled separately using the sub-projects from Level II. These approximations to the durations, including margins (+/–) for error, would be made early in the estimating process, when quick estimates are needed. Shorter, simpler jobs at deeper levels can be estimated more accurately with smaller (+/–) uncertainty.

As each lower level of the WBS is developed, a correspondingly more detailed schedule can be made with the larger number of tasks. When the individual tasks

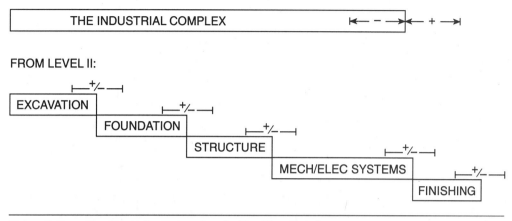

Figure 2–5   Bar Charts for Deeper Levels Give More Detail.

become simple enough for their durations to be accurately estimated, we do not subdivide the tasks any further. Such bottom-level tasks will have clearly defined objectives so that their progress and completion can be evaluated during construction.

For each of these lowest-level tasks:

- a specific crew can be assigned to achieve its objectives,
- the crew and the quantity of work determine its duration,
- each task has a natural sequence relative to other tasks.

When the "final" plan is accepted (just before commitment to construction), the "final" schedule provides

- a solid timeline for ordering all resources,
- the best start times for all tasks and, importantly,
- a forecast of cash flow for the life of the project.

Because the "final" plan is continually vulnerable to surprises and changes during construction, it must be regularly updated. Therefore, it is better to refer to your current schedule of the work yet to be done as the *latest* plan rather than the "final" one.

Responsibility and Authority

The pyramid of task areas in the WBS that expands downward from any objective defines a top-to-bottom pattern for delegating **responsibility** and **authority**. The manager at the top of the pyramid is ultimately responsible for all the tasks below.

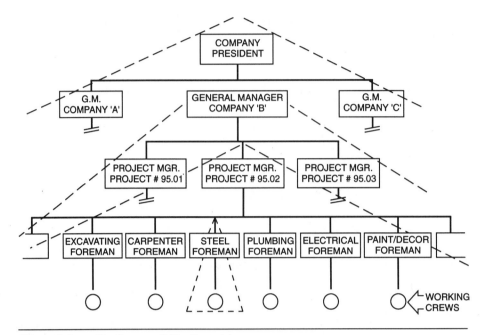

Figure 2–6   The Responsibility Pyramid.

Also, each manager at any given level has his own "tree" of tasks for which he is responsible. Figure 2–6 illustrates this chain of responsibility.

Note that any complete *level* of the WBS represents a complete description of the project and that the managers of each of these work areas are usually considered to have similar degrees of responsibility. For example, the electrical, mechanical, and carpenter foremen have equal status.

Managers with broad authority are concerned with progress measured against the upper-level objectives of the WBS. Alternatively, craftsmen (of narrow authority) are concerned about progress in terms of the tasks at the lowest, most detailed level of the WBS. When the electricians take too long with the wiring, the drywallers become concerned about delays that affect their schedule and the Project Manager resolves the issue.

Workforce Planning

The WBS illustrates the breadth of managerial responsibility and authority. A manager of a work area in Level II is ultimately responsible for all the activity expanding downward in the WBS; a unit manager lower down in the same work area is responsible for fewer workers. An example is shown in Figure 2–7.

The WBS provides senior management with a tool for estimating the requirements of supervisory manpower for the project. Of course, the number of supervi-

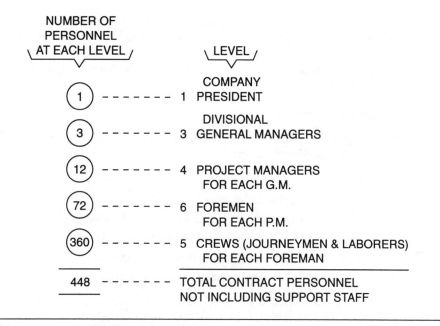

Figure 2–7   Staffing Requirements.

sors depends on the magnitude of the work in their area of the WBS; the size of the workforce is the sum of all the crew members involved in all the tasks at the lowest level of the WBS. A WBS can be the basis for constructing an organizational chart for a project. Form should follow function.

Information Flow and Progress Reporting

Generally, all the information in the WBS is not needed by every participant in the project. For example, the carpenters need to know about their assigned tasks and may be only curious about the organization of the work at other levels. Senior management, on the other hand, should have no need (and may not want) to know what the carpenters are doing (as long as they are working effectively). Information relating to the various levels of the WBS will generally be made available by management to specific groups, depending on their responsibilities and their having a "Need-To-Know."

Distribution of information must be focused on the needs of the user. If a progress report on every active task in the WBS is automatically distributed to every manager without regard to priority or need, then few will read it and fewer will understand it. Irrelevant information is discarded, often unread, by users. The WBS defines families of users who require common information.

The pyramid of responsibility not only defines the downward flow of authority, it also defines the reverse bottom-to-top direction for reporting that must flow upward in a well-managed firm. The WBS is valuable for planning a Management Information System (MIS) for the project. When all functions and projects in a company are arranged in a super-WBS, the model for a company-wide information system becomes clearer.

Document Preparation

Several typical applications for the information derived from the various levels of the WBS are suggested below:

Level

I	For the Annual Report
II	For Senior Management to manage development work
III	For the Construction Manager to manage sub-contracts
IV	For "Subs" to manage their "sub-contractors"
V	For foremen to manage the actual work

An important parallel exists between a WBS and a topic outline for a report: in a WBS we can subdivide an objective down to the smallest task; for a topic outline, we can subdivide the title of a report down to the topic sentence of each paragraph. The process is identical.

Consider a portion of the Table of Contents for this chapter (Figure 2–8). There are, at most, only three levels of subdivision after the title of the book and

. . . . . .
CONSTRUCTION PROJECT MANAGEMENT: PLANNING AND SCHEDULING
. . . .
CHAPTER TWO
. . . . . .
APPLICATIONS FOR THE WBS
. . . . .
. . . . .
Workforce Planning
Information Flow
Progress Reporting
Document Preparation
      WBS and Topic Outline
      Table of Contents
. . . .
. . . .

Figure 2–8   Table of Contents and Topic Outlines.

the title of the chapter. In the Document Preparation section the lowest level shows that one item for each paragraph governed the writing of this section. More about document preparation can be found in Chapter 13.

THE WBS FOR THE WAREHOUSE PROJECT

The Upper Levels of the WBS for the Warehouse

The first two levels of the WBS are quite straightforward because the construction seems to naturally fall into five categories that may also parallel the city's requirement for inspections. These are:

1. preparing the filled site
2. installing the foundations
3. constructing the building
4. providing the services
5. completing the site work

Most planners try to get too detailed too quickly and ignore the first level of breakdown. Often you will find that an intermediate, more general level will help in developing the next lower level. The process might be clearer if the above five task areas were preceded by three more general areas, such as Site Preparation, Construction and Landscaping. See Figure 2–9.

The Lower Levels of the WBS (Levels III and IV)

We can now focus on each objective in Level II, subdividing each one in turn. To expand "To Prepare the Site" into its components does not require considering the components of the Foundations, Structure, Services, or Finishing work areas. In this piecemeal manner you will eventually lay out all the tasks of Level III on one line. (See Figure 2–10.) As with most activities, your creativity will be keener if you focus on only one work objective at a time.

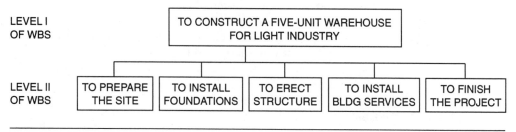

Figure 2–9   Starting the Warehouse WBS.

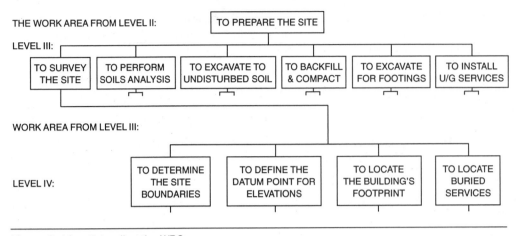

Figure 2–10   Extending the WBS.

Consider the special problems associated with preparing the site. The following tasks require special attention:

- locate the boundaries with a legal survey
- locate underground service connections
- determine the depth of the old fill
- excavate and remove the old fill
- backfill and compact the new material
- position batterboards for the excavation for the footings
- excavate for the footings

The Surveying objective (Level III) has been divided into four sub-objectives (in Level IV) which could be used to define the "Scope of Work" of a contract for a Surveyor.

There seems to be no need to attempt to develop a fifth level because it would interfere with the freedom and responsibility of the surveyor to plan his or her own work. It may be necessary to add these components later if a scheduling conflict arises with other work on the site, but for now that possibility will be ignored.

However, the breakdown of other objectives in Level II (for example, To Erect the Structure) may have to go deeper than Level IV to define the basic tasks required for the schedule. Generally, you will understand the project sufficiently when one crew can execute the task at the deepest level of the WBS; all work areas need not be subdivided down to the same level to be useful in constructing a schedule.

Outline of the Complete WBS

A graphical layout of the complete WBS is shown in Figure 2–11 to give you an idea of its size without naming all the tasks needed. This is to help you appreciate

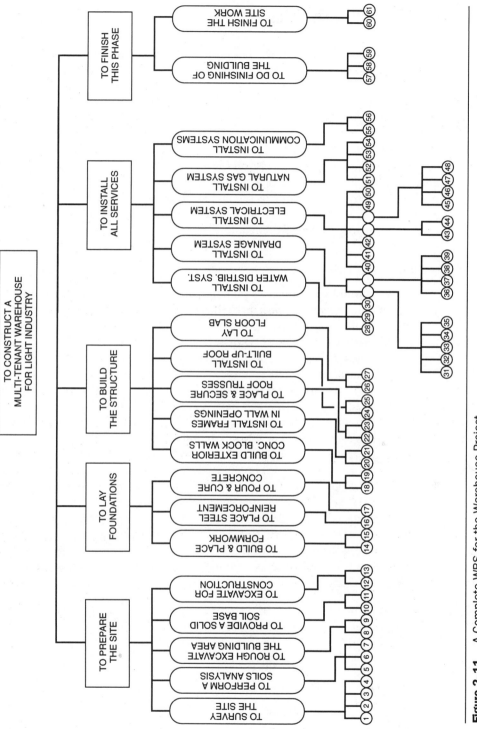

Figure 2–11 A Complete WBS for the Warehouse Project.

the large number of tasks that will be considered in later chapters. Appendix B lists all the work areas for this complete WBS of the Warehouse example, down to Level V.

SUMMARY

The actual construction tasks have now been defined via the WBS and you should be getting impatient to start work on the schedule. But before we can do that we must learn the graphical language we will need for drawing the complete project; the next chapter does this. The remaining body of the book will focus on an orderly presentation of the techniques for developing and then refining the network of tasks to give the best schedule.

EXERCISES AND PROBLEMS

1. Visit your local municipal planning office to determine the structure of its planning process. Construct a hierarchy of types of reports produced in response to a directive from the chief administrator or mayor. Ask for representative copies of reports.

2. Interview a contractor or search through the literature to compile a list of sub-contracts let for a complex contract. Endeavor to find one where there are sub-sub-contracts. For example, military contracts (for airplanes, ships, missiles, and so forth) often have many levels of sub-contracting.

3. Construct a Responsibility Pyramid for a local company or municipal offices using the organization's actual job titles.

4. Analyze a magazine article (three or four pages long) that has half-a-dozen section headings; break each section down into subtopics (use only a few words); then determine a topic for each paragraph. Arrange all these topics into a WBS, wording each one as an objective.

5. Develop a WBS to describe your objectives for reaching the goal of "To Own a Famous Sports Car." Consider carefully the meaning of all the words in the goal statement.

6. Develop a WBS of at least thirty objectives and four levels deep for a project familiar to you.

3

GRAPHICAL CONVENTIONS FOR TASKS, EVENTS, AND NETWORKS

LEARNING OBJECTIVES

After completing this chapter, you should be able to:

- Identify an activity, an event, or a milestone from a written description.
- Describe the differences between the three principal types of project diagrams.
- Identify the components of the three types of network diagrams and explain their functions.
- Identify "Milestone" events within a network diagram and be able to create and incorporate them to satisfy special purposes.
- Construct a Precedence Grid (P-G) from a set of written information and translate the data from a row or column of a P-G into written descriptions.
- Construct AON and AOA Networks from a Precedence Grid.
- Draw a Gantt Chart (not to scale) from a P-G, and from AON and AOA networks.

PREPARATION FOR THIS CHAPTER

The work in this chapter requires a thorough understanding of a WBS and your ability to develop one for a familiar project. You must recognize the difference in wording between an objective and a task. Moreover, your aptitude for relating mental concepts to graphical symbols will be a great help. Good skills in sketching and neat drawing are also necessary when it comes to expressing your ideas on paper.

INTRODUCTION

The previous chapter described a method for developing a Work Breakdown Structure with its "tree" of tasks extending the detail down to several levels. Had you been developing a WBS, you would have had to consider the method for doing each task. You would have already known a lot about the topic to start with, and as you learned more you would have confidently added more detail to the WBS. You would have realized that the WBS was also a "thought-organizer" whereby you could chart *all* your ideas about the work and combined them with the ideas from other people you consulted. To complete the WBS, you would have had to rephrase their statements into properly worded task objectives.

The next thing to do now is to determine the order of executing the tasks that have been developed in the WBS. For each task we must decide which tasks can start when the current one has been completed. The resulting sequencing data will be recorded on a grid for checking in preparation for drawing flow charts of the whole project.

As these flow charts use symbols, we must define a "language" of symbols, using rectangles, circles, and arrows containing names and data. After we have drawn the three types of flow charts using these symbols (see Figure 3–1), we can show that all three charts of the same project can evolve into one another. These diagrams are named:

Bar Charts (Gantt Charts)

"Bubble" Diagrams (Activity-On-Node Networks)

"Arrow" Diagrams (Activity-On-Arrow Networks)

TASKS, EVENTS, AND MILESTONES

The study of the WBS explained how to develop a goal and break down very general objectives into a large number of simple task objectives suitable for scheduling. Closely related to these tasks are Events and Milestones, which we will create for the three diagrams we need to draw.

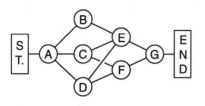

"BUBBLE" (AON) NETWORK

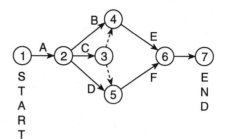

ARROW (AOA) NETWORK

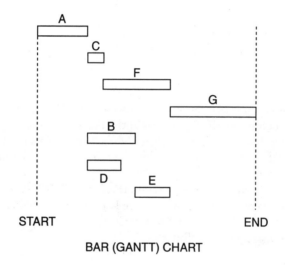

BAR (GANTT) CHART

Figure 3–1   Examples of the Three Types of Networks.

Tasks

A **task** is an activity that is directed at achieving an objective. When tasks are phrased in such a way that they exactly define the objective, every activity will have a well-defined beginning and ending. The ending event is the objective of the activity. Crossing the finish line is the event that completes your running of the race. Events are the points that mark the beginning and ending of a task.

The activity (task) of digging a ditch begins with "The Start of Digging" and is finished at "Excavation Complete," as Figure 3–2 illustrates.

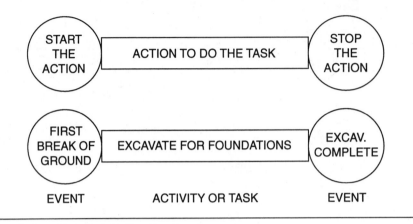

Figure 3–2   Every Activity Has Two Events.

Events

Events consume neither time nor resources and relate directly to the objectives that we defined in the WBS. "To Build the Forms" can readily be interpreted to mean reaching that point in the project when "The Forms are Complete" as much as it implies the actual activities of building them: both tasks and events can be inferred from an objective.

When two tasks follow each other, the START event of the second one is the FINISH event of the first one, but only rarely are both included in a diagram. "End the Concrete Pour" and "Begin Curing" both indicate the same point in the project, as Figure 3–3 illustrates.

Milestones

As with every task, every project must also begin and end with a **START** event and a **FINISH** event; these are examples of very special events that are named **milestones**. Milestones indicate project beginning and ending and other important times in the life of a project. A person's birth and death are the start and finish events of a life, but graduating, getting married, and having children are all milestones in that life.

Milestones are special events that advertise that major stages in the project have been reached, for example, "Project Start," "All Structures Completed," "Ready to Install Fixtures," "Electrical Inspection Approved," "Ready for Final Draw (of Money)," "Project Finished." Milestones can be inserted when several tasks all terminate at the same event within a project, indicating a major achievement. For example, "Ready for Occupancy Inspection" could follow the completion of the wiring, plumbing, weatherproofing, heating, lock-up, and so forth.

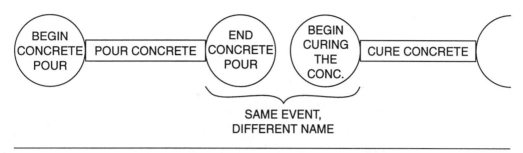

Figure 3–3   Duplicate Events Between Tasks.

NETWORKS and PRECEDENCE LOGIC

Figure 3–1 showed the three types of networks we will be working with. A **network** is a graphical array of points interconnected by lines. Note that Bar Charts are drawn with task symbols only; "Bubble" (AON) Diagrams use different task symbols accompanied by only a few Milestones. Alternatively, "Arrow" (AOA) Diagrams require tasks and events in almost equal numbers; every task arrow connects to an event circle at its ends. The lines connecting the Bubbles in an AON network indicate the sequence of the work; that is, the precedence logic obtained from your consultants.

PRECEDENCE

Even though we have spoken of the sequencing of tasks, the study of scheduling uses a more specific term for this process: **precedence**. This is one of the key words in scheduling. It is the quality of *preceding* or *coming before*. For scheduling applications precedence will specifically mean that *"a particular task must be completed before a task dependent on it can begin"*—you must finish breathing in before you can START breathing out.

To help understand a sequencing relationship between two tasks, you could ask yourself the following question: *"The task I am currently considering is waiting for which other tasks to finish so that it can begin?"*

Sequences and the Precedence Grid

When we were arranging the objectives of the WBS, we did not take any special care to arrange them in any particular order; we simply grouped them under the more general work area of the Level above it in the WBS. Now that these basic tasks have been defined, we can consider their relative order in the construction process.

Many projects are quite straightforward and the sequencing will be obvious.

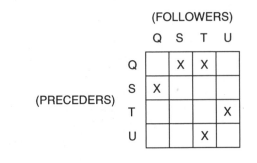

Figure 3–4   An Example of a Precedence Grid.

In many other cases, where normal procedures must be changed to accommodate a special project, you will need to discuss the issues with others. They should be people who have specific experience in how each part of the work is to be done: consultants, site superintendents, skilled tradesmen, and so forth. Your research should yield a mass of notes: some will be scribbled on file cards, some recorded on audiotape, or perhaps in the form of memos from your experts. There will be conflicting data which you must clarify before you can use it. We shall do this by recording all our collected data on one sheet of squared paper and testing it. We refer to this sheet as a **Precedence Grid** (see Figure 3–4).

In this Precedence Grid, we have marked all the precedence opinions from the workers on the job. The carpenter foreman may claim that his task S follows task Q, the mechanical work, but the Mechanical Contractor claims the opposite. In another statement, the painters want to paint, T, after Q and after the floor is finished, U, whereas the floor layers want their work to follow Q. The Precedence Grid can identify these conflicts, which you can then resolve by re-reading your notes to look for the cause of any misunderstanding or by seeking advice from your consultants.

We can save much confusion and time by using a refined version of the Precedence Grid as the basis for drawing the fundamental diagrams of a project. These diagrams (the Bar Chart, Bubble and Arrow networks) can be confusing to draw when some of the sequencing data is in conflict.

CONSTRUCTING THE PRECEDENCE GRID

A simple example project based on a familiar subject will establish the concepts and techniques for working with a Precedence Grid. Let us plan the trip across the continent for you and several friends. (It was introduced in Chapter 1.) We will present the stages of the work you would follow in planning this or any other project.

The Trip Across the Continent

You and three of your friends have decided to drive across the continent from San Francisco to New York City. You have offered to be the planner. The analysis for the trip starts with the following notes that you made at a planning session.

> The main group of three all live near San Francisco and will leave together, drive to Sacramento, then continue on to Reno, where they will stay for several days waiting for Sally's vacation to begin. Then she will fly from L.A. to meet them. Then all will drive toward Elko the next day, continuing on toward New York City.

> The *travel* activities are quite apparent and can easily be tied in with the map in Figure 3–5.

A. The group drives from San Francisco to Sacramento
B. The group drives from Sacramento to Reno
C. Sally flies from Los Angeles to Reno two days later.
D. Everybody drives from Reno to Elko, and then on to New York City.

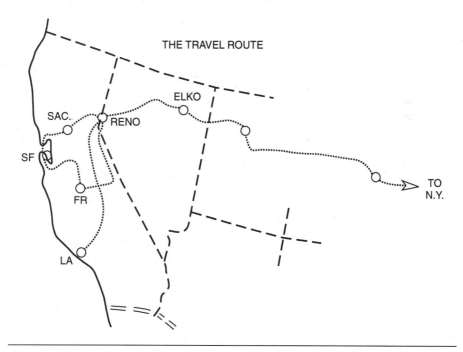

Figure 3–5   The Map and the Route Segments.

Plans must reflect the realities of a situation and be able to accommodate changes. Plans for the trip changed because Sally had her vacation delayed by an extra four-day work assignment (task E) and Bill had to visit his mother in Fresno on his way from San Francisco to Reno (tasks F and G). These three additional tasks alter the original list in the following way:

E. Sally works for four more days.
F. Bill flies from San Francisco to Fresno for an overnight stay.
G. Bill flies from Fresno to Reno.
H. Sally is delayed in Los Angeles.
I. They all drive from Reno to New York City.

The remainder of the trip (task I) can be included as one big activity until more of its details can be decided on by the group when they finally get together in Reno.

The nine statements regarding the parts of the trip (above) can be translated into a precedence list. This is shown in the first column of Figure 3–6 for all nine tasks, not forgetting the required START and FINISH milestones.

These nine activities can now be placed in sequence to answer the inverse question: "Which tasks must be completed before the one I am considering can start?" These are listed in the second column of Figure 3–6. Every task either precedes or follows another task; the **Start** and **Finish** Milestones that begin and end the project enclose the diagrams that we will draw.

The information for the trip can now be transferred to a Precedence Grid, as shown in Figure 3–7.

The complete Precedence Grid is explained in more detail in Appendix D and is copied here for reference. The reader is advised to consult Appendix D to gain

"MUST PRECEDE" LOGIC-STATEMENTS			"MUST FOLLOW" LOGIC-STATEMENTS		
START	precedes	**A**	**A,C,F, & H**	follow	**START**
A	precedes	**B**	**B**	follows	**A**
START	precedes	**C**	**C**	follows	**START & H**
START	precedes	**F**	**D**	follows	**E & C**
F	precedes	**G**	**E**	follows	**B & G**
B & G	precede	**E**	**F**	follows	**START**
START	precedes	**H**	**G**	follows	**F**
H	precedes	**C**	**H**	follows	**START**
E & C	precede	**D**	**I**	follows	**D**
D	precedes	**I**	**END**	follows	**I**
I	precedes	**END**			

Figure 3–6   Precedence Information List for the Trip.

— THESE ARE "FOLLOWER" TASKS —

	A	B	C	D	E	F	G	H	I	END
START	X	·	X	·	·	X	·	X	·	·
A	O	X	·	·	·	·	·	·	·	·
B	·	O	·	·	X	·	·	·	·	·
C	·	·	O	X	·	·	·	·	·	·
D	·	·	·	O	·	·	·	·	X	·
E	·	·	·	X	O	·	·	·	·	·
F	·	·	·	·	·	O	X	·	·	·
G	·	·	·	·	X	·	O	·	·	·
H	·	·	X	·	·	·	·	O	·	·
I	·	·	·	·	·	·	·	·	O	X
END										

PRECEDER TASKS (left label for rows A–END)

END: (nothing ever follows the END or precedes the START)

Figure 3–7   Complete Precedence Grid for the Trip.

confidence in using the method so as to be able to repeat the process for other projects.

When we are satisfied that the Precedence Grid is correct, we can begin drawing the diagrams that are the basis for developing a schedule: Bubble Network Diagrams, Arrow Networks and, lastly, Bar Charts. However, we look at the more common Bar Charts first so that we can understand why they are not overly useful to us at this stage.

NETWORKS: BAR CHARTS, BUBBLE DIAGRAMS, AND ARROW DIAGRAMS

Bar Charts are commonly used in business, mathematics, engineering, statistics, and so forth, and they appear regularly in newspapers, magazines, and annual reports. Generally, the length of the bar measures the number of things being counted. For scheduling, the length of the bar indicates a task's duration. The first leg of the trip is suggested in Figure 3–8. We assumed for this example that the trip takes 3.5 hours.

Bar charts are valuable for explaining some aspects of our project. But when we start planning, we do not yet know the durations of the activities so we cannot draw meaningful bars. Planning requires sketching and modifying a diagram until a final plan emerges: even with guessed durations, bar charts are awkward to change without redrawing the whole chart. Moreover, the required precedence relationships are difficult to show on a bar chart.

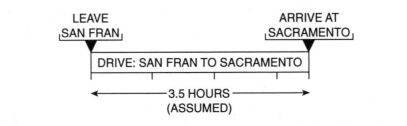

Figure 3–8   Bar Chart: First Leg of the Trip.

Constructing Bubble and Arrow Network Diagrams

Alternatively, network diagrams can be drawn using only the task names and their sequencing relative to all the other tasks; durations are not needed. Most problems—and scheduling is no exception—are better solved one step at a time rather than by trying to resolve everything at once. Therefore, we shall construct a network of all the activities of the trip using only the data from its Precedence Grid. Arrow and Bubble diagrams should be based only on data from the Precedence Grid. Never attempt to draw an Arrow network based on your view of the Bubble diagram, or vice-versa. For projects with very complex precedence relationships, it is maddening to attempt a network diagram from the research notes you received from your consultants.

Both Bubble and Arrow networks are constructed using the same basic elements: Events and Activities. But differently shaped symbols are used in each one. Let us look at our transcontinental trip as we describe each type and see how they are related. The techniques for drawing these diagrams are covered by an in-depth study in Appendix E.

Bubble Diagrams

The Bubble Diagram uses a small circle to represent each task; a line joining two task circles represents the precedence relationship. Later tasks are placed anywhere to the right of the tasks they follow. Figure 3–9 shows the Bubble Diagram for the transcontinental trip. Because lines meet at locations called "nodes," this diagram is also referred to as an "Activity-On-Node" (AON) network. Most schedulers begin with the "PROJECT START" milestone and add tasks in their natural order until they reach the "PROJECT END" milestone.

Arrow Diagrams

An alternative way of viewing the trip is to focus on the intermediate objectives of the trip: the stopping places rather than on the activity of driving. An **event** is achieved when an objective is reached, and so stopping at each town represents an

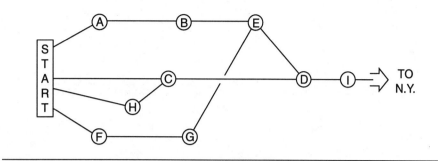

Figure 3–9   The "Bubble" (AON) Diagram of the Trip.

event; travel activities end or start at a town. Using the town names given in Figure 3–5 as the central elements in building a network produces a rather different-looking diagram from the Bubble diagram. Refer to Figures 3–10 and 3–11 for the development of the AOA diagram.

These hand-sketched "thinking pictures" can help clarify the ideas raised during the first planning meetings. In this travel example, the travelers likely drew arrows directly on a map (Figure 3–10) before developing the basic network. The draft diagrams might show arrows curling all over the diagram, but the final drawing should strive for clarity by using straight line arrows that "move" only to the right and minimize crossing other arrows by relocating the event nodes.

The line (with an arrowhead) joining Reno to Elko represents the activity (or task) of driving from Reno to Elko. This "Activity-On-Arrow" diagram (AOA) requires that activity arrows *must* have arrowheads, because arrows can be

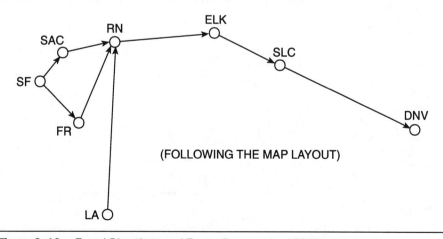

(FOLLOWING THE MAP LAYOUT)

Figure 3–10   Travel Directions and Towns Become the AOA Network.

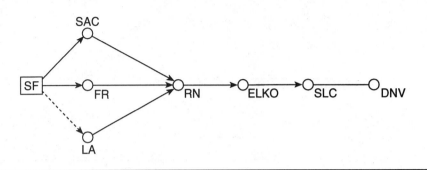

Figure 3–11   The Arrow Diagram for the Trip.

sketched in any direction, up, down, backward (left) and forward (right). Arrows need not be straight for the hand-drawn studies and can be any length needed to join the appropriate events (towns, in this example). Even for the final draft of the AOA network, where meandering lines are simplified, continue to place arrowheads on the leading end of the arrow. Place events in such a way that task arrows "move to the right" and later events are placed to the right of earlier ones.

Bar Charts

In scheduling, bar charts are called **Gantt Charts.** They are named after an early practitioner in the subject, Henry L. Gantt, who introduced the application of bar charts more than 70 years ago. To honor his contribution, bar chart schedules will be referred to as Gantt Charts throughout this book.

The Gantt Chart is the most universally and commonly understood way of

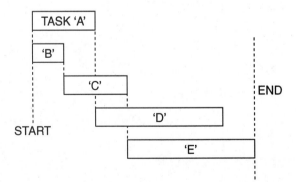

Figure 3–12   An Example of Gantt (Bar) Charts.

displaying the relative time periods for a set of tasks. When drawn to scale (for example, ¼ inch equals 1 day) a bar 1-inch long represents a 4-day duration of a task. When one task immediately follows another, the start of a following task bar is lined up with the end of the preceding task bar. The bars in the example illustrated in Figure 3–12 are not drawn to any scale.

We will reserve extensive use of Gantt Charts for explaining a final schedule to others and we shall also find them useful for illustrating and clarifying other concepts as we cover them. Gantt Charts are not practical in the early stages of planning when durations are not known and precedence data changes are frequent.

Relation Between the Three Types of Diagrams

Imagine shrinking two task bars (thus ignoring the durations) into two bubbles and drawing a line between the two task bubbles, indicating a direct sequence. See Figure 3–13. This line needs no arrowhead when all of the following tasks are placed to its right. There can be several link-lines entering and leaving a bubble for multiple followers or multiple preceder tasks.

In parallel with the above evolution, Arrow diagrams can evolve from Gantt Charts simply by adding an arrowhead to the leading end of each task bar and rearranging these arrows to connect to the other dependent task-arrows; an event symbol is placed at each such intersection. See Figure 3–14.

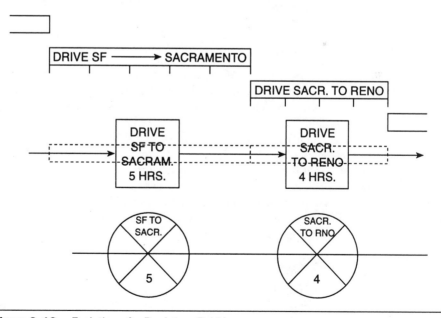

Figure 3–13   Evolution of a Bar into a Bubble.

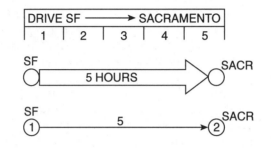

Figure 3–14   Evolution of a Bar into an Arrow.

STANDARDIZED SYMBOLS

These examples used simple shapes to represent their elements. As a general practice, however, we should adopt standard symbols so that particular shapes trigger unique concepts in our minds as we look at different networks. Standardized shapes are the language of scheduling and using them accelerates our ability to absorb the information they convey.

We will borrow the shapes for symbols more from the current computer programs than from the original manual methods found in earlier textbooks. This is a sensible approach because this book is intended to prepare students to use current software programs.

Symbols for Activities

When we drew the Bubble (AON) Diagram, we used a small circle to identify a task and wrote its name beside it. This is fine for making those initial "thinking pictures" but the small circle lacks space for its Task Number, its Duration, and the Starting and Finishing Times (or Dates). This information can be recorded manually in an enlarged, sectored circle or in a subdivided hexagon. Figure 3–15 shows these symbols.

Other symbols from the computer programs can be more useful for drawing finalized schedules but can be more awkward for some schedulers during the earlier stages of planning. It depends on your personal preferences or the standards that exist in your employer's company. In Figure 3–16, the rectangle encloses all of the relevant information of an activity.

Symbols for Events and Milestones

In Bubble (AON) diagrams, the tasks are the major symbols and only a few events are incorporated to bring attention to important "signposts" in the project: Project

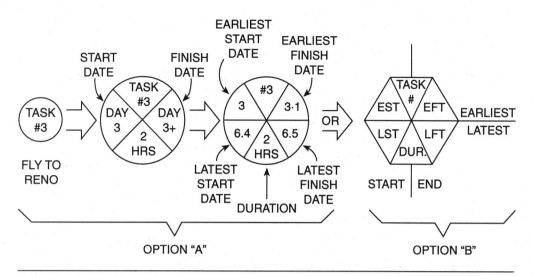

Figure 3–15   The Subdivided Bubble Symbol for a Task.

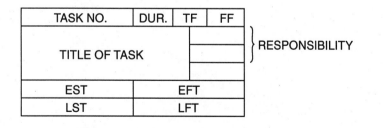

Figure 3–16   Other Symbols for Tasks.

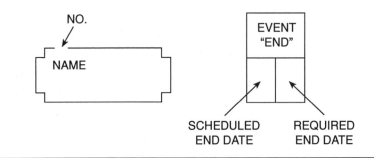

Figure 3–17   Typical Event and Milestone Symbols for AON Network Diagrams.

Start, Project Finish, Arrival of President, Building Closed In, and so forth. These special events must be eye-catching to focus on great and important achievements of the project. When round or hexagonal shapes are used to indicate tasks, rectangles are used for events. When rectangles are used for tasks, circles or double-walled rectangles can be used. Computer programs prefer rectangles because they are simpler for the program to draw. Figure 3–17 provides several examples.

Alternatively, in Arrow diagrams (AOA), the tasks are drawn as arrows and a simple shape marks the events. As every task arrow must begin and end with an event symbol, compactness and simplicity are necessary; an overly prominent event symbol would detract from the task arrows. As the only information recorded in the task symbol is its reference number, a small circle satisfies the requirement. Most graphical systems for arrow diagrams do not place any other information in the symbol; manual calculations on AOA diagrams produce time data for the events and these are shown on a small "tree" growing from each event symbol. Data about the task is recorded along the line of the arrow. These arrangements are illustrated in Figure 3–18.

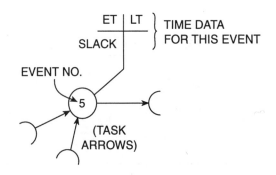

Figure 3–18   Typical Event Symbol for AOA Diagrams.

SUMMARY

We have presented two sets of graphical systems used for displaying two types of networks and showed each one for the travel example. A major concept called the Precedence Grid, which collects all the verbal precedence information in one simple format, was described. This grid helps us to remove duplicate information, identify loops in the logic, and identify precedences requiring "dummy" tasks in AOA networks.

This chapter covered a major component in the preparation of a schedule; when the durations of tasks are incorporated into a network, an initial schedule starts to take shape.

EXERCISES AND PROBLEMS

1. Identify the tasks, events, and milestones in the following description:

   Beginning at first light on Thursday, the battalion will begin to build the bridge by placing the first anchors in the near shore; the maneuver will end when the last decking piece has been bolted down.

2. Explain, supported by a diagram, why AOA diagrams have almost equal numbers of Tasks and Events. Why do most AOA's have more tasks than events?

3. From the following description, construct a Precedence Grid, then draw an AON and an AOA network from it.

   As soon as spending has been approved, task #1 can be started; #2 & #3 must wait for #1 to finish; #4, #5 & #6 can occur in series after #3 is finished: #6 also follows #2; #8 & #9 follow #6; #7 follows #2 & #8; #12 follows #9; when #8 is done, #11 can start; #10 can start right after #7; the whole site can be cleaned up (#13) when #10, #11 & #12 are done.

4. From the Bubble Diagram for the transcontinental trip (see Figure 3–9), construct a Gantt Chart. You will have to assume a realistic duration for each leg of the trip.

4

DEVELOPING NETWORK DIAGRAMS FROM A PRECEDENCE GRID

LEARNING OBJECTIVES

After completing this chapter, you should be able to:

- Prepare a draft Precedence Grid (P-G) for any Level of a Work Breakdown Structure.
- Recognize and remove redundant precedence information from a P-G.
- Identify potential AOA Dummy tasks from a P-G.
- Identify potential loops in a P-G.
- Draw Bubble (AON) Diagrams using the data from the P-G.
- Draw Arrow (AOA) Diagrams using the P-G data, correctly introducing dummy tasks and properly numbering the event nodes.

PREPARATION FOR THIS CHAPTER

You must be very familiar with the warehouse project. You have followed the development of its WBS down to a fairly detailed level and you should be able to modify and rearrange it when necessary. You are familiar with the graphical conventions for network diagramming and have the necessary tools and skills to make neat drawings. Neat free-hand lettering and sketching skills will be a bonus when you sketch the networks of this chapter.

INTRODUCTION

The purpose of this chapter is to apply the concepts and methods we have already studied to develop network diagrams for the warehouse construction project. The previous chapter covered the tools for doing this: the graphical conventions and the Precedence Grid for recording the task sequences. The next chapter (Chapter 5) will introduce time and the durations of the individual tasks; and Chapter 6 introduces these durations into the network for calculating the first time-based schedule for this project.

We are learning manual methods so that in the future we will understand what a computer is actually doing behind its screen when we command it to do something, such as "Recalculate the Schedule." We indicate throughout this book where a computer can greatly lighten the drudgery of our manual work. The learning goal is to understand the processes because blind use of a computer program without knowing what it is really doing can lead to misleading results and confusion.

PRECEDENCE GRIDS FOR THE WAREHOUSE

In analyzing any complex problem, the best approach is to develop your ideas from the "general to the specific." For example, in the transcontinental trip we began with the simple goal of "Traveling from San Francisco to New York"; we then broke it down into main divisions; and finally we added the small side trips and personal problems that refined the plan. The development of the warehouse's WBS followed this policy of increasing complexity, level by level. We shall develop a Precedence Grid for each level of the WBS for this project.

A Precedence Grid can be developed from the tasks named in each level of the WBS: each P-G becomes progressively bigger as the number of tasks increases down through the lower levels of the WBS. For our purposes, we need a network having the smallest number of tasks that can adequately describe the project for scheduling purposes. New ideas are better understood through work on simpler models. We can find such a model from among the Precedence Grids based on the several levels of the WBS.

We will develop a Precedence Grid for the family of tasks in each level of the WBS, starting at Level I and continuing down to Level IV and possibly even to parts of Level V. We will have four or five P-G's to study and compare. Starting simply and adding complexity in stages helps us to understand the project better and to select the appropriate set of tasks to be scheduled.

The WBS for the Warehouse Project was developed in Chapter 2 and the family of tasks in each level of this WBS are listed in Appendix B. These provide the names for the tasks for each Precedence Grid. We will begin with Level I (the Goal) and carry through to Levels II, III, and IV to illustrate the process.

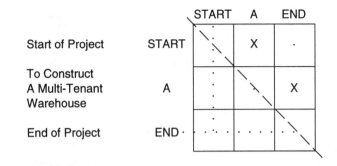

Figure 4–1   Precedence Grid for Level I of WBS (The Goal of the Project).

Precedence Grid for Level I Tasks

The Precedence Grid for Level I in Figure 4–1 is quite superficial because there is only one "task," the Goal Statement: "To Build the Warehouse." This simplest P-G reminds us that the project has a START and an END, each of which would be specifically defined in the contract. Every project must have a specified set of starting and ending conditions.

The START column and the END row will not be included in later Grids because nothing ever precedes the START or follows the END.

Precedence Grid for Level II Tasks

Level II of the WBS expands the Goal into three STAGES for the project: The Prime Construction, The Model Office, and Completion of Custom Space. Their P-G is shown in Figure 4–2 and the resulting very simple schedule, a simple end-to-end sequence, is shown in its accompanying Bubble Diagram (AON) (Figure 4–3).

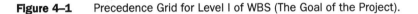

Figure 4–2   Precedence Grid for Level II of WBS (Three Stages of the Project).

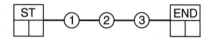

Figure 4–3   Bubble Diagram (AON) for the Level II Model.

Precedence Grid for Level III Tasks

For this example, we will consider subdividing STAGE ONE only, the major activity of the total project. Normally, all three stages must be considered at the outset, but because we are concerned with the construction schedule, the last two stages can be considered as separate projects. We have assumed that Stages 2 and 3 will not be attempted until after Stage 1 has been completed. Figure 4–3 shows this sequence. The primary construction breaks down into eight tasks (Appendix B) and the Precedence Grid for these eight Level III tasks is shown in Figure 4–4.

The precedence information is a distillation of all the information you collected from your consultants and experienced construction superintendents. You may question some of these sequencing decisions, but it is necessary to accept them as "givens" until you have an opportunity to analyze the construction processes and correct any conflicting logic.

Recall that multiple X's in a row mean these tasks can be started simultaneously (study rows 1, 3, and 5). Tasks 2 and 3 can begin as soon as task 1 is done. Alternatively, multiple X's in a column mean that the task named by the column cannot begin until all of its predecessor tasks (the X's in the column) have been completed (study columns 4, 6, and 8). For example, in column #4 (Task #4 is a follower), Task #4 cannot be started until both #2 and #3 are finished.

These are Follower Tasks

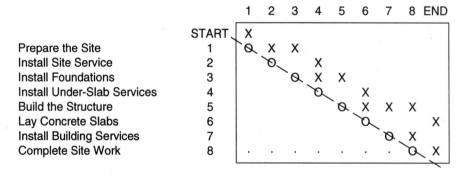

Figure 4–4   Task List and Precedence Grid for the 8-task (Level III) Model.

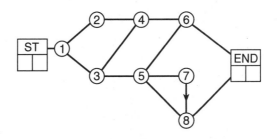

Figure 4–5   Bubble Diagram for the 8-task Model.

The simple Bubble Diagram for the precedence data of this P-G is shown in Figure 4–5 to illustrate the evolution of our method toward a schedule. Study link 5–8 to see if it is necessary.

Level IV Task Model of the Project—36 Tasks

Level IV of the WBS contains 36 tasks whose sequencing requires more careful thought than was needed for the previous 8-task model. The precedence links recorded in Figure 4–6 represent input (some conflicting) from several sources. Our purpose is to study and edit this data before attempting to draw its network.

The precedence information of these 36 tasks shows a marked improvement in detail over the P-G for Level III (8 tasks) but it is overly complex and unwieldy as a learning example. However, rather than rejecting it out of hand, we can observe several useful things from it. Item #3 in the list below is the key that allows us to modify this set of 36 tasks into a 24-task model. This 24-task model of the warehouse is the study example for the remainder of the book.

APPLICATIONS OF THE PRECEDENCE GRID

1. Find redundant precedence relationships.
2. Identify potential "dummy" tasks required for an Arrow network.
3. Identify groups of tasks that can be safely merged back into more general "super-tasks."
4. Identify potential "loops" in the networks.

Each concept in this list is described more fully in Appendix D, complete with simple but hypothetical examples. Refer to these examples and work through them; they will help you understand this discussion of the warehouse.

You should find that a Precedence Diagram is valuable for identifying and dealing with the problem areas noted above. Drawing the network after refining its P-G is much simpler than attempting to draw from the raw information. In

These Task Numbers Follow the Task List for LEVEL IV of the WBS

```
                                        (units)  |   10's   |    20's   |    30's  E
                                 1 2 3 4 5 6 7 8 9 0 1 2 3 4 5 6 7 8 9 0 1 2 3 4 5 6 7 8 9 0 1 2 3 4 5 6 N
                                                                                                         D
Project Start                    ST  X X              .              .              .              .
Conduct Legal Survey             1   O · X · X        .              .              .              .
Make A Soils Analysis            2     O X            .              .              .              .
Rough Excavate the Building Site 3       O X          .              .              .              .
Establish Structural Base (Good Fill) 4      O · · · X .              .              .              .
Trench for Site Services         5     ·   · O X      .              .              .              .
Install All Conduits, Pipes, etc. 6          O X      .              .              .              .
Connect to Municipal Services    7             O X    .              .              .              .
Backfill and Compact             8              O · · · · X · · ·     .              .    · · · · , .
Excavate for Foundations         9             O X X  .              .              .              .
Drive Piles                      10  · · · · · X O X · · X ·  · · · · · · ·     · ·   · · · · ·
Place Footings Formwork          11                O X     .              .              .
Place Reinforcement              12                O X     .              .              .
Pour Concrete                    13                  O X · · X ·   .              .              .
Apply Moisture-Proofing          14                    O · · · · ·   . · · · · · X X X · X · · ·
Trench & Bed for Under Slab Services 15 · · · · · · · · · · · O X · · · · · · · ·     .
Install Conduits, Tubes, etc.    16                      O X   ·     .              .
Connect To Site Services         17                      O X       .              .
Backfill and Compact             18                        O · · · X .              .
Build Block Walls                19                      O X       .              .
Erect Roof Structure             20  · · · · · · · · · · · · · · · · · O X · · · ·   .
Install Doors and Windows        21                          O X   .              .
Paint Wood Trim and Concrete Block Walls 22                    O · · · · · · · · · X ·
Lay Vapor Barrier for Slabs      23                            O X       ·              .
Lay Reinforcement Mesh and Rebar 24                            O X       .              .
Pour Concrete Slabs and Finish   25  · · · · · · · · · · · · · · · · · · · · O X X X X X · · X · · ·
Install Sanitary Plumbing        26                                O · · · · · · X ·
Install Storm Drains             27                                O · · · · · X .
Install Electrical System        28                              O X · · X · · X ·
Install HVAC                     29                                O · · · · X ·
Install Communication Systems    30  · · · · · · · · · · · · · · · · · · · · · · · · · O · · X ·
Install Roads and Parking        31                                    O · · X · ·
Lay Walkways                     32                                      O · · X · .
Install Area Lighting            33                                      O · · X ·
Install Fences                   34                                        O · X ·
Do Landscaping                   35  · · · · · · · · · · · · · · · · · · · · · · · · · · · · · · · O X ·
Clean-Up                         36  · · · · · · · · · · · · · · · · · · · · · · · · · · · · · · · · O X
```

Figure 4–6   Task List and Precedence Grid for the 36-task Model of the Project.

particular, AOA networks involving multiple precedence relationships can be very confusing and difficult to sort out correctly without prior thought.

Loops and Multiple Links

A violation in logic is produced by links (9,10) and (10,9): these state that task 10 must follow task 9, BUT task 9 must also follow task 10. One of these statements must be wrong, which means that you must consider the actual construction sequencing to decide which one must be removed. If the piles (#10) must be driven before the foundations excavations (#9) can begin, then link (9,10) is obviously wrong and must be removed. Such errors in the logic of precedence statements are known as **loops**.

If we search the warehouse's P-G (Figure 4–6) for multiple precedence relationships, we can identify several: they have rows and columns with multiple X's with an X at their intersection. The following cases are pairs of that type:

Row #1 and Column #3

Row #9, Columns #10 and #11

Row #10, Columns #11 and #15

Row #14 and Column #33

Row #25 at Column #29

Row #28 and Columns #29, #33, and #36

Careful study of the first set indicates that the logic is sound, because task #3 can follow #1 and #2 in either type of network. But a dummy task (1,3) will be needed in the AOA diagram (because a task arrow can start at only one event, not two). A similar argument holds for the link dictated by cell (14,33). You will find it valuable to draw a small AON and AOA mini-network to prove to yourself where the logic cannot be simplified. Use all the tasks identified in the intersecting row and column to draw the mini-networks. The complete AON network for the 36-task model shows all the links noted in the P-G. See Figure 4–7.

For AOA networks, when two (or more) tasks follow two (or more) predecessor tasks (refer to Figure 4–8) careful study is needed to incorporate dummy tasks and events. In this example, tasks #29 and #33 each follow #14 and #28; the relationships are complicated by #31 and #32 also following #14. If these latter two tasks were not there, then #33 could be connected directly to #14 and a dummy task could be added showing that #33 followed #14 as well as #28.

In the actual case where #31 and #32 also follow #14, a dummy event is needed to separate the complex dependencies and two dummy tasks are now needed. Study this example critically to appreciate the true dependencies. Look

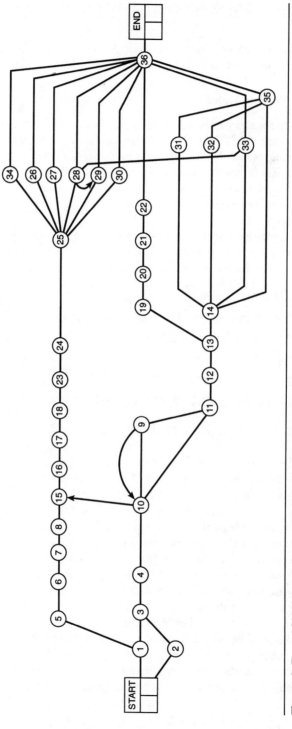

Figure 4–7   AON Network for the 36-task Model of Warehouse.

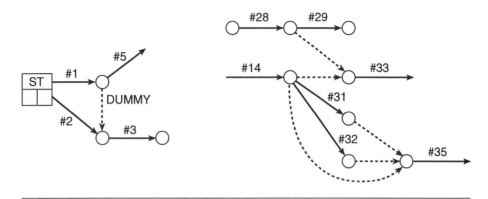

Figure 4–8   Multiple Dummy Tasks in AOA Networks.

closely at the P-G (Figure 4–6): column #33 intersects with rows #14 and #28; all contain multiple X's and the X's at the intersections identify potential dummy tasks for the arrow network—links 14,33 and 28,33.

Another idiosyncrasy of AOA networks is illustrated in Figure 4–8. Tasks #31 and #32 cannot end at the same event because they would have the same "name"; therefore a dummy event and task is introduced to circumvent this problem. Also be convinced that the dummy task linking #14 to #35 is redundant and unnecessary: compare this with the link 14,35 in the P-G.

SIMPLIFYING THE MODEL

When a single string of X's parallels the diagonal of the P-G and no other X's exist on either side of this string, the string identifies tasks that could be grouped together into a super-task. Consider the 36-task P-G for the warehouse where there are several strings.

There are several short task sequences displayed in the Grid in a line next to the diagonal: (5-6-7-8); (9-11-12-13-14); (15-16-17-18); (19-20-21-22); and (23-24-25-26). Each of these 5 sequences can be grouped together into a super-task, simplifying the P-G and reducing the total number of tasks. This can safely be done because there are no "outside" tasks linked to the intermediate tasks in each group.

Consider the first set (5-6-7-8) in Figure 4–7: #1 precedes #5, and #15 follows #8, with the simple sequence between. These four tasks are the sub-tasks of "Install Site Services" and they may be replaced in the model by this single super-task.

Another such set appears to be 9-11-12-13-14, but 14 cannot be included because 19 also follows 13, and 13 must terminate this group; only 9-11-12-13 can be merged into one super-task. See Figure 4–9. Study the sets 15-16-17-18, 19-

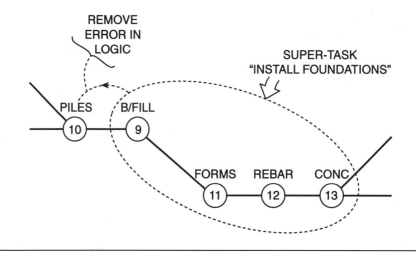

Figure 4–9   Grouping Tasks into a Super-task.

20-21, and 23-24-25-26 as additional examples. Note that 22 cannot be included after 19-20-21 because of the five other tasks that also follow 21.

To identify these sets, look for tasks that depend on each other but have no other links in their rows **and** columns; there must be blank regions on either side, and above and below the string of X's. Study the nature of these tasks to decide whether it is sensible to merge them. Sometimes a set will include all the components of the work area of the previous level in the WBS, thus simplifying the name for the set. This is not a hard and fast rule, so always study the tasks critically. The first set (9,11,12,13) becomes the "Poured Concrete Foundations" super-task.

DEVELOPING THE 24-TASK MODEL FOR THE WAREHOUSE PROJECT

These options have been pointed out to illustrate several useful applications in analyzing the 36-task P-G of the warehouse project. We will modify this 36-task P-G by merging the five sets of tasks into five super-tasks, reducing the total number of tasks by 12. The revised P-G will now have 24 tasks plus the START and END milestones. This 24-task model of the project will be the basis for our scheduling examples.

USES FOR TASKS IN LEVEL V

Most of the tasks in this detailed list are much too detailed to include in the project schedule, but some will be needed for estimating the cost and duration of their super-tasks in LEVEL IV. Each group in Level V can be treated as a small sub-project whose total duration and cost are needed by their super-tasks in LEVELS

III and IV. We can make time calculations of each small network to find its total duration, and then use that duration in the analysis for the total project.

Further breakdown of many of the 46 work areas of LEVEL V requires intimate knowledge of the techniques applied by the individual trades in executing their work. This breakdown might be very useful to certain foremen as they organize their own work but it is seldom required for organizing the total project.

THE 24-TASK MODEL OF THE WAREHOUSE PROJECT

We have grouped small families of tasks into super-tasks (actually a super-task is a sub-project) and reduced the number of tasks in our project to a more manageable level. These twenty-four activities are not all in the same Level of the WBS but this is not important because no sequencing data was ignored and no tasks were

IDENTITY	NAME OF TASK (or Milestone)
START	(likely defined by the clearance to spend money)
1	Legal Survey of the Site
2	Perform a Soils Analysis
3	Rough Excavate the Building Area
4	Provide a Solid Soil Base
5	To Install Site Services
6	Drive Piles
7	Concrete Foundations
8	To Install Under-Slab Services
9	Construct External Block Walls
10	Erect Roof Structure
11	Install Doors and Windows
12	Painting
13	To Lay Concrete Slabs
14	Sanitary Plumbing
15	Storm Drains
16	Electrical
17	Heating and Ventilating
18	Install Communication System
19	Roadways and Parking
20	Install Walkways
21	Area Lighting
22	Fencing—Gas Meter
23	Landscaping
24	Clean-Up
END	(of Stage One)

Figure 4–10   Task List for the 24-task Model.

		Units									+10									+20				E
		1	2	3	4	5	6	7	8	9	0	1	2	3	4	5	6	7	8	9	0	1	2	3	4	N D
START		X																								
Survey	1		X		X																					
Soils	2			X																						
Excav	3				X																					
Base	4					X																				
Serv.	5							X										X								
Piles	6						X	X																		
Found	7								X				X													
USlab	8											X														
Walls	9									X																
Roof	10												X		X		X	X	X							
Doors	11												X													
Paint	12																									X
Conc	13													X			X		X							
Plumb	14																									X
Drains	15																									X
Elect	16															X										
HVAC	17																			X						
Commun	18																									X
Roads	19																		X	X						
Walks	20																				X					
Lites	21																						X			
Fences	22																						X			
Landsc	23																									X
Clean	24																									X

Figure 4–11   Precedence Grid for the 24-task Model.

omitted when we developed the super-tasks from the deeper levels of the Work Breakdown Structure. The Level V tasks are accounted for as they are "submerged" in their super-tasks.

The twenty-four tasks of varying size and complexity that define our warehouse project are listed in Figure 4–10: these are the tasks to be scheduled in later chapters. The 36-task P-G has been simplified into the 24-task P-G shown in Figure 4–11.

THE AON ("BUBBLE") DIAGRAM FOR THE 24-TASK MODEL

You will find the detailed development of this network in Appendix E. Several highlights of that development are repeated here. AON networks can be developed from the START or the END milestone, depending on how your mind operates

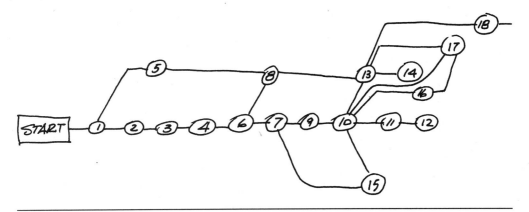

Figure 4–12   Start of the Bubble (AON) Network.

most comfortably, but beginning at the START follows the natural order of construction. Figure 4–12 illustrates the first few tasks beginning from the START.

Each Bubble contains the task's reference number from the task list in Figure 4–10. Later we will enlarge this Bubble to contain other data; but for now, our objective is only to develop a correct network. With a sketched first draft, tasks and logic lines will be placed in what will later become awkward locations; this is what a draft is for. When all precedence data from the P-G has been dealt with, then the draft is ready for its first revision: reducing cross-overs, placing all task bubbles to the right of their predecessors, and producing a more pleasing, easy-to-follow array of task bubbles. See Figure 4–13.

THE ARROW (AOA) NETWORK

The development of this different network for the warehouse project appears in Appendix D, but highlights are reproduced here for reference purposes.

The first draft is a hand-drawn "Thinking Picture," in which task arrows and events are placed according to the X's in each **column** of the P-G. See Figure 4–14. In cases where the correct task arrow must be linked to a task not yet on the diagram, shift over to links (X's) in a convenient row. When an arrow terminates too early because its end event cannot be perfectly placed, it is extended later to the correct event with a temporary dummy. See Figures 4–15 and 4–16.

SUMMARY

We have developed both the Bubble and the Arrows network for the construction project without having any knowledge of the durations of the individual tasks. The basis for this was the Precedence Matrix of the minimum number of tasks adequate

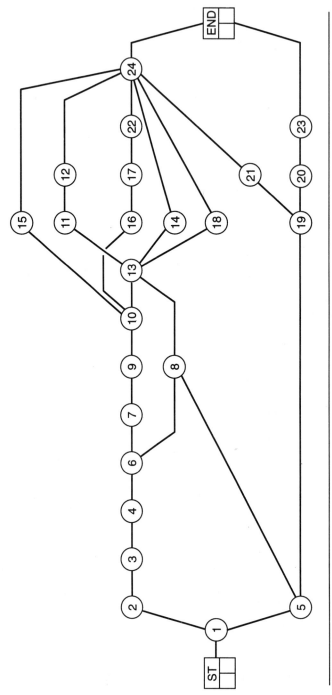

Figure 4-13 Final Bubble (AON) Network.

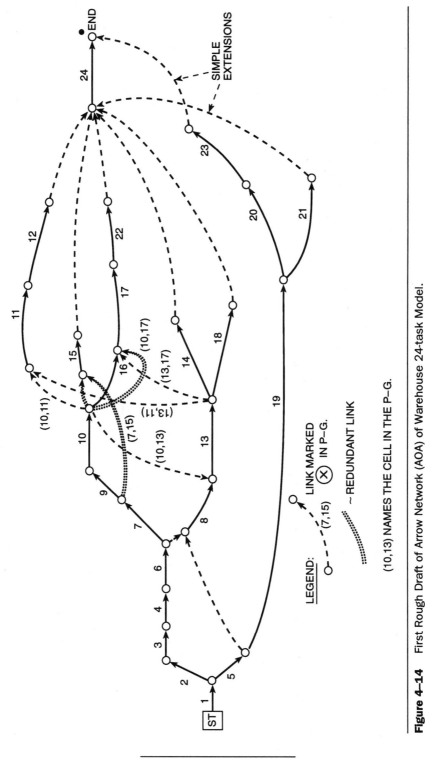

Figure 4–14 First Rough Draft of Arrow Network (AOA) of Warehouse 24-task Model.

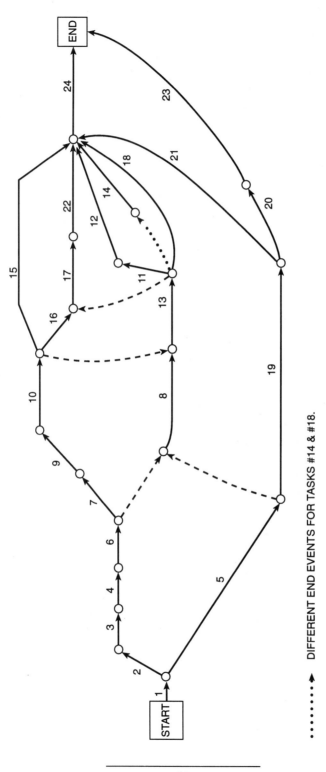

······► DIFFERENT END EVENTS FOR TASKS #14 & #18.

Figure 4–15   Improved Hand-drawn Second Draft of Warehouse 24-task Model.

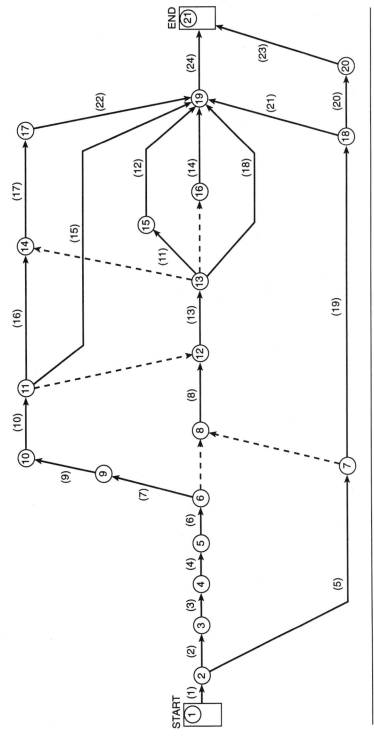

Figure 4–16 The Warehouse: Final Arrow (AOA) Network.

for the purposes of drawing these first networks. This simplest set of tasks evolved from studying the Precedence Matrices for the upper levels of the WBS and revising several work packages based on the required order of construction.

Precedence Grids were used to identify duplicate precedence logic, search for errors in the logic, and re-order the rows and columns of the P-G to simplify drawing the network diagrams. These networks are now ready to accept durations for each of the tasks and thereby the time for each event. The first draft schedule will soon be available.

EXERCISES AND PROBLEMS

1. Prepare the P-G for the following renovation project. Afterward, list the individual tasks, assign reference numbers or letters, and set up the grid on squared paper. The precedence information is:

   - Sanding and varnishing the wooden floors is the last thing to be done;
   - Just before the floors are done, the interior and exterior painting must be finished;
   - After the contract is signed, the old wallpaper can be removed, the wooden interior trim and cabinets can be removed, and the exterior wooden walls can be sand-blasted;
   - After the sand-blasting, paint the walls;
   - Replace the cabinetry after repairing the walls;
   - Lay the new kitchen tiles after the cabinets have been installed;
   - Paint the interior walls after installing the new cabinetry and laying the new floor covering.

2. The accompanying Precedence Diagram includes extraneous precedence relationships. Identify them, name the category of each one, and then correct the relationships (X). Ensure that logic needed by the Arrow diagram is not destroyed.

	A	B	C	D	E	F	G	END
START	X							D
A	·	X	X	X				
B		·			X		X	
C			·			X		
D	X			·	X	X		
E	X				·		X	
F						·	X	
G							·	X

Draw the Arrow diagram for the original data, including all the relationships given. Draw a final AOA based on your corrected P-G. You should rearrange the rows and columns so that no X's are below the diagonal.

3. Draw the AON (Bubble) diagram for your corrected Precedence Grid.

4. Create your own route for traveling from Elko to New York City. Allow for two side trips for two of your friends and allow three days to repair your car at one of the stop-over towns. From your written proposal to your friends before leaving the West Coast, make up a P-G for the total trip and then draw the AON network from your P-G.

5. Develop a P-G from the Arrow network shown below and then draw the Bubble (AON) from your P-G.

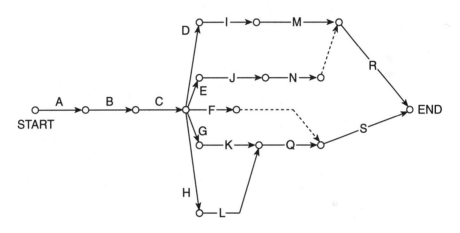

5

TIME AND THE DURATION OF ACTIVITIES

LEARNING OBJECTIVES

After completing this chapter, you should be able to:

- Understand and explain the difference between Time and Duration; Calendar Time and Project Time.
- Assemble material lists for a task based on an Estimator's Quantity Take-Off data.
- Select appropriate crews for a construction task and record productivity and related data from common references.
- Calculate the nominal duration of a task and quote the value to the appropriate numerical precision.
- Use a spreadsheet format for manual calculations.

PREPARATION FOR THIS CHAPTER

Your knowledge of the cost estimate data will be necessary in order for you to determine the duration of a task. Estimator's reports list the resources, equipment, and human expertise required to reach each task's objective. You must appreciate and understand the meaning of their terms so that you can make meaningful calculations. The formulas that direct these calculations are not complicated, but you should be able to do the simple arithmetic and mentally check each one to uncover errors.

Figure 5–1   Review of the Stages of Analysis.

INTRODUCTION

We will be estimating the durations for each of the tasks in the 24-task WBS so that we can introduce them into the network we developed in the previous chapters. In Chapter 6 we shall make the calculations that will give us our first draft of a schedule.

Before starting on this actual construction-oriented part of our work to develop a schedule, we should consult Figure 5–1 so that we can review how we reached this stage.

This process has focused on the heart of the project by selecting tasks from the highest useful level in the WBS and rejecting incorrect and superfluous information. This discipline has kept the size of the network as small as possible but has also provided adequate detail for scheduling the project, an attractive and valuable tactic for a manual analysis. This desire to maintain a simple view of the project is in conflict with the natural desire to incorporate more detail. We must always balance these opposing pressures by ensuring that the level of detail will be just adequate for our needs. We will find that segments of a schedule can be refined later to include more detail, with generally little effect on the overall schedule.

This chapter introduces time into the networks we have already prepared, adding a good deal of realism to the analysis. With the introduction of this new element, we sense that we are getting much closer to preparing a schedule. But before we do, it is necessary to clarify our ideas about the concepts of *a time* and *a duration*.

THE CONCEPT OF TIME

Albert Einstein introduced a revolutionary change in the way some people understand TIME. We have no need to study how the Theory of Relativity might affect our schedules, but we do need to consider a few ideas about time in the context of scheduling. There are two: TIME and DURATION.

We have good analogies on our wrists for these two concepts: our watches indicate the *passage of time* with the sweep-second hand; *points in time* are indicated by the apparent stationary values in the date window, the position of the hour-hand, or a digital read-out. You quote the *time* as "Twelve Twenty-Five"; but you bake a cake for "Forty-five minutes," which is the cooking duration. Seldom would you say, "Bake the cake from 12:10 to 12:55" to indicate the cooking duration.

Duration measures the passage of time and, particularly in scheduling, is the "Duration for Executing a Task." The word **time** will be used to indicate a *point in time*, such as a date or a particular time of day; say, 8:00 A.M. on August 25. In particular, we shall use such terms as "Earliest Start Time" and "Latest Finish Time" and "Early Time and Late Time," and so forth to name particular TIMES in a schedule.

On a calendar, TIME is marked by a date, which changes when one 24-hour period inexorably marches on to the next. For a project, productive effort is accumulated in discontinuous periods so that a "day's work" is generally one eight-hour shift: it has long been called "one man-day." The duration is measured between the "clock-in time" at the beginning of a working shift and the end of a shift; it may also account for short non-working periods during the day, for such things as lunch and coffee-breaks. Consider the following example: "With pick and shovel, a homeowner dug a ditch in 16 hours of work."

Thus he worked for a total of 16 hours to achieve the objective. But as few ordinary humans can dig continuously for 16 hours, we may assume that the effort occurred during shorter periods, spread over several days, as illustrated in Figure 5–2.

Many construction tasks routinely extend over several working days. If the ditch-digging example were part of a commercial construction project made up of eight-hour working days, one worker would complete the assignment in two days. The point here is that task durations govern the duration of a project. Only working periods are counted; lunch breaks, nights, weekends, and holidays are ignored.

Project Time and Calendar Time—Days and Dates

"Project" time is not the same as "calendar" time. Project time is the total count of working days from the beginning of a project; typically, one working day would be one shift. A project beginning on Monday, August 5, would accumulate 20 working days by the end of the month, twenty-six **calendar days** later. Friday, August 30, would be **Project Day** 20.

In a project's working schedule, time moves steadily through one task to another without a break, ignoring nights and holidays, as shown on the hours-based

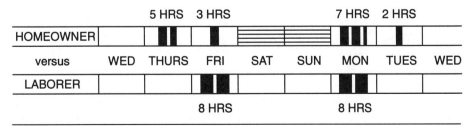

Figure 5–2   Discontinuous Work Shifts by One Worker.

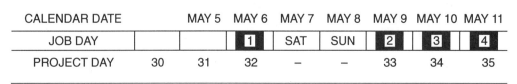

CALENDAR DATE			MAY 5	MAY 6	MAY 7	MAY 8	MAY 9	MAY 10	MAY 11
JOB DAY				1	SAT	SUN	2	3	4
PROJECT DAY	30	31	32	–	–	33	34	35

Figure 5–3   Project Days and Calendar Dates.

Gantt chart in Figure 5–2. Even though a task may occur during several shifts over several days, the analysis of a schedule counts only the total working time of a task. If durations are measured in working days (that is, one eight-hour shift per day), then the Start Time for a task, the Time of an event, is indicated by the number of Project-Days from the start of the project. Later, all the project days can be converted to calendar dates for on-the-job management. Refer to Figure 5–3.

Appropriate Units for Durations

We use units of time measurement appropriate to the application. The 100-meter dash is timed in seconds and thousandths of a second. So is the marathon (hours, minutes, and seconds), but seldom does the marathon require measurement to "the second." Sprinters race for improvements of hundredths of a second, but marathoners' concerns are with minutes. The duration of the activity affects the precision of the units used to measure it: the longer the duration, the less important are the smaller units. Construction tasks and projects follow the same policy.

Short-term projects, such as building a prefabricated assault bridge across a river for a military crossing, measure durations of tasks in minutes. Building a major highway bridge across the same river could take two years and its individual tasks might be measured in days or weeks. The choice of units depends on the duration of typical activities and on the duration of the total project. It is absurd to use minutes for a two-day task when hours are more reasonable. For example, which is the more realistic unit of measurement when you consider the equivalent durations of 2 days or 15 hours or 900 minutes? Using minutes suggests that you know the duration to within a few minutes either side of the two-day estimate.

Numerical Precision

Using units that are too small implies an extreme order of precision that is unlikely to be warranted and would be deceptive to others. Estimated durations are subject to uncertainties: when you estimate a five-day duration for a task you know it could likely vary one day either way; the "five days" is understood to be a target duration. Alternatively, when recording the actual duration of the completed task, which might have started on project day #37 and ended on day #43, you would have recorded "Six Days." If you wrote down 6.00 days, it would imply that you were sure of the duration to within one half of the last-quoted digit: that is, .005 working days or about 2 minutes. We must take into account "Significant Figures" in quoting numbers so that we pass on to the reader our degree of uncertainty regarding the number we quote:

6	implies a number between 5 and 7
6.	implies a number between 5.5 and 6.5
6.0	implies a number between 5.95 and 6.05
6.00	implies a number between 5.995 and 6.005, etc. . . .

These relative uncertainties have been graphed to scale in Figure 5–4 to illustrate the extreme precision implied when quoting a number like 6.00.

In Chapter 11 we will study the effects of uncertainty through the PERT System, in which three time estimates are required to indicate the range of possible durations for a task. We should not become hypnotized by the supposed precision of our estimated durations. Even if they are based on the best information available, we must always remember that they are only forecasts that effective managers treat as targets to be attained or surpassed.

The Importance of Good Time Estimates

Your schedule may be no better than the least accurate of your estimated durations. There are many factors affecting the actual duration of a task, and that can make your estimates easy to criticize but difficult for you to defend. A faulty estimate can divert the construction manager's attention away from other critical work areas, causing confusion on the job-site. A job does not need such surprises. If several masonry tasks were estimated to take 25 days and the masonry crew, working at their usual rate, finished in only 15 days, then the trades that follow might not be ready to start due to other prior commitments and the schedule

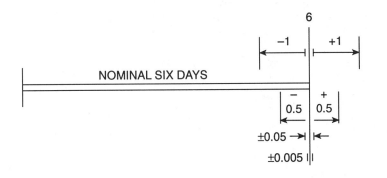

Figure 5–4   Relative Degrees of Uncertainty.

would likely "slip." Surprises like this disturb the schedule, which may require heroic corrective reactions from you and may possibly damage your professional ego and your reputation.

As your time estimates must stand up to the scrutiny of others, well-recognized reference data and the advice provided by your local experts should be used to evaluate bid estimates. Most firms collect and compile their own statistics and build up a database for future reference. This kind of data is available commercially, is updated annually, and is a good place to begin when you have little personal experience to use as your guide.

We will refer to one such reference: *Building Construction Cost Data*, published by R.S. Means Company. This reference provides hundreds of different crew definitions, along with their productivity rates, costs, and so forth. An example of information on standard crews is reproduced in Figure 5–5. Means' publications are updated annually and are widely available.

CREWS

Crew No.	Bare Costs Hr.	Daily	Incl. Subs O & P Hr.	Daily	Bare Costs	Incl. O&P
Crew B-12Q	Hr.	Daily	Hr.	Daily	Bare Costs	Incl. O&P
1 Equip. Oper. (crane)	$25.40	$203.20	$38.95	$311.60	$23.08	$35.40
1 Equip. Oper. Oiler	20.75	166.00	31.85	254.80		
1 Hyd. Excavator, 5/8 C.Y.		378.40		416.25	23.65	26.02
16 M.H., Daily Totals		$747.60		$982.65	$46.73	$61.42
Crew B-12R	Hr.	Daily	Hr.	Daily	Bare Costs	Incl. O&P
1 Equip. Oper. (crane)	$25.40	$203.20	$38.95	$311.60	$23.08	$35.40
1 Equip. Oper. Oiler	20.75	166.00	31.85	254.80		
1 Hyd. Excavator, 1.5 C.Y.		681.40		749.55	42.59	46.85
16 M.H., Daily Totals		$1050.60		$1315.95	$65.67	$82.25
Crew B-12S	Hr.	Daily	Hr.	Daily	Bare Costs	Incl. O&P
1 Equip. Oper. (crane)	$25.40	$203.20	$38.95	$311.60	$23.08	$35.40
1 Equip. Oper. Oiler	20.75	166.00	31.85	254.80		
1 Hyd. Excavator, 2.5 C.Y.		1669.00		1835.90	104.31	114.74
16 M.H., Daily Totals		$2038.20		$2402.30	$127.39	$150.14
Crew B-12T	Hr.	Daily	Hr.	Daily	Bare Costs	Incl. O&P
1 Equip. Oper. (crane)	$25.40	$203.20	$38.95	$311.60	$23.08	$35.40
1 Equip. Oper. Oiler	20.75	166.00	31.85	254.80		
1 Crawler Crane, 75 Ton		800.40		880.45		
1 F.E. Attachment, 3 C.Y.		272.40		299.65	67.05	73.76
16 M.H., Daily Totals		$1442.00		$1746.50	$90.13	$109.16
Crew B-12V	Hr.	Daily	Hr.	Daily	Bare Costs	Incl. O&P
1 Equip. Oper. (crane)	$25.40	$203.20	$38.95	$311.60	$23.08	$35.40
1 Equip. Oper. Oiler	20.75	166.00	31.85	254.80		
1 Crawler Crane, 75 Ton		800.40		880.45		
1 Dragline Bucket, 3 C.Y.		80.20		88.20	55.04	60.54
16 M.H., Daily Totals		$1249.80		$1535.05	$78.12	$95.94

Crew No.	Bare Costs Hr.	Daily	Incl. Subs O & P Hr.	Daily	Bare Costs	Incl. O&P
Crew B-17	Hr.	Daily	Hr.	Daily	Bare Costs	Incl. O&P
2 Laborers	$19.00	$304.00	$30.10	$481.60	$20.27	$31.61
1 Equip. Oper. (light)	23.40	187.20	35.90	287.20		
1 Truck Driver (heavy)	19.70	157.60	30.35	242.80		
1 Backhoe Loader, 48 H.P.		199.60		219.55		
1 Dump Truck, 12 Ton		325.00		357.50	16.39	18.03
32 M.H., Daily Totals		$1173.40		$1588.65	$36.66	$49.64
Crew B-18	Hr.	Daily	Hr.	Daily	Bare Costs	Incl. O&P
1 Labor Foreman (outside)	$21.00	$168.00	$33.25	$266.00	$19.67	$31.15
2 Laborers	19.00	304.00	30.10	481.60		
1 Vibrating Compactor		45.60		50.15	1.90	2.09
24 M.H., Daily Totals		$517.60		$797.75	$21.57	$33.24
Crew B-19	Hr.	Daily	Hr.	Daily	Bare Costs	Incl. O&P
1 Pile Driver Foreman	$25.95	$207.60	$45.25	$362.00	$24.16	$40.25
4 Pile Drivers	23.95	766.40	41.75	1336.00		
2 Equip. Oper. (crane)	25.40	406.40	38.95	623.20		
1 Equip. Oper. Oiler	20.75	166.00	31.85	254.80		
1 Crane, 40 Ton & Access.		712.80		784.10		
60 L.F. Leads, 15K Ft. Lbs.		60.00		66.00		
1 Hammer, 15K Ft. Lbs.		282.20		310.40		
1 Air Compr., 600 C.F.M.		265.00		291.50		
2-50 Ft. Air Hoses, 3" Dia.		29.60		32.55	21.09	23.20
64 M.H., Daily Totals		$2896.00		$4060.55	$45.25	$63.45
Crew B-20	Hr.	Daily	Hr.	Daily	Bare Costs	Incl. O&P
1 Labor Foreman (out)	$21.00	$168.00	$33.25	$266.00	$21.55	$34.17
1 Skilled Worker	24.65	197.20	39.15	313.20		
1 Laborer	19.00	152.00	30.10	240.80		
24 M.H., Daily Totals		$517.20		$820.00	$21.55	$34.17

Figure 5–5 Examples of Standard Crews. From *Means Building Construction Cost Data*, 1994. R.S. Means Co., Inc., Kingston, MA. All rights reserved.

CALCULATING THE DURATION OF A TASK

The cost estimate for the project was based on the quantity of work to be done for each element of the project and the method used to accomplish it. For example,

Assemble a wall 8' × 30' of 8" × 16" concrete blocks, using an inexperienced masonry crew capable of laying only 200 blocks per day.

You would have estimated the productivity of the crew (200 blocks per day) from your own experience with that particular crew or from other reliable advice.

Knowing the productivity of the selected crew and the quantity of work to be done (approximately 240 blocks), the duration is calculated by:

Duration = Quantity of Work divided by the Productivity of the Crew
= 240 blocks ÷ 200 blocks per day
= 1.2 days

As another example, assume that a "Ditching Crew" can excavate at the rate of 5400 cubic feet per day. We can estimate the duration of trenching a 2700-foot-long ditch 4 feet × 2 feet in cross-section by dividing the volume to be trenched by the daily productivity of the crew:

(2 × 4 × 2700) ÷ 5400 = 4.000 days (from the calculator screen)

Precision of Quoted Values

The question arises how to quote the duration that we have just calculated. Is it 4.000 or 4.0 or just 4? Quoting 4.000 announces that we are confident that the duration lies between 3.9995 and 4.0005 days; this is absurd because .0005 days is 14 seconds. If we believe that these nominal dimensions of the cross-section (2 feet × 4 feet) can vary within 5 percent, then the area of the cross-section could be as small as 90 percent and as large as 110 percent of the nominal value of 8 square feet. The volume to be excavated could then vary between 78,000 and 95,000 cubic feet:

0.90 × 8 × 2700 = 78,000 cu ft
1.10 × 8 × 2700 = 95,000 cu ft

Using these limits, the duration would vary between 3.6 and 4.4 days. Because of the uncertainty of the excavated volume, we cannot quote the above duration with any greater precision than 4 days (not 4. or 4.0, and certainly not 4.000).

Worker Productivity and Cost of a Task

Whereas the Crew Productivity determines the duration of the task, the Worker Productivity is found by dividing the Crew Productivity by the Crew Size.

In the ditching example, if there were 3 workers in the crew, the Worker

Productivity would be 5400 ÷ 3 = 1800 cubic feet per day per worker; or, in a more abbreviated fashion, 1800 **cu ft/man-day**. Three workers toiling for four days results in 12 man-days of human effort; if a worker's average pay is $135 per day ($135/man-day), the direct cost of labor for the task is 12 man-days × $135/man-day = $1,620.

If working conditions reduce the productivity of each worker, then the crew productivity is reduced and the task's duration increases. Because the worker is still paid $135 per day, the job's direct labor cost increases. If cool weather reduces the worker's efficiency by 15 percent (output is reduced from 1800 to 1530 cu ft/man-day), then the crew's output would be reduced to 4590 cu ft/day and the task's duration would increase from 4 days to 4.7 days and its cost from $1,620 to $1,903.

We will use the Worker Productivity concept when we study the cost penalties of accelerating tasks to shorten a project.

DURATIONS IN FIXED-PRICE CONTRACTS

The direct method of estimating the **nominal duration** of a task is based on the amount of work to be done and the "best" crew for doing that job. However, in the majority of cases the construction project has been won through bidding on a fixed-price basis. In this case a different approach is used to determine the required duration of a task: the bid amount combined with the daily direct cost determines the duration required to be "On Time and On Budget" for that task. If all tasks of a project were On-Time-and-On-Budget then the project would also be. Thus when durations are determined from the budget estimates, the resulting schedule has an added dimension that is of concern to management: COST.

The Bid Amount was compiled from the sum of all costs to the contractor of each element of work to be done. If, for example, the direct labor cost of constructing the masonry walls was $20,000 and the labor cost of the crew is now $850 per day, then the job *must* be finished in less than 24 days or the company will lose money on this important component. If the estimate was rationally developed using the most efficient crew, then the duration based on cost should satisfactorily agree with the basic duration using Volume of Work Crew Productivity. If it does not, then the task will require special attention before and during construction to maintain budget and time targets.

We will pursue the effects of this constraint on the duration later, when we consider ways to shorten a single task to reduce the duration of the project.

OBTAINING DURATIONS FROM QUANTITY TAKE-OFF DATA

The amount of work to be done, the kind of materials required, and the method for doing the job determine the selection of the ideal crew to do it.

The **Quantity Take-Off** worksheet lists the materials and the method, and the

UCI CODE	DESCRIPTION	COMMENTS	QUANTITY	UNITS
412	Masonry, West Wall	Standard	4180	SF
412	Masonry, S. Wall	Ribbed	770	SF
412	Masonry, North Wall	Ribbed	378	SF
412	Masonry, North Wall	Standard	152	SF
412	Masonry, East Wall	Standard	1204.5	SF
412	Masonry, East Wall	Ribbed	581.5	SF

Figure 5–6   A Portion of an Estimating Sheet.

WBS names the packages of work that will consume these resources. There should be little need for the scheduler to refer back to the detail drawings of the structure.

As an example, a portion of the Materials List for our warehouse has been copied from the Appendix B to Figure 5–6. The concrete masonry block walls appear in six entries under section 412 of the Unified Construction Index code.

There are 5536.5 square feet in surface area of standard blocks and 1729.5 square feet of ribbed blocks. A review of the drawings and the WBS indicates that the construction of these walls constitute one task and there is an appropriate crew to do it.

Referring to the Means catalogue of crews shows that Crew #D-8 is appropriate for this task; it can lay 345 blocks (8 " × 16 ") per day. And since each assembled block occupies one square foot of surface area, there are 7266 blocks to be assembled. Hence, the estimated duration of this task is 7266 blocks ÷ 345 blocks per day = 21.06 days, which we would quote as 21 days because 21.06 "rounds-off" to 21 (since 0.06 is less than the precision of 0.5). Depending on your confidence in the productivity estimate of your crew, you might feel more confident in quoting 20 or 25 days instead of 21.

Tabular Method for Calculations

This type of calculation will be repeated for every task identified in the WBS and shown in the network of tasks. Expediency and efficiency dictate that we must become organized when making repetitious calculations and especially when many such calculations must be made. Ultimately, you will do this type of calculation by computer, but we will begin here with manual methods to develop skills and to become familiar with tabular methods.

Line-by-line calculations (above) are adequate to explain a single calculation, but repetitive calculations should always be recorded in a table to make it easier to check them, compare them with the other results, and find errors. A calculation table for durations (Figure 5–7) is set up with the following columns:

CALCULATING TASK DURATIONS FOR ROOFING SUB-PROJECT

TASK NO. (1)	UCI NO. (2)	MATERIAL NAME (3)	QUANTITY (4)	UNITS (5)	CREW NO. (6)	PRODUC- TIVITY (7)	UNITS (8)	DURATION (9)
1	521	TRUSSES	22	Tons	E-7	10	Tons	2
2	531	DECKING	6650	SF	E-4	980	SF	7
3	720	INSULATION	6650	SF	G-1	3500	SF	2
4	733	CLADDING	2172	SF	G-3	1000	SF	2
5	610	OVERHANG	1577	BM	F-2	450	BF	4
6	733	SOFFITS	802	SF	2 CARP	210	SF	4
7	751	FLASHING	1650	SF	2 Shee	280	SF	6

Figure 5–7   Spreadsheet Headings for Duration Calculations.

Column 1 is assigned by you from the definition of the tasks and the WBS. The data for Columns 2 through 5 are taken from the Quantity Take-Off sheets; columns 6, 7, and 8 are from the Means crew catalogue; column 9 is found by dividing the total quantity in column 4 by the productivity value in column 7.

Tabular calculations improve your efficiency because you fill out one complete column at a time with the same kind of data. By doing so, your mind can focus on one process, such as looking up crew data from reference material, before moving to the next column to execute a different mental process. In the line-by-line calculation your mind changes function at every step, which—when repeated hundreds of times—accelerates mental fatigue and leads to errors.

Another value in using tabular methods is that they serve as an introduction to computerized spreadsheets. Programs such as Supercalc and Lotus 123 and others have revolutionized accounting methods, allowing the easy manipulation of large amounts of grouped data. Our current topic requires analysis of large amounts of quantity take-off data by grouping materials data associated with each construction task and accumulating amounts of like materials; the computer can do this sorting effortlessly. Since we will pursue this further in Chapter 12, become accustomed to using the tabular methods presented in this chapter.

DURATIONS FOR SUB-CONTRACTED TASKS

Sub-contracts are let to specialty contractors (for example, electrical, mechanical, painting, and so forth) because of the expertise and the specialized suppliers of materials available to them. General contractors do not usually find it economical to retain workers of all trades as permanent employees. Firms that provide Construction Management expertise sub-contract out all of the work and will apply their own forces only under exceptional conditions. In agreeing to a sub-contract, the Construction Manager would require a time estimate for the duration of the work and would mark (SUB) in the calculation spreadsheet.

Estimating the Duration of a Sub-Contractor's Job

The Crew Productivity data applies to clearly identified tasks, not combinations of tasks. We must therefore work with the much greater number of tasks at the lowest level in the WBS, not the fewer, general work areas at the higher levels. For example, "To Build the Roof" involves several different trades. The only way to obtain durations of these general task areas is to accumulate the durations of their component tasks. When we let sub-contracts we leave the accumulating up to the sub-contractor, who then quotes the duration of his work in the contract.

Therefore, if we want to use a network model of our project using fewer, more general task areas, we must either

1. use the sub-contractor's duration; or
2. treat each as a sub-project composed of several simpler tasks, using the more accurate durations of these components to calculate the duration of the sub-project.

DURATIONS FOR TASKS OF THE WAREHOUSE PROJECT

The relevant data for this project is found in the Take-Off list in Appendix B and the Task List in Chapter 2. The durations for the twenty-four tasks are known as the NORMAL DURATIONS; they represent the time required to execute the stated task by the OPTIMUM CREW which, by definition, is the most efficient combination of skilled tradesmen. It should have the most economical direct labor costs but it does not imply that this is the shortest duration. Later, we will want to shorten several of these *normal* durations by increasing the supply of certain resources and thereby reduce the duration of the project.

DURATIONS OF MORE GENERAL AREAS OF WORK—SUPER-TASKS

As noted above, we may want to find the duration of the general task area, "Erect Roof Structure" (task area #20). This is a super-task made up of seven basic-level tasks. We will use this small project-within-a-project as the example for recording referenced data and calculating the durations. The list of all 36 basic-level tasks (Level V of the WBS) appears in Chapter 2 and Appendix B.

Detailed Tasks for Task Area #20—"Erect Roof Structure"

Place and Secure Roof Trusses

Install Roof Deck

Install Vapor Barrier

| TASK NO. | IDENTIFICATION NAME | MEANS REF. NO. | MATERIAL TYPE | QUANTITY | UNITS | CREW DESCRIPTION | | PRODUCTIVITY | | TASK DURATION |
						TYPE	MEANS NO.	VALUE	UNITS	
1	Install Roof Trusses	5.2-40	Steel	33	Tons	Steel Workers	E-7	17	Tons	1.9 days
2	Install Roof Deck	6.1-35	2 × 6 T&G 3"wood	6650	sq-ft	Carps (3 crews)	F-2	320 × 3	sq ft	6.9
3	Install Vapor Barrier	7.4-09	Membrane	6650	sq ft	Roofers	G-1	3000	sq ft	1.5
4	Install Built-Up Roof	7.4-09	Tar & Grav	6650	sq ft	Roofers	G-1	3000	sq ft	2.2
5	Install Canopy + Cladding	7.6-33	Steel	105	Brackets	St Wrkrs	E-7	25	Brackets + Cladding	4.2
6	Install Soffits	7.6-33	Alum	2160	sq ft	St Wrkrs	E-7	500	sq ft	4.3
7	Install Flashing	7.6-33	Steel	1400	lin ft	St Wrkrs	—	240	lin ft	5.8

Figure 5–8 Task Duration Spreadsheet.

Install Roof Cladding

Construct Overhang

Install Soffits

Install Flashing

Each of these seven tasks can be assigned a standard crew and we can estimate the duration for each one using the table in Figure 5–8.

Example Use of a Spreadsheet for Tabulated Calculations

We do *not* simply sum the seven durations (27 days) to find how long the crews take to assemble the roof because several tasks can be worked on simultaneously: for example, the overhang can be constructed while the deck is being installed. Because we have not yet studied the time calculation technique, we will make an informed estimate of 21 days and update the duration later. The duration should be marked with an (*) to remind us to correct it later (after Chapter 6).

SUMMARY

A large amount of information has been presented in this chapter so that we will be prepared to calculate our first schedule in the next chapter. We reviewed several concepts of time as they apply to this subject and have learned how to differentiate between TIME and DURATION. We saw where we could find universal data on productivity of crews doing specific work and how to quote our calculated results in such a way as not to mislead our readers. We gained an understanding of the value of making repetitive calculations using tabular methods and we used this layout to develop and record the durations.

You should review this chapter until you feel comfortable with the new concepts and are able to proceed to the next chapter with confidence.

EXERCISES AND PROBLEMS

1. Take a current calendar and determine the duration of a task that was scheduled to begin on August 17 (or the nearest working day thereafter) and to end on September 7 (or the closest working day thereafter).
2. A project that started on February 4 is currently actively proceeding on July 18. What is today's Project Day?
3. The dimensions of a rectangular building are 47'9" by 213'3". It has a perimeter foundation and two cross walls that divide it into three compartments. If two carpenters can each erect 35 feet of forms per day, what duration should be allowed for this task?
4. Make a strip calendar by marking 31 equal divisions along a line to represent the days of July. Mark each division with the day of the week (M, T,

W, Th, F, Sat, Sun, etc.), based on your current calendar. How many regular (8:00 A.M. to 4:00 P.M.) working days are there for a job that was considered to start at 1600 hours on the first Friday and to end at the same hour on the last Wednesday of the month?

5. A large pile of earth from a swimming pool excavation must be removed by trucks nominally holding 15 cu. yds. By measuring the dimensions of the excavation you calculate the volume to be 185.0 cu. yds. If your linear measurements could have been consistently low by 4 percent,

    a. what should the volume be corrected to and to what precision would you quote the volume?

    b. how many truck loads would you budget for? ($1.04 \times 1.04 \times 1.04 = 1.13$)

6

TIME CALCULATIONS FOR BUBBLE AND ARROW NETWORKS

LEARNING OBJECTIVES

After completing this chapter, you should be able to:

- Incorporate durations and other time data into networks.
- For an AON Network, calculate the EARLIEST and LATEST STARTING TIMES for every *task* and hence identify the CRITICAL PATH(s) through the Bubble diagram.
- For an AOA Network, calculate the EARLIEST and LATEST TIMES for every *event* in the Arrow diagram and hence identify the critical path(s) through the Arrow diagram.
- Draw a Gantt Chart using the times derived from AON or AOA systems.
- Determine Task Floats (Total and Free) from Bubble diagrams, and Slack times from Arrow diagrams.

PREPARATION FOR THIS CHAPTER

You should be able to construct Arrow and Bubble networks from the Precedence Grid and be able to differentiate between event and task symbols on those diagrams. You should also be able to identify a cluster of tasks, group them into a sub-project, and construct its network.

INTRODUCTION

The primary goal of this chapter is to develop the initial schedule from the information covered in the earlier chapters. We developed a network for the 24-task model of the warehouse project and calculated the durations of its basic tasks, but we could only approximate the durations of its super-tasks. This chapter shows how to calculate the durations of these sub-projects and then the duration of the full 24-task project.

The previous chapter dealt with time and the durations of basic-level tasks; it alluded to how we would determine the duration of the ROOF STRUCTURE, a super-task made up of seven basic-level tasks. We will use this sub-project as the example "project" for this section. We will work completely through the time analysis of its Bubble (AON) diagram before concentrating on its related but quite different Arrow (AOA) diagram.

THE SUPER-TASK: "ERECT ROOF STRUCTURE"

The WBS outline in Chapter 4 lists seven tasks that define the work area, "Roof Structure." These seven basic-level tasks are as follows (the durations are from Figure 5–8):

Task No.	Task Name	Duration
1	Place and Secure Trusses	2 days
2	Install Roof Deck	7
3	Apply Vapor Barrier	2
4	Apply Roof Cladding	2
5	Construct Roof Overhang	4
6	Install Soffits	4
7	Apply Flashing	6

The AON network was developed in Chapter 4 and the durations for each of these seven tasks were estimated in Chapter 5. Using the six-sector circle for the task symbol (introduced in Chapter 3), the up-dated AON Network for this sub-project is shown in Figure 6–1. Note the legend for defining the use of each of the sectors in the large bubble: the Earliest Times occupy the upper half and the Latest Times, the lower; starting times are on the left half and finishing times on the right half.

To illustrate the meanings of these times, we will construct the Gantt Chart for this sub-project and then concentrate on making the calculations directly on the AON diagram after these new concepts have been covered. Recall that "Bar Chart" is the common name for a Gantt Chart in which the length of each bar represents the duration of a task. The bar for a four-day task will be twice as long

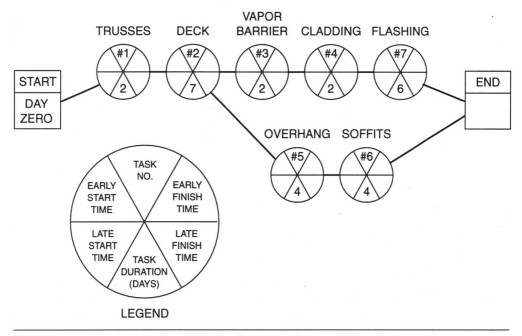

Figure 6–1   The AON Network for the Roof Construction.

as the bar for a 2-day task. In Figure 6–2, task #1 is 2 units long and task #2 is 7 units long.

Based on Earliest Start Times

The first task starts at time zero and extends to the right for 2 units, which represent the 2 days' duration of task #1. Each task starts at its earliest possible time, which is the end of its predecessor task. Task #2 starts at the instant task #1 ends, and then #3, #4, and #7 carry on in succession. Note that task #7 ends at the end of working day 19, which defines the duration of this sub-project: that is, the Roof can be installed in 19 working days. Tasks #1, #2, #3, #4, and #7 govern the total duration; tasks #5 and #6 do not and they have what is called "float." That is, they each have a few spare days during which they can be executed. The other five tasks have zero "float" and are called "critical" because their individual durations are critical to the duration of the total project. If any one of these tasks took one day longer, the project's duration would also be extended one day.

Regarding the two tasks with "float," task #6 could be delayed two days so that it would end at the same time as task #7 (end of day 19), and the bar for task #5 could be placed just before it. These two tasks would occur in their latest time

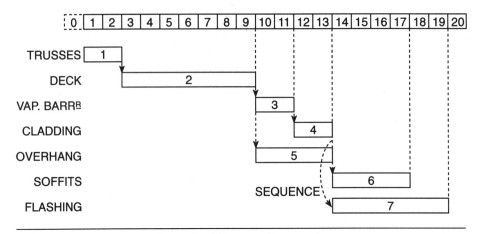

Figure 6–2   Gantt Chart for the Roof Structure Super-task.

period without affecting the project's duration. This arrangement defines the LATEST START TIMES for these two tasks. Note that the five critical tasks have no scheduling flexibility and their Earliest and Latest Start Times are the same; their floats are zero.

We could have constructed a Gantt Chart based on the *latest* finishing time for each task. We would have begun this chart from the END milestone and worked backward to the START milestone, thereby determining the project's duration. However, we are usually more concerned with the earliest rather than the latest starting times for tasks so we normally add the Late Finish Time marks to the "Early Start" Gantt Chart. The latest times are usually shown on the "earliest start" Gantt Chart, where the "floats" can be clearly shown. The completed Gantt Chart appears as Figure 6–3. The two types of floats are discussed later.

Earliest and Latest Start Times for all Tasks

The start and finishing times can be seen directly by referring to the Gantt Chart, but since we will be calculating directly on the AON diagram, we must understand the basis for these calculations. Once the durations are entered into the bubbles, the Times are readily calculated:

Start Time = End Time of Its Predecessor*

and

End Time = Start Time + Its Duration

(*When there is more than one predecessor task, select the latest ending time of these predecessors.)

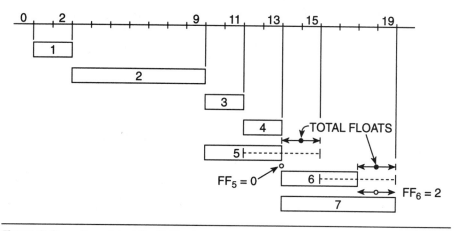

Figure 6–3   Completed Gantt Chart.

CALCULATING THE EARLIEST STARTING AND FINISHING TIMES

Earliest Starting Time (EST) and Earliest Finishing Time (EFT) are special terms and their abbreviations are used frequently in this text. Time is measured from the "START" Milestone (the Time of "START" is zero), and any task that follows "START" must begin at Time = 0. Recall that we mark points in time at the *end* of the day. Tasks finish at the end of a project-day and the next task begins at the same instant (that is, the end of that same day), even though the actual work begins at 8:00 A.M. the next work day.

Hence, Task #1 begins at the end of an artificial day, Day "Zero." This allows easy calculation and appreciation of Times, because Task #1 will finish at the end of Day Two (Day 0 + 2 Days). Refer to the Gantt Chart in Figure 6–2.

For Task #1: (Duration, 2 days)

EARLIEST FINISHING TIME = (starting time) + (its Duration)
End of day zero + 2 days = End of Day #2

For TASK #2: (Duration, 7 days)

EARLIEST START OF TASK #2 = EARLIEST FINISH of TASK #1
                             = Day #2
EARLIEST FINISHING TIME   = Day #2 + 7 days = End of Day #9

Note that Task #3 and #5 can both start when Task #2 is finished and therefore both have the same Earliest Start Time, Day #9. Hence Task #3 has an EFT of Day #9 + 2 Days = Day #11, and Task #5 has an EFT of Day #9 + 4 Days = Day #13.

CALCULATING THE LATEST STARTING AND FINISHING TIMES

Recall that we abbreviate Latest Finishing Time to LFT in this text. Knowing the Project Finishing Day, we calculate backward from the END milestone to sequentially calculate the Latest Finishing Times for each task. The LFT of any task is the LST of its follower task(s). This calculation is often called "The Backward Pass."

LATEST STARTING TIME = (Latest Finishing Time) – (Its Duration)
LST for Task #6 = End of Day 19 – 2 days
= End of Day 17

Ensure that these concepts are clear by studying the Gantt Chart in Figure 6–3, because we shall apply these same rules to calculations on the Bubble (AON) diagram. The technique used with the Arrow diagram is very similar.

THE RULES FOR TIME CALCULATIONS ON BUBBLE DIAGRAMS

The "Forward" Calculation for Earliest Start Times (EST)

Follow this discussion on the example AON diagrams of Figures 6–4 and 6–5. For any task (for example, we will call it Task "i"), its Start Time and its Duration determines when it finishes:

Earliest Finishing Time = (Earliest Starting Time) + (Duration)
$EFT_i = EST_i + DUR$ of i

and the next following task begins as soon as its predecessor is finished:

Earliest Starting Time of a Task = Earliest Finishing Time of its preceding Task

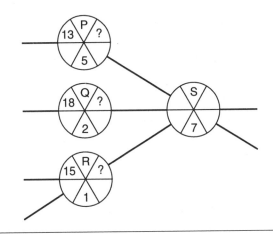

Figure 6–4   Earliest Finishing Time of a Task.

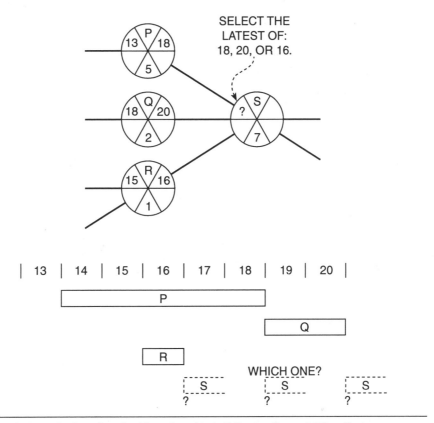

Figure 6–5   Earliest Starting Time for a Task Following Several Other Tasks.

that is,

$$EST_j = EFT_i$$

But, when more than one task precedes, select the task with the *latest* EFT.

These rules can be visualized using Bubbles and their corresponding Gantt Charts for each case. Study the Gantt Chart in Figure 6–5.

"Latest Times" Calculation on an AON Diagram

The **"Backward" Calculation** is illustrated in Figure 6–6. For Task E, for example:

(Latest Starting Time) = (Latest Finishing Time) minus (its Duration)

that is,

$$LST_B = LFT_B - \text{DURATION OF Task "B"}$$

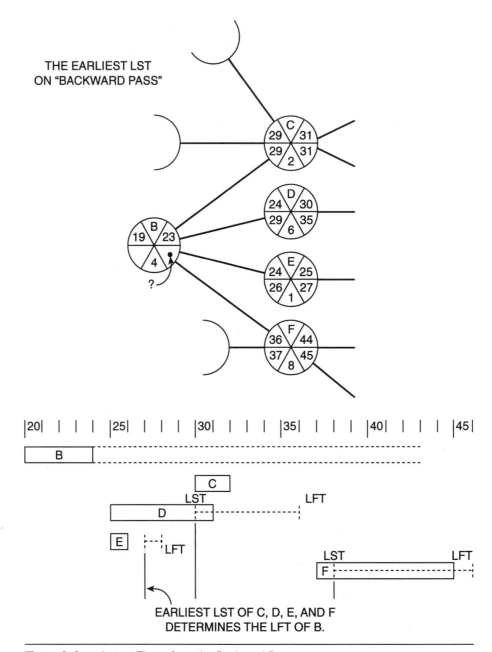

THE EARLIEST LST ON "BACKWARD PASS"

EARLIEST LST OF C, D, E, AND F
DETERMINES THE LFT OF B.

Figure 6–6   Latest Times from the Backward Pass.

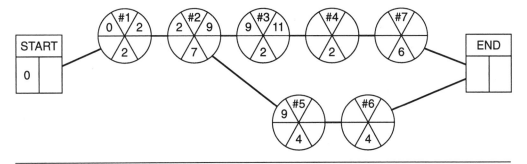

Figure 6–7   Earliest Times from the Forward Pass Calculation.

When several tasks must follow a task in the network, you must consider all their Late Starting Times before deciding which one governs the latest finishing time of the task they all follow. When working backward through a network, remember that time still goes forward through the network even though you are working backward through it. None of the several following tasks can begin until the preceding one has finished; therefore, the task having the *earliest* Late Starting Time determines the Late Finishing Time of a predecessor.

Latest Finishing Time = Earliest of the Latest Starting Times of the several tasks following the task. Therefore, LFT_B = Earliest of the LST of C, D, E, or F. In Figure 6–6, Day 24 is the Earliest LST of its followers.

When you are calculating directly on a Bubble Diagram, discipline your mind to remember the patterns of the bubble segments used in the calculation. Continue to ask yourself questions such as "Which is the last task to finish (so I can select its EFT for the EST of this next task)?"

The bubble diagram for the seven-task Roofing sub-project is shown in Figure 6–7 with some of its Early times calculated. Check these times and fill in the remaining EST's by completing the calculation.

Similarly, several of the LATEST times from the "Backward Pass" are shown on the AON diagram (Figure 6–8). You should check these and complete the calculation as before. Note that we begin at the END using the project's duration (19 days) derived from the "Forward Pass" calculation.

Once you have become familiar with the process, you should find the following slogans useful during the calculations on an AON Diagram:

Forward Pass Calculation: "LATEST OF THE EARLY FINISHERS"

Backward Pass Calculation: "EARLIEST OF THE LATE STARTERS"

FLOAT

We noted after presenting the first Gantt Chart (Figure 6–2), that tasks #5 and #6 have flexible scheduling periods and we introduced the term "FLOAT." We noted that Task #6 could finish as late as Day 19, instead of its regular earliest finish time

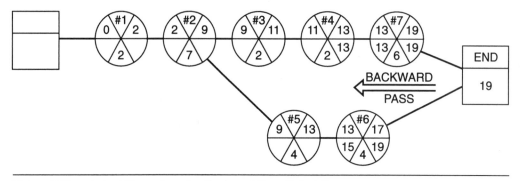

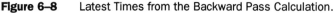

Figure 6–8   Latest Times from the Backward Pass Calculation.

of Day 17. This task is said to have a FLOAT of two days, which would allow it to be scheduled to finish on any one of Days 17, 18, or 19. This scheduling flexibility is called **Total Float** (TF), which is the difference between its EST and LST. Task #5 also has 2 days of Total Float.

However, there are special circumstances that relate to Task #5. Just because it has two days of Total Float does not allow it to be rescheduled without considering the scheduling of Task #6. If Task #5 is allowed to start one day late, it will end on Day 14 and it will clash with Task #6, which was supposed to start on Day 13.

In order to warn us of potential clashes like this one, we define a second type of float that is more restrictive than the one described above: it is called **Free Float** (FF) and it is the amount of time available for rescheduling a task WITHOUT AFFECTING THE SCHEDULE OF ANY OTHER TASKS. In the above network, Task #6 could be delayed two days without affecting the schedule (FF=2). But if Task #5 were delayed (from its EST), Task #6 would also have to be delayed; thus Task #5 has ZERO FREE FLOAT. Both have TF=2. These terms are illustrated on the Bubble Diagram and Gantt Chart in Figure 6–9.

Note that the FF is a special case of TF. There may be a long string of tasks having the same Total Float, but the last one's Free Float will depend on the EST of the task following it. The FF of all the preceding tasks in the string of tasks will be zero. A task's FF can never be larger than its TF.

THE CRITICAL PATH

Float is a measure of the flexibility available for re-scheduling a task or a string of tasks making up a path through the network. We have studied the path having a TF of two days but we must now focus on the other path where the TF is ZERO. If the duration of any one of those tasks (1, 2, 3, 4, and 7) were increased by one day, the duration of the project would be extended by one day. Therefore, these five tasks are

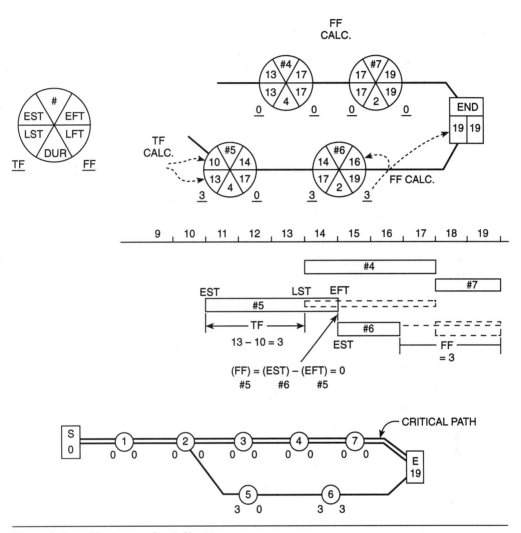

Figure 6–9   Floats on a Gantt Chart.

critical to the duration of the project and the "path" through them is called the **Critical Path.** It is the path through the tasks having ZERO TOTAL FLOAT.

This concept is central to an appreciation of scheduling, because the duration of the project is sensitive to the duration of each critical task. The duration of such tasks should be scrutinized in the planning stage and monitored closely during construction to protect the schedule. Often critical tasks (TF=0) can be accelerated to shorten a project's duration.

The critical path should always be identified on a network diagram. On an AON network, the links can be drawn as double lines, as shown in Figure 6–9. Care must be taken not to ignore other paths that have low values of float which can become critical if a few days are lost during construction. Tasks assessed as having unreliable estimated durations require more study to reduce the risks. The PERT system (see Chapter 11) is useful for identifying this risk.

TIME CALCULATIONS ON ARROW NETWORKS

We have found that the AON network and the AOA network for the same set of tasks are quite different, even though they describe the same project. With Arrow networks, we focus our attention on events rather than activities. Task Arrows are identified by the event numbers at each end; the Project TIMES of those events are the objective of the calculation, rather than the Start and Finish Times of the tasks. In many ways the time calculations for an Arrow network are much simpler, but an AOA diagram also has its idiosyncrasies.

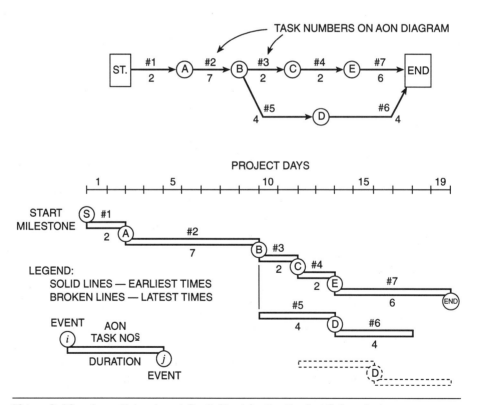

Figure 6–10   Arrow Network and Gantt Chart for the Roofing Sub-project.

The Arrow network for our ROOFING sub-project in Figure 6–10 evolves from the precedence information in Figure 6–1. Its corresponding Gantt Chart is included for reference. For emphasis, we have marked the events on the Gantt Chart, using the same "numbering" as on the AOA Diagram. We have used the alphabet to name the events to lessen confusion with the numerical information copied from the AON network. The Start and End milestones are treated as regular events.

EARLIEST TIME OF AN EVENT

When calculating times on an Arrow Diagram it is helpful to *not* think about Bubble Diagrams. You must concentrate on events, which often do not correspond

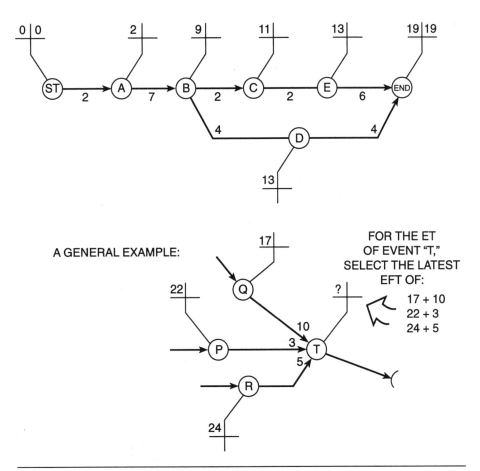

Figure 6–11   The Early Time of an Event in an Arrow Network.

to the EST's and EFT's of the tasks. We will show how to obtain these Start and Finish Times a little later.

The EARLIEST TIME of an event is readily determined by adding the duration of the intervening task to the Early Time of the preceding event. Figure 6–11 shows the method. When there are multiple task-arrows terminating at the event, use the latest (largest) EFT of the preceding tasks (ET & DUR).

LATEST TIME OF AN EVENT

After determining the EARLIEST TIME of the last event, which is the END Milestone of the project, make the Backward Calculation through the Arrow network. The LATEST TIME of preceding events is simply the LATEST TIME of the current event *minus* the duration of the preceding task. In Figure 6–12, the LT of Event "E" is Day 19 – 2 = Day 17. When there are several task-arrows leaving the target event, select the earliest (smallest) LATE START TIME: the LT of Task "B" is determined from the earlier of the LST's of tasks "C" or "D."

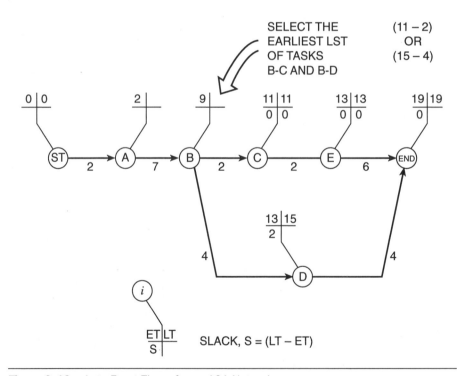

Figure 6–12 Late Event Times for an AOA Network.

SLACK TIME

The tasks of Bubble networks have FLOAT and the events of Arrow Diagrams have SLACK. These terms are not the same but we shall find a way to relate them.

Slack is simply the difference between the LATEST TIME and the EARLIEST TIME of an event. For example, the date of Easter Sunday occurs on the first Sunday after the first full moon that follows the Spring Equinox. Since there is a new moon every 29 or 30 days, Easter Sunday can occur only between March 22 and April 25; therefore, for any year, the TIME for Easter Sunday would have a SLACK TIME of 35 days.

If a task arrow connects two events, each with zero slack, then that task is critical; but if one of those events has some slack, the task has float. If both events have slack then the task's float needs closer scrutiny.

In Figure 6–13, only a portion of a larger network is shown; the ET's and LT's of both events were determined by other tasks of the complete network.

The earliest time the task can begin is on Day 6 and therefore its earliest finishing time is on Day 11 (6 + 5), which is derived by adding the duration to the ET. The latest that the task could end is Day 19 and therefore its Total Float is 8 days (19 – 11). A more direct calculation is made by subtracting the Duration (D) from the difference between the LT at the arrowhead from the ET at the start of the task:

$$\text{TOTAL FLOAT} = (LT_j - ET_i) - D_{ij}$$

Recall that FREE FLOAT is the amount a task can be delayed without affecting the schedule of any subsequent task. For this example, the task could end as late as Day 12, the ET of its terminating event, without delaying the start of a subsequent task. Since its Earliest Finishing Time was Day 11 (above), the task has a FREE FLOAT of 1 day. The formula for making the calculation subtracts the duration from the difference between the ET's:

$$\text{FREE FLOAT} = (ET_j - ET_i) - D_{ij}$$

Note that the LT of the first event ("i") does not affect the values of the floats; that is, if Event "i" has zero slack, the task is not critical unless Event "j" also has zero slack. In that case, the task would be critical. Observe also that the difference between Total and Free Float is the difference between the LT and ET of the last event ("j"), which is the slack of Event "j." This should be used for checking your float calculations.

$$(\text{TOTAL FLOAT})_{ij} - (\text{FREE FLOAT})_{ij} = (LT_j - ET_i - D_{ij}) - (ET_j - ET_i - D_{ij})$$
$$= (LT_j - ET_j)$$

Thus, when indicating the Critical Path of *tasks* through an Arrow network (Figure 6–14) we must ensure that the tasks actually have zero float by ensuring

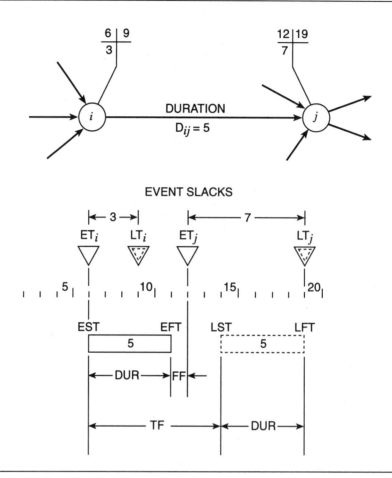

Figure 6–13   Task Floats and Event Slack.

that *both events* of a task arrow have zero slack. In order to mark an unbroken line through the project, it may be necessary to mark dummy tasks as part of the critical path (CP) in tracing through all the events with zero slack.

RELATIONSHIPS BETWEEN AON AND AOA RESULTS

Both ways of drawing the networks produce the same schedule for the tasks of a project; the critical tasks are the same and the durations of the project are the same. The AON produces the times for the tasks while the AOA produces times for the events and the results from one type can be transformed into the results of the other. The Early Time of an event will be the same as the Earliest Start Time for all of the tasks starting at that event.

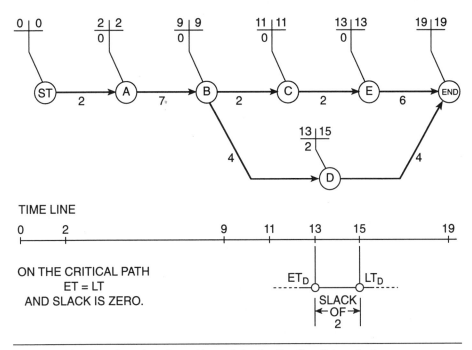

Figure 6–14   The Complete Arrow Network for the Roofing Sub-project.

The floats of a task (ij) are readily found by first evaluating the EFT of a task ($ET_i + DUR_{ij}$) and subtracting it from either the ET_j for the Free Float, or the LT_j for the Total Float.

For the example project in Figure 6–14, the EFT of task BD is 13 (9 + 4); the Free Float is $ET_D - DUR_{BD}$ (13 – 13), which is zero; the Total Float is $LT_D - DUR_{BD}$ (15 – 13), which is 2.

THE WAREHOUSE PROJECT: AON and AOA NETWORKS

The Precedence Matrix for the Warehouse construction was developed in Chapter 4 and the durations for its tasks were determined in Chapter 5 and above, in this chapter, for the ROOF sub-project. Once the durations are recorded on the elements of the networks, the calculations can be quite quickly but carefully done. See Figures 6–15 and 6–16.

Manual calculations are best done by selecting the numbers to be added (or subtracted) based on a pattern rather than by trying to think through the construction processes. Figure 6–17 shows these useful patterns. But it is also a good practice to continually remind yourself of the basic definitions of the terms that you are calculating.

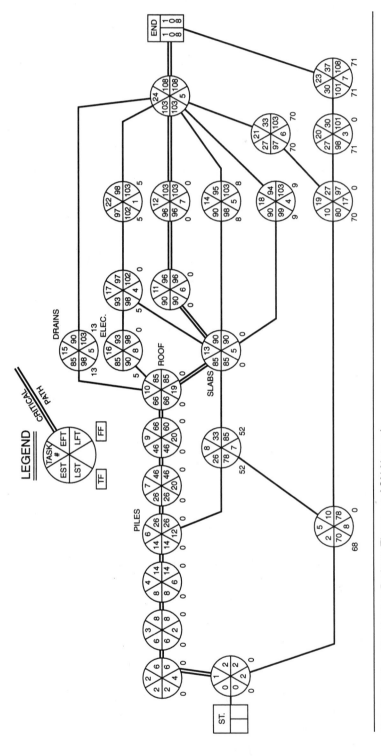

Figure 6–15 Warehouse Project: Times on AON Network.

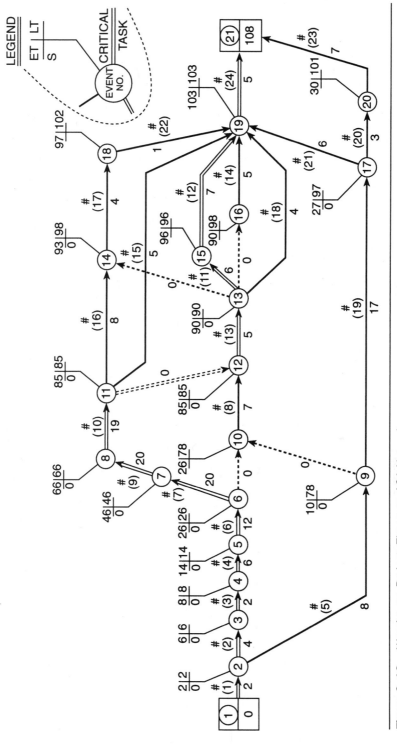

Figure 6–16 Warehouse Project: Times on AOA Network.

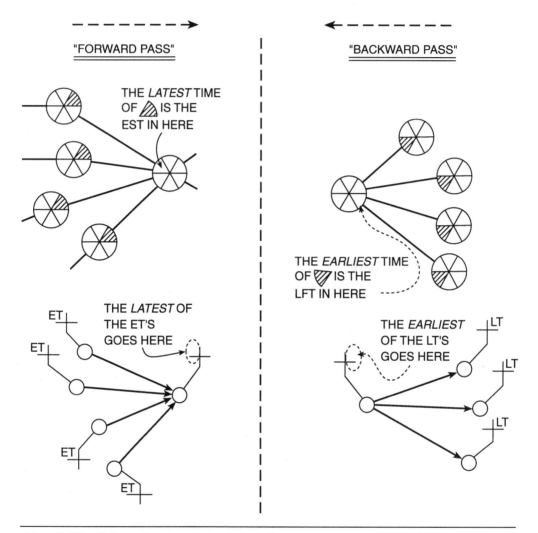

Figure 6–17 Patterns for Manual Time Calculations.

SUMMARY

We have presented a number of important new techniques that will require practice to master. The concept of scheduled time periods for a task with its early and late start times defined its Total and Free Float. The events and task-arrows of the AOA network may have been an abrupt departure from the apparent simplicity of the Bubble Diagram. The AOA system has advantages that can outweigh its idiosyncrasies in applications later in this book, for example, the PERT system, which is covered in Chapter 11.

EXERCISES AND PROBLEMS

1. For the ROOF SUB-PROJECT (Figure 6–1) insert the following revised durations for its seven tasks and recalculate all Times on the Bubble Diagram, including both types of Floats.

Task	Duration
1	4
2	8
3	2
4	4
5	12
6	6
7	7

2. Repeat Problem 1 but use the Arrow Diagram for the sub-project (Figure 6–10). Compare the Floats (TF and FF), obtained from the AON and AOA calculations.
3. Draw the Gantt Chart for the revised sub-project, showing the earliest and latest time slots for each task, and indicate the Total and Free Floats for each task.
4. For the 24-Task Model of the Warehouse project, redraw the AON and AOA Networks and insert the revised durations listed. Recalculate the Times and Floats for each and compare the Floats from each calculation.

**WAREHOUSE PROJECT REVISED DURATIONS FOR 24-TASK MODEL—
SPECIAL VALUES FOR PROBLEM 4 (CHAPTER 6)**

Task	Revised Duration	Task	Revised Duration
1	3	13	5
2	6	14	6
3	1	15	4
4	6	16	10
5	15	17	7
6	16	18	7
7	15	19	28
8	20	20	8
9	15	21	9
10	13	22	4
11	6	23	12
12	5	24	4

7

DELAYS AND OTHER CONSTRAINTS

LEARNING OBJECTIVES

After completing this chapter, you should be able to:

- Estimate, from weather records, the probability of adverse working conditions occurring during a particular type of work.
- Estimate the number of days a task's effective duration is expected to be extended due to the chance of adverse conditions.
- Calculate the delay expected from a combination of several adverse working conditions occurring simultaneously.
- Incorporate Series and Parallel Dummy tasks into AON and AOA networks.

PREPARATION FOR THIS CHAPTER

You will have developed your first draft schedule using the network, durations, and methods covered in the previous several chapters. You must be familiar enough with the processes of every task to decide which will be sensitive to external conditions outside of your control: for example, "Will rain prevent or slow down excavation?" or "Do I expect that the temperature will be too cold (or too hot) to pour and cure concrete?"

You must be comfortable with making tabular calculations because we shall assemble data and make calculations using a spreadsheet format.

INTRODUCTION

The scheduling procedures presented in this book are based on the idea of starting with a simple basic schedule and developing it into a realistic one by adding real-life complexities, one at a time.

We begin with a first draft of a schedule; it is comprised of only construction tasks that were chosen to describe the project. At first sight, this may appear to be sufficient to schedule a project, but in actuality it fails to consider many time-consuming effects that will extend the duration of the project. Such things as the acquisition of materials, labor problems, and uncooperative weather can cause delays.

The effects of items such as these can be represented by artificial "tasks" to account for the time they might consume in delaying actual construction tasks. These "dummy" tasks and their estimated durations will be inserted into the basic network to produce a more realistic schedule. The dummies representing these effects will enlarge the initial network and complicate the schedule.

SCHEDULING CONTINGENCY

Many construction contractors include a time cushion at the end of the schedule to account for time slippage and other delays that creep into the project; it is called a "contingency" allowance. This is a realistic approach for dealing with unforeseen problems, but when weather conditions are expected to disrupt progress, it is prudent to identify sensitive tasks and allow for them in the schedule.

Anticipating specific phenomena allows you to prepare alternate plans to offset their effects should they occur. To ignore conditions that are likely to occur is foolhardy, because surprises can lead to increased direct and overhead costs. For example, interest at 7% on $1,000,000 for two weeks is $2,700. Added to this is the increased cost of labor that results from the attempt to make up for lost time. Surprises cause confusion and reduce profit. Granted, preparing alternative plans costs extra money, but it should be evaluated as a trade-off against the chance of the problem actually occurring. Mindful of contingencies, military planning requires that a "Plan B" always be ready for deployment.

This chapter deals primarily with delays caused by bad weather; suggestions for dealing with other interruptions are mentioned at the end of the chapter. A separate chapter is devoted to scheduling the acquisition of the resources required for executing each task: materials, equipment, labor, and so forth. Adding artificial delays can help to clarify schedules when certain tasks display excessive floats.

USING DELAYS REDUCES EXCESS FLOAT

We can introduce the use of dummy tasks into the network by dealing with the case in which a task with a large float needs to be scheduled into a more specific time slot. A useful schedule should be more specific so that the manager knows when a certain task will be done within narrower time limits than calculated from the initial network. Tasks with huge floats can lose their importance and be treated lightly by sub-contractors.

Consider a task to build an access road; it has 62 days of float for 8 days of work. The manager can schedule this task into a more attractive time slot by adding a pair of dummy "tasks" into the network to reduce the calculated float to a practical value. This modified network produces revised times (and a smaller float) for the job, thereby improving the working schedule. This action may seem artificial, but it represents a manager's control over the schedule: tasks are "scheduled" into better time periods. Once the manager has dealt with it, he can move on.

For the road project, let us assume that the 8-day task can be scheduled to start sometime between May 16 and August 25, which represents a total float of 62 working days. Figure 7–1 shows this on a time line.

The manager prefers a more specific start time in early July, when the site is not so busy and the weather should be more reliable. This float can be reduced from 62 days to (say) 12 days by incorporating 50 days in two dummy tasks: one before the construction task (that schedules its EST to early July) and another after it (to reduce the float to 12 days). The manager added a dummy of 35 days to delay the EST to July 5 and a 15-day dummy before the next successor task to advance the LFT to August 22.

The first dummy task "lags" the start by 35 days and the second one "leads" the initial Latest Finish Time by 15 days, to August 22; this refinement has been called "Incorporating LAGS and LEADS."

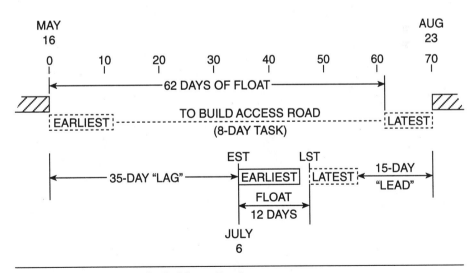

Figure 7–1   Time Line for Building a Road.

WEATHER DELAYS

Predicting the weather is the realm of atmospheric scientists. Their work relies on theories of movement of large masses of air. Mathematical models of the atmosphere are programmed into huge computers and, when combined with actual measured properties of the air, result in weather forecasts for the next few days. The masses of data collected over several years also define the average weather for every day, week, and month of the year for most parts of the world. This history of the weather defines the climate.

Historical weather records provide average conditions of precipitation, temperature, and wind for any day of the year. Specific forecasts provide the chance of certain weather conditions occurring in the short term based on actual current conditions: for example, "There is a 70 percent chance of heavy rain tomorrow." The weather is of such concern to so many different parts of the population that television Weather Channels have significant commercial value. "Good" weather is a boon to the travel industry and all types of "bad" weather have special significance to contractors.

Construction companies with contracts to build oil refineries in different parts of the world rely on weather and climatic data when they plan their projects. Building conditions in Saudi Arabia, Northern Canada, or near the Gulf of Mexico have radically different climates and plans for projects must be tailored to the unique local conditions for their projected construction dates.

Bad Weather

"Bad weather" describes weather conditions that interfere with our planned activities. Some activities can proceed but others cannot. Some are slowed down while others are shut down. What is good weather for some is bad weather for others. Rain and cold can make the workplace dangerous for some tasks; and even when work can continue, the bad weather slows down workers physically and psychologically and their productivity falls. Government regulations prevent high riggers from working in high winds. When the temperature is too high, without protection concrete can dry before it sets, some metal parts cannot be assembled, and paint will not dry properly. Extremes of weather cause problems and either the work is delayed or special protection must be provided: both cost money and many consume time.

WEATHER STATISTICS

The table in Figure 7–2 lists the historical (40-year) average number of days of rain for each month of the year for a West Coast city. The number of bad days per month are converted to probability (percent) by dividing by the number of days in the month. The probability of GOOD days is the difference between 100% and the probability of BAD days. January had 18 rainy days out of a monthly total of 31

AVERAGE MONTHLY RAINY DAYS
(Typical for the Pacific Northwest Region)

MONTH	NUMBER OF BAD DAYS	PROBABILITY OF BAD DAYS (Percent)	PROBABILITY OF GOOD DAYS (Decimal Fraction)
January	18	58%	0.42
February	16	57%	0.43
March	16	52%	0.48
April	13	42%	0.58
May	10	33%	0.67
June	11	37%	0.63
July	5	16%	0.64
August	7	23%	0.77
September	8	27%	0.73
October	13	42%	0.58
November	17	57%	0.43
December	19	61%	0.39
AVERAGE	153	42%	0.58

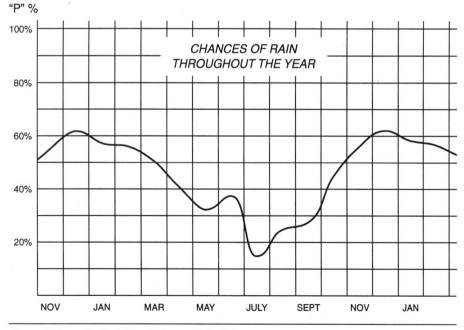

PROBABILITY OF "BAD" DAYS

Figure 7–2   Probability of Measurable Rain.

days. When 18 is divided by 31, the result shows that there was a 58 percent chance of rain, which translates into a 42 percent chance of good weather (100% − 58%).

Thus, on any day in January there will be a better than 50-50 chance of rain, making January not a good month to dig an excavation or deck a roof. Not until April could you expect to have more "good" days than "bad" ones. Even though there is no guarantee that the weather next January will follow this statistical pattern, you can reasonably expect that your work will be affected by rain more than half the time.

These statistics relate to *measurable* rain, which includes light drizzle, occasional showers, and downpours. Based on the sensitivity of a particular task, you will need to make subjective decisions for allowing higher probabilities for good weather from the above data. When scheduling work in January, you must take into consideration that outside painting cannot be done in any sort of rain (42% Good Days), whereas pouring concrete foundations can be done in even moderate rain (say, 70% Good Days). Fine finishing of concrete slabs may be allowed in only a light drizzle (say, 55% Good Days).

Estimating the effect of weather on a task is not an exact science, but you need to allow for *expected* bad weather to produce a more realistic schedule with fewer surprises. The average weather quoted for a particular month (say, January) means that for every January when the weather is better than normal, there will be another January when the weather will be worse.

ESTIMATING A WEATHER DELAY

The probability of bad weather in a month does not differentiate between holidays and working days; the 58% for January applies to any day in January. During the whole month of January (31 days), on average there should be 18 days of rain. There are 17 working days in January (accounting for holidays and weekends), and we should expect (on average) to have 10 rainy days (58% of 17) and 7 days without rain to do our work (42% of 17 or 17 − 10).

These average conditions do not guarantee that there will be only 7 days available for work on sensitive tasks. "Average" means a 50% probability of having 7 days; there could be more or fewer, but the average is 7. Actual records show that there has never (yet) been a January when there were fewer than 3, or more than 29, rainy days; the average is 18 days (58%).

BUILDING THE ROOF IN JANUARY—AN INTRODUCTORY EXAMPLE

Before considering all the weather effects, let us see the effect of only one. For the "Roofing" sub-project, the superintendent has reported that the Decking requires 5 non-raining days for safety. Let us assume that it was scheduled to begin on

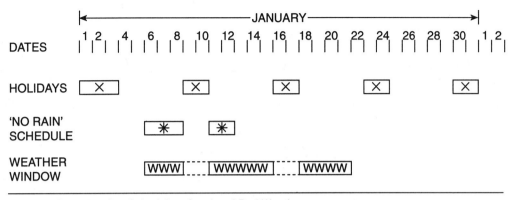

Figure 7–3   Roofing Schedule—Good and Bad Weather.

Wednesday, January 6, at 8:00 A.M. The time-line in Figure 7–3 shows the dates, holidays (X), and the working schedule (*) for the 5-day Decking task.

THE WEATHER WINDOW

The objective of the first calculation finds what we call the **"Weather Window"** (symbol **"W-W"**), which is the total number of GOOD plus BAD days needed to accomplish a task. We want to estimate how many GOOD days we can expect in the period of average January weather. Historical records suggest that it will rain for 58% of the period in January when we wish to this job; therefore, 42% of the period will be "GOOD" days available for Decking. And, since we need 5 GOOD days: $0.42 \times$ (W-W) = 5 Good Days.

Recalling a bit of algebra, the duration of this Weather Window (W-W) is calculated by *dividing* the required number of Good Days (duration of the task), by the probability of GOOD weather.

(W-W) = $5 \div 0.42$ = 12 days of average January weather

Checking the calculation to make sure:

Time for working on the task: 12×0.42 = 5 days

and

Time for rain: 12×0.58 = 7 days

The duration of the Weather Window is shown (WWWWW) on the last line of the bar chart. Thus, we should allow for 12 working days in order to complete the Decking task on the roof; it could start as early as 8:00 A.M. Wednesday, January 6, and should be completed by the end of January 21. We do not know which days may be rained out, but we expect, **on average**, that we will not complete the task until January 21, with 7 days of rain scattered throughout that period.

INCLUDE ALL WEATHER-SENSITIVE TASKS

We should include all weather-sensitive tasks in the analysis so that we can evaluate the overall effect for the total project. This may seem pessimistic and artificial, but recall that according to the 40-year weather records, the weather was worse for 20 of the Januarys and better for the other 20. The January of our schedule could have better or worse weather than the average quoted here.

The uncertainty about the duration of lost working time should not cause concern when a long project is being planned. Some months will be good for work and others will not. The lost time caused by extra delays during one especially bad month could be gained back by tasks carried out during another especially good month. However, the duration of a short project will be more at the mercy of the weather because there will be fewer opportunities for compensating savings of time.

COMBINED CONDITIONS

The previous example considered one task with one weather constraint. How can we deal with several conditions that affect a task?

Wind would also interfere with the decking activity and determining its effect is straightforward. If there is a 15% probability of excessive wind during January, then we apply this factor to the actual days when work would be progressing on the deck. We are not concerned if the wind blows on rainy days when there is no work, just on the days when the crew is on the roof. We have assumed that these two weather conditions are unrelated, which may be only partly true.

Thus a Weather Window for wind is: $5 \div 0.85 = 6$ days, which means that there would be a one-day delay due to wind. When we combine several effects, we must be careful to accumulate only the *delays* incurred and *not* the Weather Windows which include work days and "BAD" days.

For combined rain and wind, the total *delay* is $(7 + 1) = 8$ days.

The Weather Window resulting from both effects is the Duration of the Task *plus* the Total Weather Delay from all effects.

$$W\text{-}W = DUR + D_R + D_W + \ldots \ldots$$

Thus

$$\text{TOTAL WEATHER WINDOW} = 5 + (7 + 1) = 13 \text{ days}$$

MECHANIZED CALCULATIONS (Tabulated on a Spreadsheet)

The possibility of confusing a Weather Window with a Delay will decrease with familiarity with the concept. In order to reduce thinking to a minimum, it is valuable to mechanize these calculations and calculate the DELAYS directly. We will use the following symbols for conciseness:

Where "W-W" means Weather Window

"DUR" is the Duration of the Task

"p"   is the probability of BAD conditions; there can be any number of conditions affecting a task.

and   "D"   is the Delay.

A formula for calculating the total weather delay appears below. "F" is an intermediate result, useful for the calculations. Only three weather conditions appear in the formula; additional conditions would just extend the formula.

$$F = [\{p/(1-p)\}_{RAIN} + \{p/(1-p)\}_{WIND} + \{p/(1-p)\}_{other}]$$
and the Total Delay, "D" = F × DUR
and the Total Weather Window, "W-W" = DUR + D

Repetitive calculations such as these are less prone to errors and are easier to check if the data and the calculations are recorded on a worksheet, such as Figures 7–4 and 7–7A.

INCORPORATING WEATHER EFFECTS INTO THE NETWORKS

The SERIES Case

In the simplest case, the dummy task for a DELAY is inserted into a network *after* its related construction task; that is, it is placed in SERIES with it. It acts like an extension of the task, keeping the EST unchanged but allowing more time for it to get finished. It is misleading to place it before the task, because that would imply that the task cannot start until the weather delay occurs. The task should be scheduled to start on its original EST but may require more days to be completed. The delay actually adds in a few days of float to a weather-sensitive task and it is more conventional to place the delay after its task.

> **WARNING:** *Never* change the duration of the construction task to include the delay. That would alter the allocation of resources to the task. Delays consume no construction resources and must be incorporated as separate dummy "tasks." A 5-day task that consumes $1,000 in materials still consumes $1,000 in materials even when 12 days are assigned for its completion because of bad weather.

Any construction tasks originally following the weather-sensitive task must be linked to the end of the delay, *not* to the task. *Before* and *After* cases for Bubble (AON) Diagrams are illustrated in Figure 7–5.

SPREADSHEET FOR TABULAR CALCULATIONS OF WEATHER DELAYS

TASK IDENTIFICATION		DUR'N	INITIAL EST	MID DATE OF TASK	PROBABILITY OF *BAD* CONDITIONS				TOTAL FACTOR	TOTAL DELAY	WEATHER WINDOW
NO.	NAME				DECIMAL FRACTIONS						
					p1	p2	p3	p4			
①	②	③	④	⑤	⑥	⑦	⑧	⑨	⑩	⑪	⑫

COLUMNS ①, ②, ③, & ④ ARE BASIC DATA

COLUMN ⑤ IS ⑤ = {0.5 × ③} + ④ CONVERTED TO CALENDAR DATE

COLUMNS ⑥, ⑦, ⑧, & ⑨ ARE YOUR INTERPRETATION OF WEATHER FORECASTS AND THE SENSITIVITY OF THE TASKS TO THEM.

$$\text{COLUMN } ⑩ = \left\{ \frac{⑥}{1.0 - ⑥} + \frac{⑦}{1.0 - ⑦} + \frac{⑧}{1.0 - ⑧} + \frac{⑨}{1.0 - ⑨} + \frac{\cdots}{\cdots} + \frac{\cdots}{\cdots} \text{ etc.} \right\}$$

COLUMN ⑪ = ③ × ⑩

COLUMN ⑫ = ③ + ⑪

Figure 7–4   Columns Needed for Tabular Calculations.

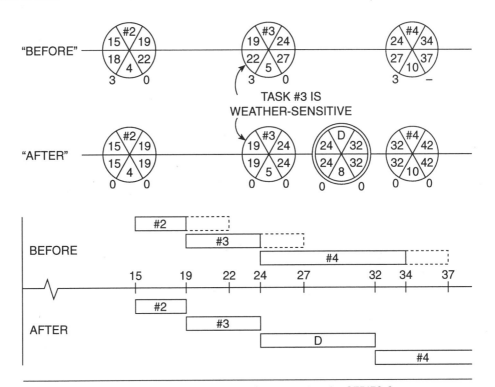

Figure 7–5   Placing Weather Delays into AON Networks: the SERIES Case.

The PARALLEL Case

When a string of linked tasks are all weather-sensitive, their total delay can be combined into one DELAY at the end of the group as though the group were a sub-project. This single delay is preferable to incorporating an individual delay for each one of the sensitive tasks. However, there is an alternative method (and often a better one) that brackets the group with a single Weather Window (rather than a delay) placed parallel to the group of sensitive tasks. Figure 7–6 shows the method, which emphasizes the total effect of the delay by showing the Weather Window in which the tasks must be completed.

This is called the PARALLEL METHOD because it introduces a new path parallel to the sensitive tasks. The Weather Window has a duration equal to the sum of the durations of the tasks it straddles plus the combined delays of the tasks. On Bubble Diagrams, the Weather Window "task" is linked to the tasks preceding and following the string, not to the end tasks in the string. If the original tasks were on the critical path, the CP now passes through the Weather Window because its duration is greater than through the string of tasks it parallels.

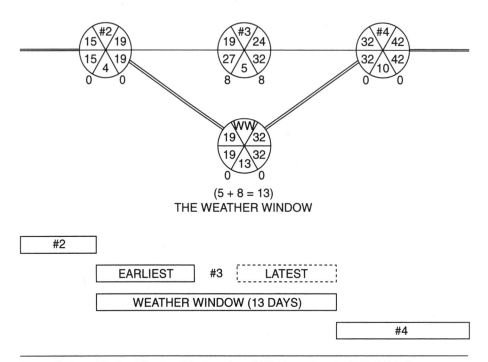

Figure 7–6   Placing Weather Windows into AON Networks: the PARALLEL Case.

This method draws attention to the fact that the Weather Window contributes to the duration of the project. For a SERIES weather delay, it is not always clear which tasks contribute to the weather delay.

APPLYING THE METHOD TO THE ROOFING SUB-CONTRACT

After studying the seven tasks of this small project, it was decided that the Trusses(1), Overhang(5), and Flashing(7) were sensitive to wind; Vapor Barrier(3) and Cladding(4) were sensitive to rain; Vapor Barrier(3), Cladding(4), and Flashing(7) were sensitive to low temperatures. The Decking(2) and Soffits(6) were not sensitive to any of these weather conditions.

The probabilities for these weather conditions to occur during the construction tasks in January were determined and entered into the spreadsheet (Figure 7–7A). These calculations may be done manually using the format of Figure 7–4, but the results for this example, shown in Figure 7–7A, were calculated "automatically" using a popular computer spreadsheet program.

The modified Bubble Diagram is shown in Figure 7–7B. A delay is added after tasks #1 and #5 and a single Weather Window brackets tasks #3, #4, and #7. If

COMPUTER SPREADSHEET FOR TABULAR CALCULATIONS OF WEATHER DELAYS

a	b	c	d	e	f	g	h	i	j	k	l
TASK IDENTIFICATION		DUR'N	INITIAL EST	MID DATE OF TASK	PROBABILITY OF BAD CONDITIONS				TOTAL FACTOR	TOTAL DELAY	WEATHER WINDOW
NO	NAME										
1	TRUSSES	2	0	1	0	.15		0	0	0	2
2	DECKING	7	2	5.5		.15			0	1	8
3	VAP BARR	2	9	10	.58	.15	.2		2	4	6
4	CLADDING	2	11	12	.58		.2		2	3	5
5	OVERHANG	4	9	11		.15			0	1	5
6	SOFFITS	4	13	15					0	0	4
7	FLASHING	6	13	16		.15	.2		0	3	9

Note: The computer uses the fractional values calculated for "j".

Where Total Factor, "j" = f/(1-f) + g/(1-g) + h/(1-h) + i/(1-i);

Total Delay, "k" = (c × j)

Weather Window, "l" = (c + k)

Figure 7–7A Calculation for the Roofing Sub-project.

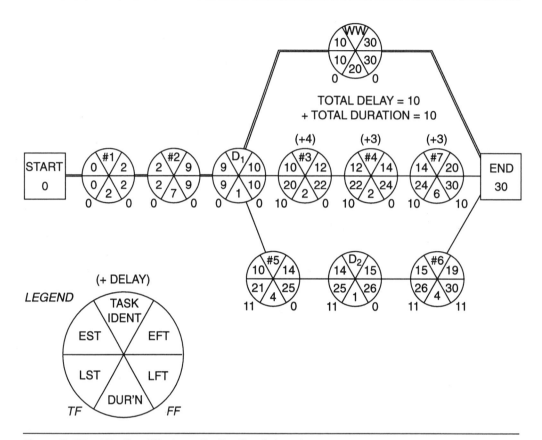

Figure 7–7B   Weather Effects on the Roofing Sub-project.

task #2 had a weather delay, it would have to be incorporated as an individual delay; it could not become part of the Weather Window because task #5 is also dependent on the duration of task #2.

Note that the Critical Path passes through the Weather Window, which draws attention to the tasks it brackets. You might prefer to place a single delay of 9 days after task #7 instead of using the Weather Window, but the emphasis will be weaker if you do.

MODIFICATIONS TO ARROW (AOA) NETWORK DIAGRAMS

Incorporating Delays or Windows into an AOA network is a little different than the methods described above. A dummy DELAY arrow is drawn after the sensitive task, requiring one new event. When a Weather Window encloses a string of several tasks, its dummy arrow connects the events bordering the string. If you

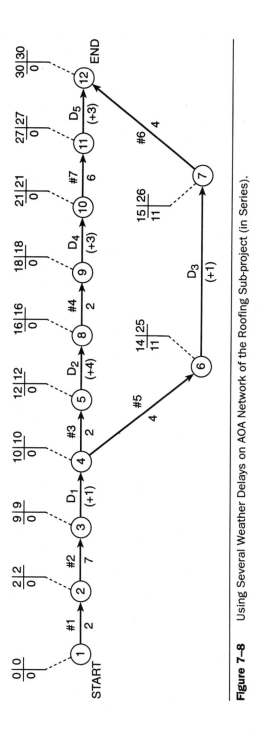

Figure 7–8 Using Several Weather Delays on AOA Network of the Roofing Sub-project (in Series).

want to place a Weather Window dummy parallel to a single task you will need to add another event to prevent the new dummy task from having the same event identity as its related construction task. Recall that only one arrow can connect two events.

Modifications to the AOA network for the Roofing sub-project are shown in Figure 7–8. Note the additional events required and compare the Delay Method (in series) with the Weather Window (in parallel). The Weather Window for the string of tasks #3, #4, & #7 is included for comparison with the modified AON network case (see Figure 7–9). No extra event is needed because the weather window arrow straddles more than one task arrow.

OTHER KINDS OF DELAYS

A schedule is a statement of a plan for organizing clearly defined construction tasks and statistically expected phenomena like the weather. Minor unpredictable effects can be allowed for with a contingency factor. There can be another class of effects that will delay a project: forest closures due to a summer fire hazard, religious observances that affect construction sites in different parts of the world, strikes resulting from breakdowns in bargaining, and wild-cat strikes. Some of these can be anticipated and others cannot.

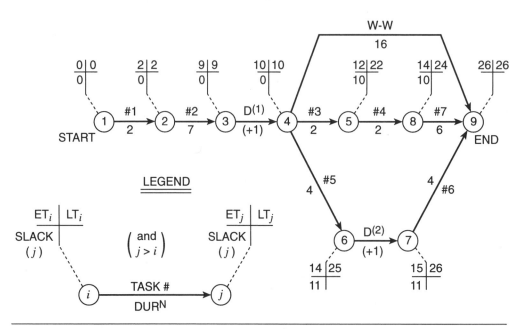

Figure 7–9   Using a Weather Window on AOA Network of the Roofing Sub-project.

In most cases, the duration of such happenings cannot be estimated but their timing may be known. For example, if a union contract is due to expire on August 15 and the mood is negative for its resolution, tasks that are scheduled into the period following August 15 need to be re-planned. In fact, a broad review of the entire project is required with studies made of various alternatives. Some risks are predictable. It is known, for instance, that the forest fire season is weather dependent and that the local humidity governs forest closures. Therefore, certain construction tasks may be rescheduled early to minimize risk when threatening conditions become apparent.

A complete shut down of a project for an indeterminate period effectively divides the project into two smaller ones. The network would simply show this with a milestone at the point where all the tasks in the first half of the project would terminate. All tasks in the second half would begin at this new "START" milestone. New tasks would be incorporated on both sides of this milestone, reflecting the activities of shutdown and startup. Good plans cannot include allowances for every possible surprise; good planning systems must be able to adapt to changes, large and small.

SUMMARY

We have determined average delays expected for tasks known to be sensitive to unfavorable weather conditions. We realized that actual conditions could vary widely from the average values used in the analysis but that actual conditions might be self-compensating during construction. We learned of two methods for inserting dummy "weather" tasks into AON and AOA networks and saw how the critical path is affected by these non-construction tasks that consume time. We were careful to keep separate the durations of the weather delay and its related construction task to keep the costs of each quite independent.

EXERCISES AND PROBLEMS

1. Using the historical weather data on page 107, determine the probability of measurable rain in mid September. If 20% of this rain were just a light drizzle (and 80% heavy rain) and one of your tasks could not tolerate heavy rain, find the probability of losing a working day at this time of year.
2. You have a contract to repair a portion of the Golden Gate suspension bridge and you estimate that it will take 8 days to do it. The work is exposed to wind and rain and the location is dangerous. You must do the work in October, when there is a 30% chance of rain and a 60% chance of wind at this location.

    a. Find the delay caused by the wind only.

    b. How many days should you set aside for this job due to both conditions? (*Hint:* Find the weather window.)

3. The AON and AOA networks for the 24-task model of the Warehouse can be found in Chapter 6 in Figures 6–15 and 6–16. Incorporate weather delays if the project is planned to start on August 1st. Do it for both networks for the following cases of rain-sensitive tasks.

    a. Tasks 2, 3, and 4

    b. Tasks 19, 20 and 23

    c. Tasks 10 and 13

C H A P T E R

8

SCHEDULING RESOURCE PROCUREMENT

LEARNING OBJECTIVES

After completing this chapter, you should be able to:

- Prepare a resource/task list.
- Tabulate a list of all resources needed for a task.
- Estimate the duration for each procurement step.
- Calculate the total procurement duration for a task and find the Project Day (or Date) for initiating the ordering.
- Decide which procurement activities should be incorporated into the network, and then be able to incorporate the appropriate activities.
- Set up a "Tickler Sheet" for monitoring procurement.

PREPARATION FOR THIS CHAPTER

You will have prepared draft schedules for your project and will have evaluated the refinements covered in the previous chapters. You should be able to name the principal resources needed for every task of a project, and you may know who can provide the required information. For example, designers and contractors can provide details of the construction processes and the equipment needed for those processes.

You should be comfortable with arranging data on a spreadsheet and you should be increasingly curious and impatient to start using computer software for much of this kind of analysis. Computer methods are referenced where they apply, but you should work through this chapter using a pencil and paper to ensure that you understand the details of the analysis before applying a computer to the task.

INTRODUCTION

The eventual success of a project depends directly upon each task being executed on schedule. All the resources for each task should be on-site by the task's Earliest Start Time; they *must* be there by its Latest Start Time. If any resource is delivered after the task's LST, time is lost and the project's finishing date slips. Tasks on the Critical Path must start when scheduled because they have no float to absorb lost time from late deliveries.

To ensure that all resources are accounted for, we must identify all of them: the construction materials, the equipment needed for assembling them, the workers (skilled and unskilled, managers, etc.), the equipment to be installed (wiring, piping, machinery, etc.)—a very large list indeed.

PROCUREMENT

The whole process of ensuring that the correct resources will be on-site and on-time for each task is called **procurement**. It begins with the contractor identifying each resource, writing its specification, selecting a supplier, and ordering it. The supplier may have to prepare working drawings, make a prototype and have it inspected, manufacture the complete order, and then have it delivered. Several different groups are involved and the project manager has little direct control over many of these activities of procurement.

The contractor depends on others for timely deliveries, but he does not ignore the procurement process after orders have been placed. The project manager designates someone to make continual contacts with all the suppliers. This person is called an **expediter** and his or her job is to monitor the suppliers at important milestones during the procurement process. Typically, the duties of the expediter consist of inquiring whether a supply contract has been issued, the supplier has a prototype model ready for inspection, the work is complete, and the order has been shipped. Finally, the expediter informs the manager when items have arrived on-site.

These and other milestones identify the events of a small sub-project related to procuring a resource. Thus, every resource has its own unique schedule based on this simple network. These events of procurement (and their related activities) are common to almost every resource. The basic procurement network is shown in Figure 8–1.

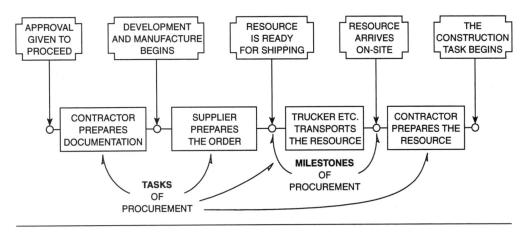

Figure 8–1   A Generalized Procurement Sub-project.

THE TICKLER SHEET

As planner, you would prepare one schedule for each resource needed for the project. When all these small schedules are arranged together, the collection is called a "Tickler Sheet." Because the scheduled time for each milestone triggers a phone call to a supplier, it acts as a tickle to the expediter's and supplier's memory—hence the name.

Because there will likely be very many resources, setting up the Tickler Sheet is a formidable task without a "system" available to provide guidance. This chapter proposes a way to go about doing this large job. It leans heavily on the need for computerized ways of handling the immense amount of data, for the volume of information can truly be enormous.

The expediter measures a supplier's success in achieving each milestone in the Tickler Sheet and continually reminds, cajoles, or threatens the supplier to keep to the schedule. When actual delivery problems are suspected, the manager may receive sufficient warning to prepare alternate plans that minimize the effect of late deliveries on the project's schedule.

EFFECTS ON THE CONSTRUCTION SCHEDULE

Monitoring the procurement process is a large and active job. But there is another effect caused by the procurement process that can alter the construction schedule: awkward procurement times can prevent a construction task from beginning when scheduled. For example, if the concrete forms are to be placed in position on Project Day 12 but the special forms that are needed take 18 days to get, how do we account for this in the construction schedule? As well as needing a "system" for setting up a Tickler Sheet, we now need another for updating the schedule to account for awkward procurement durations. We will find that both these systems interact with one another.

Before we can consider the updating of the schedule, we need a list of all the resources for the project.

TYPES OF RESOURCES

Listing resources is simplified by classifying them by type. There are **commodities** that are commonly available that can be ordered "off the shelf" and there are **key** materials that require special order. There is **equipment** for installation and there is support equipment to assist in the construction process. And most central to any project is the **human expertise** which is provided by the crews of workers: skilled journeymen and laborers, supervisors, administrators, record-keepers, consultants, inspectors, and so forth.

A methodical system minimizes the chance for errors and omissions. By completing a task list for one task at a time, you can tabulate all its resources at once. For checking afterward, you could follow the "shotgun" approach, by asking such questions as "Which tasks need gravel?" The table headings in Figure 8–2 help you focus your attention on one task at a time. The figure lists the major resources needed for erecting the roof structure (Super-Task #10) of the 24-task model for our project.

This table forces you to deal with one task at a time. Columns #1 and #2 number and name a super-task, while Column #3 lists its simpler component tasks. If the tasks in Column #3 required a further breakdown to reach still simpler tasks, then another column could be added to the table. Columns #4 to #9 categorize the five types of resources used here; other projects might have different types.

TASK AREA # NAME (1) (2)	SUB-TASK NAME (3)	CONSTRUCTION MATERIALS COMMODITIES		EQUIPMENT		EXPERTISE	
		OFF-THE-SHELF (4)	KEY (5)	INSTALLED (6)	SUPPORT (7)	CREW (8)	SUPRVSR (9)
10 Erect Roof Structure	Trusses Decking Vap Barr Cladding Overhang Soffits Flashing	Pads Metal Decking Kraft Glue Asph Roll Sealant Framing Alum. Soffit Nails Galvan. Sheet Gunk	Trusses		1-T Crane 1-T Crane 1-T Crane 1-T Crane	Elec 4 Fram 2 Carps 2 Carps 2 Fram 2 Carps 2 Sht Mtl 2	

Figure 8–2   Tabulated Resources for a Task.

In later tabulations we shall abbreviate these names and categories in order to condense the data on a spreadsheet.

The list of a dozen or so resources in Figure 8–2 covers only one of the twenty-four tasks of the project. If all the tasks were included, the list would become too large and unwieldy for the purposes of this book. For our example, we will use only eleven of the above set: six off-the-shelf items, three key materials, and two key pieces of equipment.

PROCUREMENT DURATIONS

The completed resource list is the basis for a second table used for estimating the procurement dates for each resource. For example, if a supplier takes 20 days to prepare and ship our order, then it should be ordered at least 20 working days before it is needed on the site. A procurement duration must be estimated separately because it depends on your experience with the supplier, the type of resource, and the shipping distance. However, similar types of resources are procured in the same way and it is helpful to estimate their procurement durations together. We could sort the resources by type and group each type together.

Commodities like lumber, gravel, nails, and so forth are obtained on an as-needed basis once a supply contract has been arranged with a supplier. Most commodities are "just a phone call away" and can be obtained with a couple of days' notice. Ordering Key Materials and Equipment and setting up initial supply contracts for commodities usually require more time. Obviously, if a rare electronic positioning instrument is needed on the first day of a project, finding one and getting it to the site has the highest priority. "Surveying the Site" may have been the first task of the basic construction network but "Getting the Instrument" will effectively become the first task, because Task #1 cannot begin until its resources are available.

EVENTS AND MILESTONES IN THE PROCUREMENT PROCESS

The procurement of a resource is a mini-project (see Figure 8–1). It has events and the activities required to reach them. For the supplier, the events are milestones to be achieved; for the construction manager, they are target dates to be monitored. Figure 8–3 lists four general milestones and a dozen specific events that might be encountered in practice, depending on the nature of a particular resource.

Many resources follow this string of events to reach the project. The progress of specially designed components might need monitoring through every one of these events; delivery of commodities such as common lumber require only a few. To find dates, we shall need to name procurement *activities*, estimate their durations, and calculate the Times of the events in the small network.

For the majority of resources, only three or four contacts may be sufficient for

EVENTS OF PREPARATION
1 Specification and Quantity documented
2 Purchasing Department alerted to begin procurement
3 List of pre-approved suppliers prepared
4 Bidding documents prepared
5 Bids invited (advertised)
6 Bids received and Contract awarded

EVENTS OF DEVELOPMENT
7 Supplier presents a prototype for evaluation
8 Prototype evaluated and approved
9 Supplier completes manufacture of all items

EVENTS OF DELIVERY
10 Supplier ships all items
11 All items delivered intact to the site

EVENTS ON THE SITE
12 Storage period begins
13 Installation of components begins

Figure 8–3   List of Typical Procurement Events.

monitoring a supplier's progress. We will use the following four milestones that apply to all procurements.

Four Universal Milestones

1. Procurement Documentation Completed (by contractor)
2. Resources Prepared (by supplier)
3. Order Delivered (by supplier's agent)
4. Construction Started (by us)

Activities of Procurement

To reach these four milestones requires four activities:

1. PREPARATION (by your company)
2. DEVELOPMENT and MANUFACTURE (by supplier)
3. DELIVERY (by supplier's agent)
4. LEEWAY (estimated by the manager)

The durations for these activities are estimated on the basis of your experience and information from the supplier. The LEEWAY is your private contingency cushion covering the whole process. The reputation of the supplier and your purchasing department, the manufacturing complexity of the item ordered, delivery distances, and so forth all contribute to the Leeway contingency.

RESOURCE		TIMES FOR RESOURCE PROCUREMENT								DATA FOR CONSTRUCTION TASK			
		PREPARATION		DEVEL/MANUF		DELIVERY		LEEWAY					
NAME (1)	TYPE (2)	DATE (3)	DUR (4)	DATE (5)	DUR (6)	DATE (7)	DUR (8)	DATE (9)	DUR (10)	EST DATE (11)	TF (12)	NAME OF TASK (13)	NO. (14)
Conduit	K	94:07:06	8	94:07:18	9	94:07:29	6	94:08:08	4	94:08:12	2	Install Conduit	#94

Figure 8–4   Tabular Layout of a Tickler Sheet.

Calculating the Event Times

Calculating the date for starting the procurement process is straightforward. The EST of the Construction Task and the total procurement duration determines the date to start the procurement process. For example, if special conduit is scheduled to be installed starting at 08:00 hrs on Monday, August 15 (= Friday, the 12th at 5:00 P.M.) and you estimate its procurement will take 27 working days, then you should order the conduit after 5:00 P.M. on July 6. Be sure that you count only working days, because suppliers usually observe both weekends and holidays.

These calculations are best made on a spreadsheet, whether it is filled out by hand on paper or typed into a computer. Figure 8–4 shows the basic concepts.

In the example in Figure 8–4, the total duration of the procurement process for some conduit is (8 + 9 + 6 + 4) = 27 working days. Note that the metric convention is used here for writing dates: YY/MM/DD, but the year (YY) could be omitted for conciseness. You can use any date-writing system, but it should be defined on your worksheets.

The durations derive from your company's experience (PREPARATION and LEEWAY) and commitments by the supplier (DEVEL/MANUF and DELIVERY). The dates are determined from a calendar of working days; 27 days before August 15 at 08:00 hrs ("94:08:12") is July 6 ("94:07:06").

COUNT TIME IN "PROJECT DAYS"

Calculations using calendar dates can be awkward when the analysis is done manually. Computer programs "can be told" all the non-working days in the year and can make these calculations effortlessly. However, manual calculations are best done using **Project Days** instead of calendar days: for example, Project Day #145 is the 145th working day since the project began. In the above conduit example, if the construction task was scheduled to begin on Project Day #145, then the conduit must be ordered on Project Day #118 (145 – 27). Recall that event times mark 5:00 P.M. on the quoted day, therefore the first construction

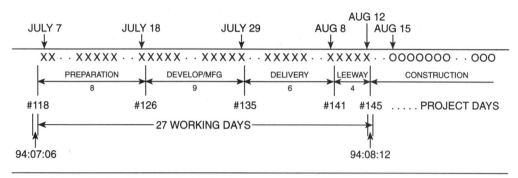

Figure 8–5 Project Days and Calendar Days.

activity actually begins at 8:00 A.M. on Project Day #146. Study Figures 8–4 and 8–5, noting that construction begins on August 15 with the first of a series of "xxxxxxxx's."

Generally, it is simpler to use Project Days rather than Calendar Dates on a tickler sheet because unforeseen holidays, strikes, or other shut-downs do not necessarily require changing the "dates." "Project Days" are working days from the start of the project and these do not change when a few more non-working days intervene. Aware of this reminder about time, we can proceed to construct the Resource Ordering Spreadsheet for a portion of the warehouse project.

THE 24-TASK WAREHOUSE PROJECT—PROCUREMENT

For this example, we will schedule the procurement of nine resources for the Roofing Task (#10), a surveying instrument for the "Site Survey" (Task #1), and an order of piles for "Drive Piles" (Task #6). Our objective is to identify those resources that impact on the basic schedule to update start times of all 24 construction tasks. We will modify the basic schedule developed in Chapter 6 and recorded on the AON Network of Figure 6–15.

We can assemble the relevant data on an extended form of Figure 8–4, The Tickler Sheet. The EST and TF for the three construction tasks is taken from Figure 6–15 and the resources are taken from Figure 8–2, augmented by the Instrument and Piles mentioned above. The result of this first step is shown in Figure 8–6.

Each resource requires a separate row of data and so we copy the construction task data into eight more rows to accommodate all nine resources associated with this task. Ditto marks cannot be used because we will want to sort these rows later into different orders and these marks would lose their meaning. Tasks #1 and #6 have only one resource each and repeated rows are not needed for them.

Estimating the duration for each of the activities constitutes the second step. Once these durations have been estimated (from your experience and promises

FOR PART OF THE PROJECT: "THE 24-TASK MODEL FOR THE WAREHOUSE"
Listing the Basic Data

RESOURCE		TIMES FOR RESOURCE PROCUREMENT								DATA FOR CONSTRUCTION TASK			
		PREPAR		DEVEL/MFG		DELIV		LEEWAY					
NAME (1)	TYPE (2)	DATE (3)	DUR (4)	DATE (5)	DUR (6)	DATE (7)	DUR (8)	DATE (9)	DUR (10)	EST (11)	TF (12)	NAME OF TASK (13)	NO. (14)
Equipment	KE									0	0	Site Survey	1
Piles	KM									14	0	Drive Piles	6
Trusses	KM									66	0	Erect Roof	10
Crane	KE									66	0	Erect Roof	10
Pads	C									66	0	Erect Roof	10
Decking	C									66	0	Erect Roof	10
Vap Barr	C									66	0	Erect Roof	10
Cladding	C									66	0	Erect Roof	10
Steel Frm	C									66	0	Erect Roof	10
Soffit	C									66	0	Erect Roof	10
Flashing	C									66	0	Erect Roof	10

Figure 8–6   The Resource-Ordering Spreadsheet: Step 1.

from the suppliers), they are entered into Figure 8–7, in columns 4, 6, 8, and 10. The event times are calculated by subtracting a duration from the later event to its right in the table, starting with the EST of the construction task and working to the left. Recall that any activity begins and ends with an event. The results of these calculations are shown in Figure 8–8.

Because the trusses are needed on Day #66 and you felt a Leeway of 15 days is

FOR PART OF THE PROJECT: "THE 24-TASK MODEL FOR THE WAREHOUSE"

RESOURCE		TIMES FOR RESOURCE PROCUREMENT								DATA FOR CONSTRUCTION TASK			
		PREPAR		DEVEL/MFG		DELIV		LEEWAY					
NAME (1)	TYPE (2)	DATE (3)	DUR (4)	DATE (5)	DUR (6)	DATE (7)	DUR (8)	DATE (9)	DUR (10)	EST (11)	TF (12)	NAME OF TASK (13)	NO. (14)
Equipment	KE		3		0		1		0	0	0	Site Survey	1
Piles	KM		3		17		2		5	14	0	Drive Piles	6
Trusses	KM		22		23		13		15	66	0	Erect Roof	10
Crane	KE		15		2		1		1	66	0	Erect Roof	10
Pads	C		10		12		1		5	66	0	Erect Roof	10
Decking	C		8		4		6		5	66	0	Erect Roof	10
Vap Barr	C		8		2		1		2	66	0	Erect Roof	10
Cladding	C		15		6		6		4	66	0	Erect Roof	10
Steel Frm	C		8		3		2		4	66	0	Erect Roof	10
Soffit	C		7		1		1		2	66	0	Erect Roof	10
Flashing	C		3		1		1		3	66	0	Erect Roof	10

Figure 8–7   Durations for Resource Procurement: Step 2.

FOR PART OF THE PROJECT: "THE 24-TASK MODEL FOR THE WAREHOUSE"

| RESOURCE | | TIMES FOR RESOURCE PROCUREMENT | | | | | | | | DATA FOR CONSTRUCTION TASK | | | |
| | | PREPAR | | DEVEL/MFG | | DELIV | | LEEWAY | | | | | |
NAME (1)	TYPE (2)	DATE (3)	DUR (4)	DATE (5)	DUR (6)	DATE (7)	DUR (8)	DATE (9)	DUR (10)	EST (11)	TF (12)	NAME OF TASK (13)	NO. (14)
Equipment	KE	–4	3	–1	0	–1	1	0	0	0	0	Site Survey	1
Piles	KM	–4	3	–1	17	9	2	11	5	14	0	Drive Piles	6
Trusses	KM	–7	22	15	23	38	13	51	15	66	0	Erect Roof	10
Crane	KE	47	15	62	2	64	1	65	1	66	0	Erect Roof	10
Pads	KM	38	10	48	12	60	1	61	5	66	0	Erect Roof	10
Decking	C	43	8	51	4	55	6	61	5	66	0	Erect Roof	10
Vap Barr	C	53	8	61	2	63	1	64	2	66	0	Erect Roof	10
Cladding	C	35	15	50	6	56	6	62	4	66	0	Erect Roof	10
Steel Frm	C	49	8	57	3	60	2	62	4	66	0	Erect Roof	10
Soffit	C	55	7	62	1	63	1	64	2	66	0	Erect Roof	10
Flashing	C	58	3	61	1	62	1	63	3	66	0	Erect Roof	10

Figure 8–8   Start Times for Resource Procurement: Step 3.

safe enough, the Expected Delivery Day is Day #51, found by subtracting 15 from 66. All the preceding event times are found by calculating from right-to-left; it is a Backward Pass through this little network. The procurement for the trusses is calculated to start on Project Day #7.

ORDERING BEFORE PROJECT START

Note that the preparation of the order for the Trusses must start 7 days before the construction begins, which would become an issue if your company decided to commit company resources before financial approval was received. For this example, we will be conservative and assume that no approval can be given to the project manager, and therefore we have a scheduling problem to deal with: How do we cope with start times earlier than the START Time of the project?

The project starts on the day commitments can be made; this defines Day 0. Therefore, the trusses can be ordered on Day 0, when the project starts. For the case of a single negative start time, we could see the project being extended by 7 days to a revised duration of 115 days (from the original 108). Refer to Figure 6–15 for the original schedule.

In a complete analysis that includes all the resources for all the tasks of the project, many tasks will have non-zero Floats (Column #12). For these, a negative Order time in Column #3 may not cause a problem if there were adequate float in the construction task to absorb the early start. That is, if the number in Column #12 is greater than the one in Column #3, then that problem may be easily resolved.

In the present case (Figure 8–8), the surveying instrument, the piles, and the trusses all display negative start times (–4, –3, and –7) but only the piles have sufficient float to absorb this early start.

UPDATING THE SCHEDULE

In complex cases that include several resources with a negative start day, simplistic decisions about the effect on the schedule should not be made. To confidently evaluate this kind of situation, a new task representing *each* awkward procurement should be incorporated into the basic construction network. Crucial procurement activities should now be considered to be part of the construction project. The basic network of Figure 6–15 has been modified to include these crucial procurement tasks, as shown in Figure 8–9.

The three awkward resource procurements showing the negative start times can be readily inserted into the basic network by adding a task bubble between Project Start and the construction task needing the resource. This assumes that any resource could be ordered as early as Day 0, but that one showing a negative order time will probably have to start at Day Zero. Once the network has been enlarged, the usual time calculation can be performed; this has been done in Figure 8–9. The construction duration is seen to have increased by seven days, to a total of 115 days.

UPDATING THE TICKLER SHEET

These revised dates (and floats) from the updated schedule are next inserted back into columns #11 and #12 of the tickler spreadsheet and the event times for the ordering process are updated. This revised spreadsheet becomes the Tickler Sheet that the expediter will use to monitor the progress of the suppliers in meeting the delivery dates. See Figure 8–10.

Note that no start times are negative even though there are three EST's of zero; these must be zero because any task immediately following Project Start will have an EST of zero. Only one has its LST also at zero: the trusses. Note also that the ordering times for all these resources have been set back by 7 days. This is not a general rule; to be safe, recalculate the revised network with all the negative start resources included.

There is an advantage to rearranging the rows of this tickler sheet to assist the expediter. In Figure 8–11, Column #3 has been used to sort the rows so that the earliest Start Prep times appear at the top; in fact, all the times in that column are arranged in increasing order. This is an arduous manual job. It would be made slightly easier if each row of the tickler sheet were written on sticky tape so that it could be peeled off and moved to another location, but the best way is to sort the rows on the values in column #3 by using a computer spreadsheet to do the work. Fewer than half-a-dozen key strokes will do it.

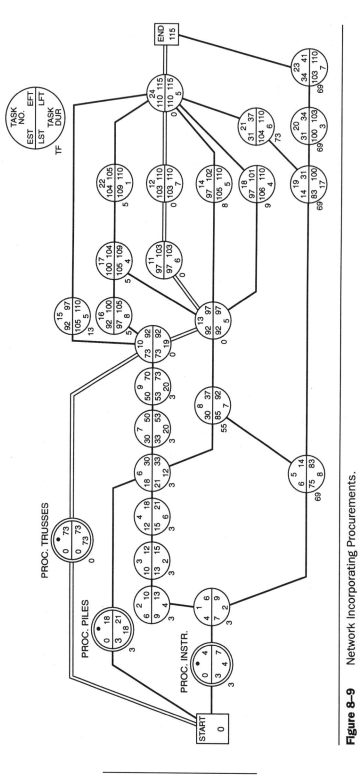

Figure 8–9 Network Incorporating Procurements.

FOR PART OF THE PROJECT: "THE 24-TASK MODEL FOR THE WAREHOUSE"
Using the Revised EST's from Updated Network: Figure 8.9

RESOURCE		TIMES FOR RESOURCE PROCUREMENT								DATA FOR CONSTRUCTION TASK			
		PREPAR		DEVEL/MFG		DELIV		LEEWAY					
NAME (1)	TYPE (2)	DATE (3)	DUR (4)	DATE (5)	DUR (6)	DATE (7)	DUR (8)	DATE (9)	DUR (10)	EST (11)	TF (12)	NAME OF TASK (13)	NO. (14)
Equipment	KE	0	3	3	0	3	1	4	0	4	3	Site Survey	1
Piles	KM	0	3	3	10	13	2	15	3	18	3	Drive Piles	6
Trusses	KM	0	22	22	23	45	13	58	15	73	0	Erect Roof	10
Crane	KE	54	15	62	2	71	1	72	1	73	0	Erect Roof	10
Pads	KM	45	10	55	12	67	1	68	5	73	0	Erect Roof	10
Decking	C	50	8	58	4	62	6	68	5	73	0	Erect Roof	10
Vap Barr	C	60	8	68	2	70	1	71	2	73	0	Erect Roof	10
Cladding	C	42	15	57	6	63	6	69	4	73	0	Erect Roof	10
Steel Frm	C	56	8	64	3	67	2	69	4	73	0	Erect Roof	10
Soffit	C	62	7	69	1	70	1	71	2	73	0	Erect Roof	10
Flashing	C	65	3	68	1	69	1	70	3	73	0	Erect Roof	10

THIS
DATA FROM
FIGURE 8–9

Figure 8–10 The Basic Tickler Sheet: Step 4.

FOR PART OF THE PROJECT: "THE 24-TASK MODEL FOR THE WAREHOUSE"
Using the Revised EST's from Figure 8–9 — "Revised Network Diagram"

RESOURCE		TIMES FOR RESOURCE PROCUREMENT								DATA FOR CONSTRUCTION TASK			
		PREPAR		DEVEL/MFG		DELIV		LEEWAY					
NAME (1)	TYPE (2)	DATE (3)	DUR (4)	DATE (5)	DUR (6)	DATE (7)	DUR (8)	DATE (9)	DUR (10)	EST (11)	TF (12)	NAME OF TASK (13)	NO. (14)
Piles	KM	0	3	3	10	13	2	15	3	18	3	Drive Piles	6
Trusses	KM	0	22	22	23	45	13	58	15	73	0	Erect Roof	10
Equipment	KE	0	3	3	0	3	1	4	0	4	3	Site Survey	1
Cladding	C	42	15	57	6	63	6	69	4	73	0	Erect Roof	10
Pads	KM	45	10	55	12	67	1	68	5	73	0	Erect Roof	10
Decking	C	50	8	58	4	62	6	68	5	73	0	Erect Roof	10
Crane	KE	54	15	69	2	71	1	72	1	73	0	Erect Roof	10
Steel Frm	C	56	8	64	3	67	2	69	4	73	0	Erect Roof	10
Vap Barr	C	60	8	68	2	70	1	71	2	73	0	Erect Roof	10
Soffit	C	62	7	69	1	70	1	71	2	73	0	Erect Roof	10
Flashing	C	65	3	68	1	69	1	70	3	73	0	Erect Roof	10

*

THESE
ARE
UPDATED

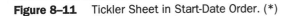

Figure 8–11 Tickler Sheet in Start-Date Order. (*)

FOR PART OF THE PROJECT: "THE 24-TASK MODEL FOR THE WAREHOUSE"
Using the Revised EST's from Figure 8–9 — "Revised Network Diagram"

| RESOURCE | | TIMES FOR RESOURCE PROCUREMENT | | | | | | | | DATA FOR CONSTRUCTION TASK | | | |
| | | PREPAR | | DEVEL/MFG | | DELIV | | LEEWAY | | | | | |
NAME (1)	TYPE (2)	DATE (3)	DUR (4)	DATE (5)	DUR (6)	DATE (7)	DUR (8)	DATE (9)	DUR (10)	EST (11)	TF (12)	NAME OF TASK (13)	NO. (14)
Cladding	C	42	15	57	6	63	6	69	4	73	0	Erect Roof	10
Decking	C	50	8	58	4	62	6	68	5	73	0	Erect Roof	10
Steel Frm	C	56	8	64	3	67	2	69	4	73	0	Erect Roof	10
Vap Barr	C	60	8	68	2	70	1	71	2	73	0	Erect Roof	10
Soffit	C	62	7	69	1	70	1	71	2	73	0	Erect Roof	10
Flashing	C	65	3	68	1	69	1	70	3	73	0	Erect Roof	10
Equipment	KE	0	3	3	0	3	1	4	0	4	3	Site Survey	1
Crane	KE	54	15	69	2	71	1	72	1	73	0	Erect Roof	10
Piles	KM	0	3	3	10	13	2	15	3	18	3	Drive Piles	6
Trusses	KM	0	22	22	23	45	13	58	15	73	0	Erect Roof	10
Pads	KM	45	10	55	12	67	1	68	5	73	0	Erect Roof	10

*

THESE
ARE
UPDATED

Figure 8–12 Tickler Sheet in Order of Material Type. (*)

The advantage of this arrangement is that the expediter can start the procurement for each resource from the top down and work down the list more or less in order.

This simple example for only one task area of the project becomes a very large job when all resource procurements are assembled into one large spreadsheet. The previous spreadsheet can become easier to monitor by collecting all the Key Materials, Key Equipment, and Commodities in separate groups. A computer alphabetic sort on Column #2 is shown in Figure 8–12. Within each category, the Start Procurement dates remain in order of earliest first from the previous sort.

USING THE TICKLER SHEET

After the spreadsheet has been expanded to include all the resources for the whole project and has been updated by including the negative-start procurements, it is ready to be used to monitor the suppliers. The expediter contacts each supplier as due-dates come up and incorporates any newly reported times or durations into the spreadsheet. Periodically, as durations and actual dates are changed in the construction schedule, the expediter should put these changes into the network, recalculate the revised times, and change the task data in the tickler sheet. This keeps the tickler sheet current and dependable.

FOR PART OF THE PROJECT: "THE 24-TASK MODEL FOR THE WAREHOUSE"
Using the Revised EST's from Figure 8–9 — "Revised Network Diagram"

RESOURCE		TIMES FOR RESOURCE PROCUREMENT								DATA FOR CONSTRUCTION TASK			
		PREPAR		DEVEL/MFG		DELIV		LEEWAY					
NAME (1)	TYPE (2)	DATE (3)	DUR (4)	DATE (5)	DUR (6)	DATE (7)	DUR (8)	DATE (9)	DUR (10)	EST (11)	TF (12)	NAME OF TASK (13)	NO. (14)
Cladding	C	~~42~~	~~15~~	~~57~~	~~6~~	63	6	69	4	73	0	Erect Roof	10
Decking	C	~~50~~	~~8~~	~~58~~	~~4~~	62	6	68	5	73	0	Erect Roof	10
Steel Frm	C	~~56~~	~~8~~	64	3	67	2	69	4	73	0	Erect Roof	10
Vap Barr	C	~~60~~	~~8~~	68	2	70	1	71	2	73	0	Erect Roof	10
Soffit	C	62	7	69	1	70	1	71	2	73	0	Erect Roof	10
Flashing	C	65	3	68	1	69	1	70	3	73	0	Erect Roof	10
Equipment	KE	~~0~~	~~3~~	~~3~~	~~0~~	~~3~~	~~1~~	~~4~~	~~0~~	4	3	Site Survey	1
Crane	KE	~~54~~	~~15~~	69	2	71	1	72	1	73	0	Erect Roof	10
Piles	KM	~~0~~	~~3~~	~~3~~	~~10~~	~~13~~	~~2~~	~~15~~	~~0~~	18	3	Drive Piles	6
Trusses	KM	~~0~~	~~22~~	~~22~~	~~23~~	~~45~~	~~13~~	~~58~~	15	73	0	Erect Roof	10
Pads	KM	~~45~~	~~10~~	~~55~~	~~12~~	67	1	68	5	73	0	Erect Roof	10

THESE
ARE
UPDATED

Figure 8–13 Tickler Sheet Showing Status of Procurement.

As the suppliers report that they have met their milestones, completed procurement activities are blanked out so that current status is identified. If the Tickler Sheet is displayed on paper, a marking pen can neatly indicate the status. Figure 8–13 shows how Figure 8–12 should appear on Project Day 60.

SUMMARY

The Four Steps to a "Tickler Sheet"

1. Copy the original EST data of the construction tasks into the draft Tickler Sheet and calculate the Start Procurement Dates for all the selected resources.
2. Select those resources showing negative dates and, for each one, create a procurement task in the project network.
3. Recalculate the Early and Late Times for the augmented network.
4. Copy the revised EST's into the Tickler Sheet and recalculate the final dates for its Milestones for all the resources.

Where procurement problems appear to delay the start of a construction task, check its float: for a non-critical task the apparent delay may be absorbed by its construction task.

In some cases we might be judicious in reducing the stated leeway and absorbing it in the Total Float. This practice must be used carefully. If there is any question about the reduced size of the leeway, do not change anything. In cases where there is a huge Total Float then no leeway was required anyway.

NOTE: It is imperative during all the detailed manipulations with the network to keep a clear eye on what you are trying to achieve and then make only simple and constructive changes.

EXERCISES AND PROBLEMS

1. Refer to the 24-task AOA network for the warehouse project (Figure 6–16) and prepare a tickler sheet for the resources needed for construction tasks #3, #7, and #8. Select a total of twelve realistic resources, including at least two different crews and at least one from each of the other resource types listed in this chapter.

9

RESOURCE LEVELING

LEARNING OBJECTIVES

After completing this chapter, you should be able to:

- Draw a histogram displaying the daily requirements of a resource.
- Determine the total usage of a resource over the duration of a project.
- Recognize a clash in the use of a scarce resource.
- Apply re-scheduling ploys to eliminate a clash in the use of a resource.
- Smooth a manpower loading histogram.

PREPARATION FOR THIS CHAPTER

In the previous chapter you learned how to set up a schedule for timing the ordering of resources needed for a construction project. Your familiarity with the resources will be extended in this chapter as you draw graphs of their utilization and relate parts of some of the graphs to actual activities on the construction job.

You should have some background knowledge about the construction industry, the state of labor relations, and the local economy to appreciate that problems of supply may restrict your ability to obtain the resources you need when you want them.

You should be very familiar with the construction sequences of a project and the physical layout of the site so that you will know whether certain crews and equipment would be able to work in close proximity with one another.

INTRODUCTION

We saw that resource procurement can affect the construction schedule; we will now see how competition for a resource in short supply (for example, gypsum board or a crane) can have similar effects. An evaluation of when resources are used will reveal that many are irregularly used over the course of the project. This chapter discusses why and how we should smooth these irregularities. This process is called "Leveling," "Smoothing," or "Balancing."

In developing the most up-to-date schedule in the earlier chapters, we unconsciously assumed that we had an unlimited supply of all the resources needed for the tasks, but the real-world situation may be very different. The single crane we budgeted for may be needed for two construction tasks at the same time; or the carpentry crew may be required to work on two or more different tasks at the same time; or the carpentry crew may be scheduled for work on two or more overlapping tasks; or the painting crew will not be allowed to work alongside the electricians in a confined space.

In retrospect, we intentionally were unconcerned about these issues because our philosophy in this book is to improve a network and schedule one step at a time until we reach a realistic model for the project. We have reached the point where we can superimpose onto our network the constraints that result from scarce resources.

Other than resolving resource clashes, we must try to smooth the wide swings in the daily application of certain resources, especially work crews. For example, the carpentry crew might be assigned work on a four-day task and then be left idle for three days, which would disrupt its working momentum, decrease its efficiency, and complicate management of the job. Management's objective is to achieve a steadily working crew by rescheduling certain tasks by altering or adding precedence links into the network. These adjustments tend to complicate the network and lengthen the project.

EXAMPLES OF CLASHES: THE WAREHOUSE PROJECT

The 24-Task model of the Warehouse Project is a useful example for a resource analysis. Its AON network, from Chapter 6, provides the construction precedence information and its related Gantt Chart (Figure 9–1) shows the time slots for each task.

We are not using more recent schedules from the two preceding chapters because those versions were not completely updated. For an actual project in which all of the refinements were incorporated, you would use the latest schedule. Because all of the refinements we make are interrelated, the refining process ends only when you are satisfied or run out of planning time.

Tasks Starting at the Same Time

When the schedule shows two tasks requiring the same piece of equipment at the same time, the manager decides which task should use it first by comparing the total floats of both tasks. Their floats determine the priorities.

For example, in Figure 9–1, Tasks #13, #15, and #16 have the same EST:

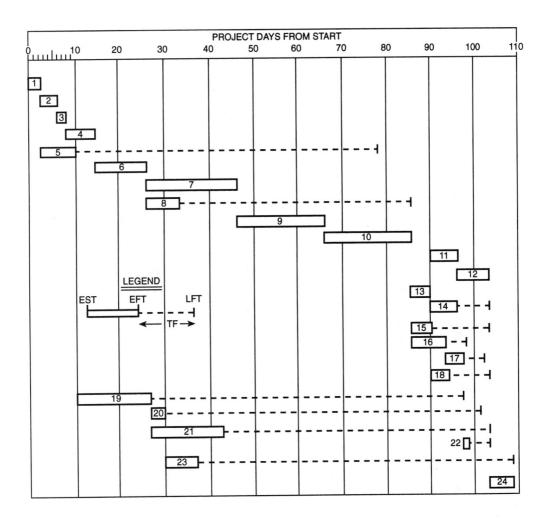

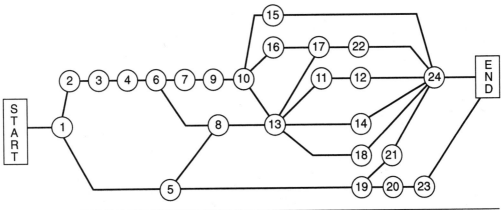

Figure 9–1   Gantt Chart and AON for 24-task Warehouse Project.

work on all three is scheduled to start simultaneously on Day #85. Two of them require the same crew of laborers: the Foundation Drains (#15) and Preparing the Slabs (#13). This is an easy decision for the manager, because Task #13 (Slab) has zero total float whereas Task #15 (the Drains) has 13 days TF.

Clearly, the work on Task #13 should start first, with the labor crew moving on to Task #15 when they finish #13. The sequencing of these two tasks can be arranged on the network by forcing #15 to follow #13 by adding a sequencing arrow between them. The link has an arrowhead to emphasize the sequence; it can be seen in Figure 9–2.

With this precedence added (#15 follows #13), it is clear that Task #15 has its EST pushed back by 5 days (the duration of #13) to Day #90 and its TF would be reduced from 13 to 8 days. Task #15 now has the same start time as tasks #11, #14, and #18, and we discover that a new conflict may have been caused. Let us assume that a major piece of equipment is needed by these four tasks. They should be executed in order of their total floats: #11 is first, followed by #14 or #15, and then by #18. As before, we use arrows superimposed on the existing network to rationalize the use of this overloaded piece of equipment. Figure 9–2 shows these refinements as dotted-line arrows on a portion of Figure 9–1.

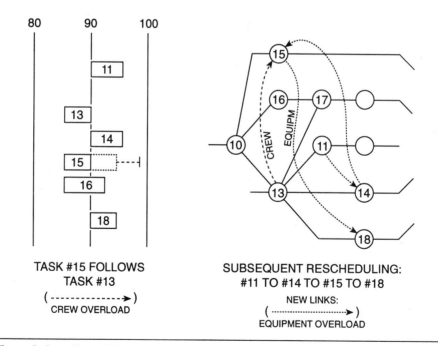

TASK #15 FOLLOWS TASK #13

(------------>)
CREW OVERLOAD

SUBSEQUENT RESCHEDULING: #11 TO #14 TO #15 TO #18

NEW LINKS:
(·····················>)
EQUIPMENT OVERLOAD

Figure 9–2   Forced Sequencing by Adding Links.

An Alternative Way to Prioritize Tasks

Reviewing the data for the four tasks listed below in the table, we see that the tasks could be prioritized in the order of their Late Start Times with the same result.

Task No.	Total Float	LST
11	zero TF	Day #90
14	8 days	Day #98
15	8 days	Day #98
18	9 days	Day #99

Recall the relationship [EST + TF = LST]. Because all four tasks have the same EST, the LST could serve equally well as a criterion for defining the order in which these tasks are to be rescheduled. When tasks have the same TF (as is the case for tasks #14 and #15), select the one that fits better into the schedule.

Problems of a Crowded Work Area

A third type of constraint relates to separating tasks that can confuse progress if allowed to occur together. An example is the work on the Foundations (Task #7), laying the Underslab Services (Task #8), and the development of the Road Beds (Task #19). All three are scheduled to start on Day #26. The manager wants the important Foundation work to proceed unimpeded, therefore tasks #8 and #19 are required to start afterward. The delays are not a problem because the TF's can absorb them and no major schedule disruptions are caused.

All of the above alterations to the basic schedule have been incorporated into the basic network and appear in Figure 9–3. The forward pass calculation shows the project's duration to be changed to 115 days, caused solely (in this case) by the equipment clash; its effect completely engulfs the delay from the crew overload. Note the revised critical path.

Possibilities for Shared Use

In cases where several tasks are competing for the use of a piece of equipment (as above), such use is rarely 100 percent allocated to any task over its whole duration. Its use might be shared among all the competing tasks, thereby reducing or eliminating any loss of time. A crane, for example, is often needed for a short time at the beginning of a task to place materials, after which it would be free for other applications. Such shorter use periods would be sequenced. Some computer scheduling programs accept resource allocation rates to allow for shared use. Our manual system could account for shared used if each task were subdivided into two sub-tasks: one being the time period for using the equipment, and the other being the regular construction activity. This is illustrated in Figure 9–4.

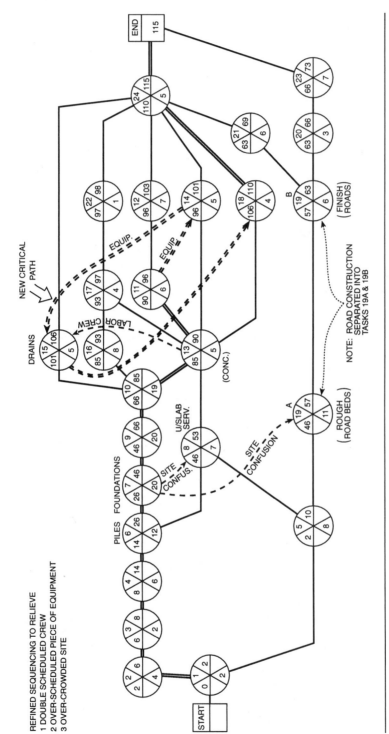

Figure 9–3 Revised Network Showing the Forced Sequences.

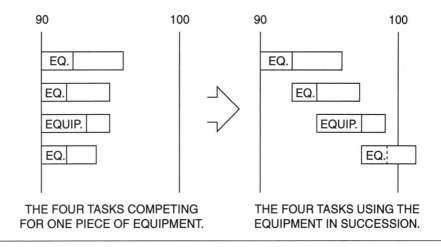

THE FOUR TASKS COMPETING
FOR ONE PIECE OF EQUIPMENT.

THE FOUR TASKS USING THE
EQUIPMENT IN SUCCESSION.

Figure 9–4   Subdivided Tasks Share a Resource.

These new tasks and links are simply hand-drawn into the network or added to the data in the computer program. Depending on the float available, the revised time calculations *may* change the times and the floats. But when the TF's are small and large changes are made in the calculated schedule, you must decide whether to increase the amount of the resource available (lease another crane or hire more workers), or allow the schedule to be stretched out. The difference in costs will help you decide.

To "Crash" or Not to "Crash"

"Crashing" is adding resources to save time. Irrespective of the pressures to avoid falling behind in the schedule, the option to add more resources may not exist. They can be in limited supply due to external factors such as a busy construction season or very long delivery schedules. Crashing is an important technique and we shall study it separately in Chapter 10. Revised delivery durations have already been studied in Chapter 8. Keeping to the principle of fixing the schedule one step at a time, we will not consider crashing here but will make changes while keeping the rate of supplying resources unchanged.

SMOOTHING RESOURCES

One goal of good management is to apply human resources in an effective and efficient manner because on-again, off-again work periods are unsatisfactory to the workers in a crew. We will use an example to illustrate such situations, define the terminology, and explain the graphical aspects.

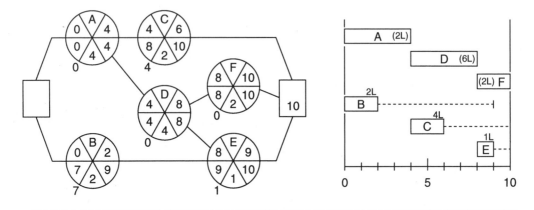

Figure 9–5 AON and Gantt Chart for a Small Project.

The basic Gantt Chart for a small project in Figure 9–5 shows when action is being taken on each task and when specific resources are being used, in this case, laborers.

Resource Histograms

The number of workers needed by each task is written in each bar of the chart. Using this manning data, we can construct a time-based graph showing the total number of workers needed on each day of the project. This is called a resource histogram. A separate histogram is needed for each resource, crane utilization and labor assignments. The histogram is based on every task starting at its Earliest Start Time and the resource being used for the complete duration of the task. Figure 9–6A is the histogram for laborers.

The total height of a box on the Gantt Chart indicates the total number of workers needed from day to day, obtained by summing the number of workers from each task for that day. It is useful to show the contribution from each task as a separate block on this histogram because this will help later in planning where to relocate a particular task in the histogram.

Total Effort and Average Crew Sizes

A resource histogram provides another function as well: the area inside the graph represents the total number of man-days required for the project. For example, Task "A" needs two workers for 4 days; the effort required is 8 man-days (2 workers × 4 days). Therefore, all the tasks in this small project require a total of 45 man-days over the 10 days of the project, an average of 4.5 workers per day. This gives us a target for smoothing the workforce to less variable levels. Obviously we

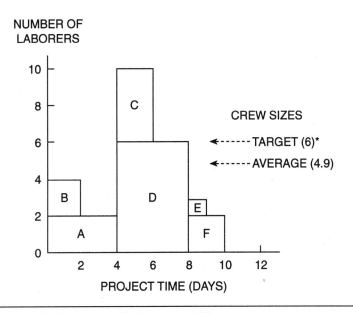

Figure 9–6A   Daily Requirement for Laborers: A Histogram.

cannot have half-a-worker so we must be content with a theoretical target of a constant crew of five workers. After making changes, we must ensure that the total effort is the same as before the changes, 45 man-days.

Smoothing the Daily Crew Allocations

In the example, we should strive to level each day's crew to the five-person target, but we may have to accept six as more realistic. At any rate, the 10 workers scheduled for Days 5 and 6 are unacceptable. To resolve this overload, we need to re-schedule several tasks to start later than their initially calculated Earliest Start Times. We can accomplish this in two stages:

1. "Freeze" the critical tasks (TF = 0) in their original time periods; then re-schedule the others within their floats, starting with the task having the least float. Note that tasks with TF = 0 have priority ONE. They are "frozen" in time and are scheduled first (that is, in their original time period).

2. If the crew size is still too large, re-schedule certain of the critical tasks to minimize the increase in the duration of the project.

In our example, the priorities based on the Total Floats of the tasks are shown in the table below. (Remember that smaller floats equate to higher priorities and earlier re-scheduling.)

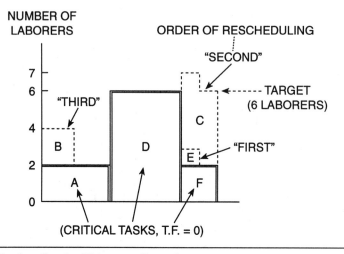

Figure 9–6B Leveling the Histogram: Stage One.

TASK NAME	A	B	C	D	E	F
TOTAL FLOAT	0	7	4	0	1	0
PRIORITY	1	4	3	1	2	1

The technique works like this: Freeze Tasks A, D, and F; then re-schedule E, C, and B (in that order). With E left where it is (the number of workers is below 6) and C scheduled to start after D is finished, then the original clash of C and D is fixed but a new one is caused between C and E. Day 9 is now overloaded by one worker.

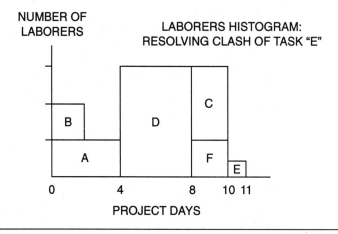

Figure 9–6C Resolving the Second Clash.

These changes are displayed in Figure 9–6B. Often, a "frozen" task must be moved to a later time slot to preserve the proper sequencing.

One way to satisfy the six-man requirement is to start E after F is finished, causing E to become critical and extending the project by one day (see Figure 9–6C). In this case, E must be linked to both C and F to ensure that E cannot clash with either one if C or F slips with a longer duration. Alternatively, blindly placing C after F would solve the overload but would lengthen the project by 2 days and cause an irregular crew size.

Projects normally start with a small crew, increase to a maximum near the middle, and then fall off near the end. In this example, we could start Task "B" 2 days late (to start the project "slower") with 2 workers for the first 2 days, followed by a fixed crew of 4 for the rest of the project, ending with one on the last day. This final plan is shown in Figure 9–6D, together with an updated AON

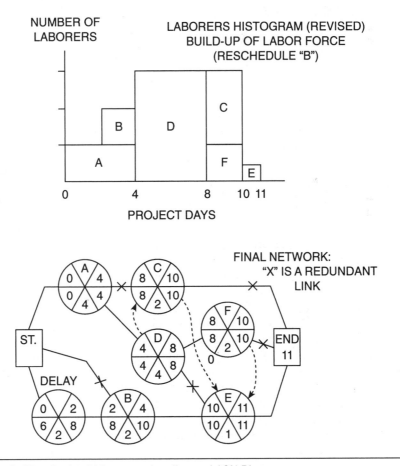

Figure 9–6D   Revised Manpower Loading and AON Diagram.

network showing the new precedence links and the new Delay task; several original links have become redundant.

Conflicting tasks are re-scheduled only by adding precedence linkages to the network. Never use a dummy Delay task to reschedule a clashed task. The real delay wanted for Task "B" has a different objective. To prevent a clash, the re-scheduling requires that one task must follow another independent of the actual durations during construction. A dummy "delay" tactic will break down if one of the tasks slips and takes longer than expected, causing another clash. The completion of the preceding task really signals that the crew can be transferred to the next task; a precedence link ensures this sequence. In the example, if a four-day delay is placed before Task "C" and Task "D" ends on Day 7 instead of Day 6, then the two tasks still overlap on Day 7.

STRETCHING OUT A TASK

To lower peaks in the loading (and also to fill in the valleys) it may be possible to stretch out a particular task by reducing its crew size and extending its duration. You may be able to tolerate a lower crew efficiency in order to get the benefits of a reasonably constant crew size; each compromise requires that you exercise good judgment. Task "D" requires 24 man-days of effort (6 workers × 4 days), which could be modified to 4 workers for 6 days or 3 workers for 8 days, each of which results in 24 man-days of effort. This stretching technique is useful if an extended project duration is acceptable. The small project we have been using as an example has been stretched; it is shown in Figure 9–6E.

A TABULAR METHOD FOR SMOOTHING

The graphical approach for resolving clashes works well for small projects but is unwieldy for large ones. However, we have a tabular method to help with solutions. Figure 9–7A is the worksheet for resolving the resource issues of the Warehouse. This worksheet is developed from the basic Gantt Chart (Figure 9–1), with the size of the labor crew placed inside the task bars and specific task data listed to the left of the Gantt Chart.

For the Warehouse, the much-simplified crew data is listed for each task: only Equipment Operators (EO), Carpenters (C), Painters (P), Plumbers (PL), Masons (M), and Laborers (L) are considered. Among the others not included are journeymen, supervisors, special equipment operators, and managers.

For a specific day, we can add up the number of crew workers and record the sum in one of the bottom rows under the Gantt Chart, with one row for each resource. Similarly, we can sum the total number of man-days for each task (that is, along a row) and enter this value in the appropriate column at the right-hand side of the Chart.

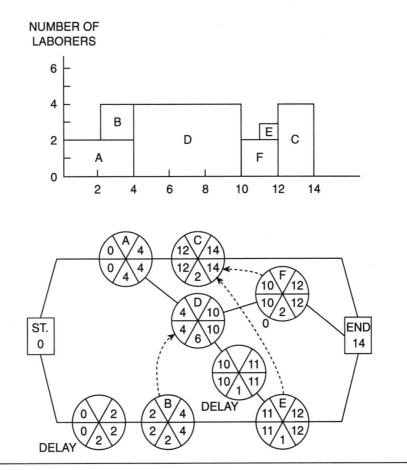

Figure 9–6E   Stretching out a Task—Its Gantt Chart.

The manpower loading histogram (Figure 9–7B) for laborers was constructed from the daily loading values on the worksheet. For example, on Day #86, tasks #13 and #15 are in-work requiring 3 and 2 laborers, respectively. Thus 5 laborers are required on Day #86. (Note that sub-contractors are responsible for their own resources.) It shows how the daily requirement for laborers varies over the 108-day life of the project.

The daily manning levels vary quite dramatically, from 8 (on Day #30) to 2, a few days later, and then falling to zero, rising again to 3, and staying at that level to the end. It should be possible to smooth these variations closer to the average of 4 by thoughtful re-scheduling of some tasks.

You may be considering which tasks to re-schedule to improve the wide

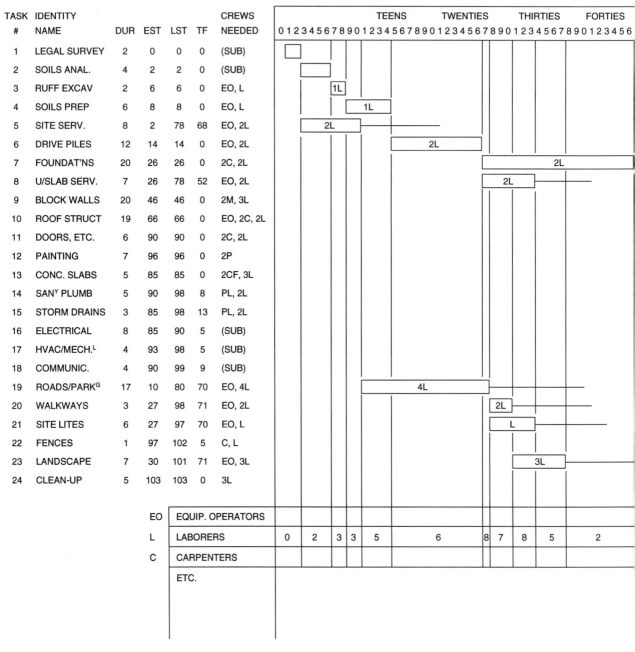

Figure 9–7A Worksheet for Resource Leveling.

FIFTIES	SIXTIES	SEVENTIES	EIGHTIES	NINETIES	HUNDREDS	MAN-DAYS:	LABOR CREW
7 8 9 0 1 2 3 4 5 6 7 8 9	0 1 2 3 4 5 6 7 8 9	0 1 2 3 4 5 6 7 8 9	0 1 2 3 4 5 6 7 8 9	0 1 2 3 4 5 6 7 8 9	0 1 2 3 4 5 6 7 8 9		

Chart rows (MAN-DAYS / LABOR CREW):

MAN-DAYS	LABOR CREW
—	1
—	2
2	
6	4
16	
24	6
40	
14	8
60	
38	10
12	
—	12
15	
10	14
6	
—	16
—	
—	18
68	
6	20
6	
1	22
21	
15	24

Labeled bars in chart: 3L, 2L, 2L, 0, 3L, 2L, 2L, SUB, SUB, SUB, 6, 3L

Totals row: 3 | 2 | 5 3 | 4 | 4 4 2 0 1 | 3 | 360

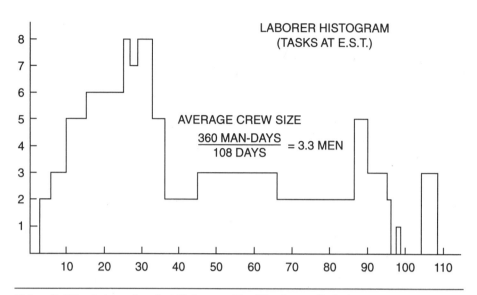

Figure 9–7B   Laborer Loading Histogram: The Warehouse Project.

swings in the labor crew, but let us now study the worksheet and then peruse the re-scheduling techniques in detail afterward.

For bookkeeping purposes, note that task #3 needs 1 laborer for 2 days, for a total effort of 2 man-days; task #4 has 1 laborer for 6 days (6 man-days); and task #5 has 2 laborers for 8 days (16 man-days). These three values are entered in the last column of the worksheet.

Step-By-Step Method

You must first decide where to begin. The first task to be "frozen" in the new schedule is the one with the earliest LST. The rest are "frozen" in the order of earliest LST. To assist this selection process, it is useful to sort the list of tasks in order of LST and TF and then work down the list. Figure 9–7C shows the 24 tasks sorted in this new order (using spreadsheet software). Note that the first 8 tasks have zero TF; these cannot be re-scheduled without lengthening the project but this is often necessary.

Scheduling the first eight tasks incurs no changes from before, but the next three (#8,#5, and #19) can be placed anywhere between their EST and LST as long as their precedence logic is *not* violated (an easy mistake). Because #8 must occur after #5 finishes, #8 cannot be scheduled without considering the revised timing for task #5.

One re-scheduling solution is shown on the worksheet of Figure 9–7D, with its

WAREHOUSE PROJECT: 24-TASK SCHEDULING MODEL
Sorted in Order of Late Start Time and TF

#	TASK NAME	DUR	EST	LST	TF	CREWS NEEDED	PRECEDING TASKS
1	LEGAL SURVEY	2	0	0	0	(SUB)	Start
2	SOILS ANAL	4	2	2	0	(SUB)	1
3	RUFF EXCAV	2	6	6	0	EO,L	2
4	SOIL PREP	6	8	8	0	EO,L	3
6	DRIVE PILES	12	14	14	0	EO,2L	4
7	FOUND'NS	20	26	26	0	2C,2L	6
9	BLOCK WALLS	20	46	46	0	2M,3L	7
10	ROOF STRUCT	19	66	66	0	EO,2C,2L	9
8	U/SLAB SERV	7	26	78	52	EO,2L	5 & 6
5	SITE SERV	8	2	78	68	EO,2L	1
19	ROADS/PARK	17	10	80	70	EO,4L	5
13	CONC SLABS	5	85	85	0	2CF,3L	8 & 10
11	DOORS, ETC	6	90	90	0	2C,2L	13
16	ELECTRICAL	8	85	90	5	(SUB)	10
12	PAINTING	7	96	96	0	2P	11
21	SITE LITES	6	27	97	70	EO,L	19
17	H-VAC MECH	4	93	98	5	(SUB)	13 & 16
14	SAN PLUMB	5	90	98	8	PL,2L	13
15	STORM DRAINS	3	85	98	13	PL,2L	10
20	WALKWAYS	3	27	98	71	EO,2L	19
18	COMMUNIC	4	90	99	9	(SUB)	13
23	LANDSCAP	7	30	101	71	EO,3L	20
22	FENCES	1	97	102	5	C,L	17
24	CLEAN-UP	5	103	103	0	3L	12,14,15,18, 21 & 2

Figure 9–7C   Tasks Sorted Ready for Re-scheduling.

resulting histogram in Figure 9–7E. This shows improvement in the earlier stages of the project, but some further refinement is needed. Perhaps a constant workforce of four laborers could cope with the work after Day #86; later in the project, actual schedules may be different from this early plan and laborers can be reassigned more flexibly.

Rules for Re-Scheduling to Smooth Resource Allocations

The previous discussion about resolving resource over-use did not provide explicit rules for doing it. A fundamental rule governs the process: freeze tasks with zero TF and then re-schedule conflicting tasks in order of their LST's. The set of rules below should lead you to a successful smoothing of resources.

WAREHOUSE PROJECT: 24-TASK SCHEDULING MODEL, Sorted in Order of Late Start Time and TF

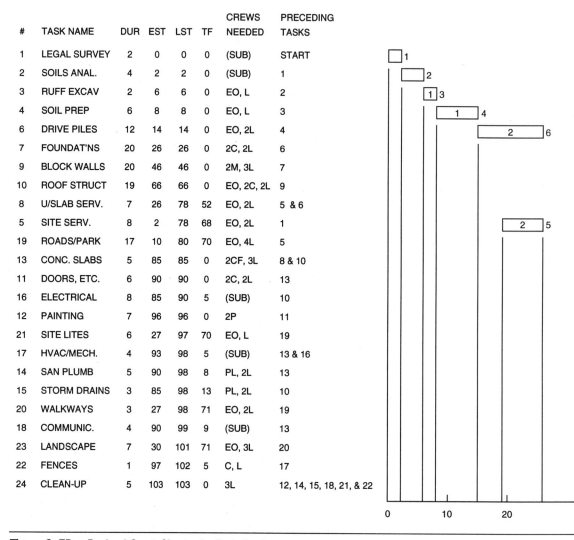

#	TASK NAME	DUR	EST	LST	TF	CREWS NEEDED	PRECEDING TASKS
1	LEGAL SURVEY	2	0	0	0	(SUB)	START
2	SOILS ANAL.	4	2	2	0	(SUB)	1
3	RUFF EXCAV	2	6	6	0	EO, L	2
4	SOIL PREP	6	8	8	0	EO, L	3
6	DRIVE PILES	12	14	14	0	EO, 2L	4
7	FOUNDAT'NS	20	26	26	0	2C, 2L	6
9	BLOCK WALLS	20	46	46	0	2M, 3L	7
10	ROOF STRUCT	19	66	66	0	EO, 2C, 2L	9
8	U/SLAB SERV.	7	26	78	52	EO, 2L	5 & 6
5	SITE SERV.	8	2	78	68	EO, 2L	1
19	ROADS/PARK	17	10	80	70	EO, 4L	5
13	CONC. SLABS	5	85	85	0	2CF, 3L	8 & 10
11	DOORS, ETC.	6	90	90	0	2C, 2L	13
16	ELECTRICAL	8	85	90	5	(SUB)	10
12	PAINTING	7	96	96	0	2P	11
21	SITE LITES	6	27	97	70	EO, L	19
17	HVAC/MECH.	4	93	98	5	(SUB)	13 & 16
14	SAN PLUMB	5	90	98	8	PL, 2L	13
15	STORM DRAINS	3	85	98	13	PL, 2L	10
20	WALKWAYS	3	27	98	71	EO, 2L	19
18	COMMUNIC.	4	90	99	9	(SUB)	13
23	LANDSCAPE	7	30	101	71	EO, 3L	20
22	FENCES	1	97	102	5	C, L	17
24	CLEAN-UP	5	103	103	0	3L	12, 14, 15, 18, 21, & 22

Figure 9–7D Revised Gantt Chart—An Early Draft.

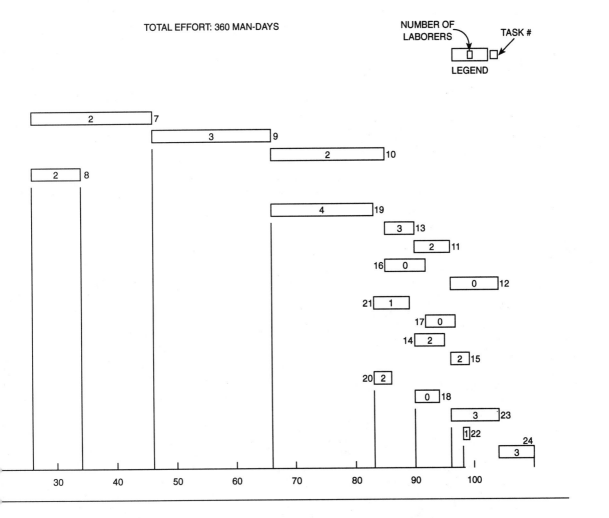

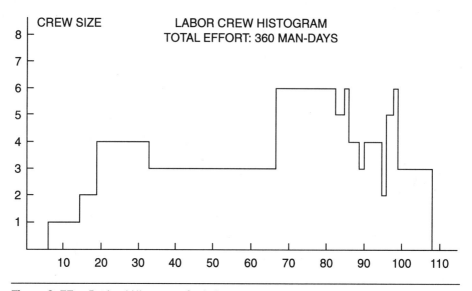

Figure 9–7E   Revised Histogram for Laborers.

1. Record your changes graphically on the spreadsheet (by relocating the task bars).
2. Check the AON network to ensure that the sequence of tasks is not violated (adding new links where required).
3. Keep a constant check-sum at the bottom of the spreadsheet.

THE TECHNIQUE: STEPS FOR RESOURCE LEVELING

For a group of tasks contributing to an Overloaded Resource:

1. Schedule the task having the EARLIEST Late Start Time (this gives priority to the earliest critical task—for critical tasks, LST = EST) and then re-schedule the task having the next earliest LST, and so on.
2. When several tasks have the same LST, give priority to the one having the smallest Total Float.
3. Schedule each task as *early as possible* without violating any of the precedence requirements for the project. When a critical task slips, any task following it must also start later. Refer continually to the network or Precedence Matrix to maintain the order of construction. You can ensure that construction sequencing is not violated by adding links to the network based on the sequencing dictated by your smoothing objectives.

4. Ensure that the total amount of each resource scheduled does *not* exceed the prescribed limit; it measures the total effort expended by a crew.

Smoothing More Than One Resource at a Time

This introduction to "smoothing" focused on smoothing only one resource: laborers. Realistically, there will be more than one type of manpower and equipment that clash among themselves and must be smoothed. Realistic multiple clashes are practically impossible to smooth to their ideal levels because re-scheduling one could cause a clash in another. Compromises must be made. The manager must decide which resource should be "smoother" than the others. If smooth manpower loading is preferable to the smooth use of machinery, then this criterion will guide the re-scheduling of tasks.

In Figure 9–7A, between Day #28 and #33, tasks 8, 20 and 21 each require one Equipment Operator. Re-scheduling any of these three tasks may cause a clash with other tasks for EO's or any other resource. This illustrates the complexity of attempting to level several resources simultaneously.

Checking Your Work: Bookkeeping Checks Reveal Errors

As we re-schedule a task, its resource bar (and its man-day count in the last column) will be moved along the row and therefore the sums in the bottom row will change; the sum in the last column will *not* be changed. We must remember to keep track of the effort for each resource each day and record the totals in the lower rows at the bottom of the page. When we have finished, we can check our accuracy by summing the totals of the last column and comparing it with the sum of values in the bottom row. They should be the same. An example is shown in Figure 9–8, which is based on the small example project described in Figure 9–5.

And just as important, the terms in the last column must be the same as they were before you re-scheduled. If not, then you made mistakes. These values in the last row and the last column represent the effort expended for each task on any given day; the total in the lower right corner is the total effort required for the project. This is so because the fundamental assumption of this method is to re-schedule—*without changing the* TOTAL *resources of any task!*

Updating the Network

Because you re-scheduled on a Gantt Chart/Worksheet, you should update the AON network to record a consistent set of data. If you worked carefully on the worksheet and did not violate any existing precedence links, there may be very few adjustments to be made. Check each task from the task order on the worksheet and compare this sequencing with the original AON's, making corrections and

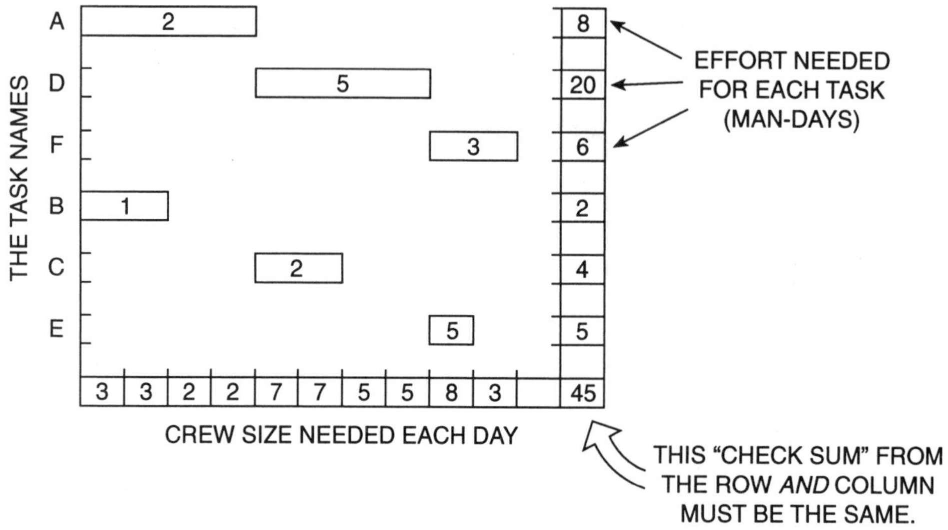
THE TASK NAMES
A
D
F
B
C
E
2
5
3
1
2
5
8
20
6
2
4
5
3 3 2 2 7 7 5 5 8 3
45
EFFORT NEEDED
FOR EACH TASK
(MAN-DAYS)
CREW SIZE NEEDED EACH DAY
THIS "CHECK SUM" FROM
THE ROW AND COLUMN
MUST BE THE SAME.

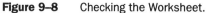

Figure 9–8 Checking the Worksheet.

additions where necessary. You may find errors in the worksheet. This has been done for leveling the laborer crew and the revised AON is shown in Figure 9–9.

Computer Assistance

The methods of this chapter can be quite challenging to execute with pencil and paper. Thankfully, several scheduling programs are capable of "automatically" leveling resources as part of the services that they offer to the human scheduler. To refer to this part of the software as "Black Art" would be unfair to the programmers who devised it; but it is quite unnerving to manually level a project at considerable emotional expense and then repeat it on the computer by simply pressing a few keys and waiting. Regardless of all the other services supplied by a good scheduling program, this leveling function alone justifies its purchase.

SUMMARY

There is much in this chapter about leveling resources by modifying the schedule of individual construction tasks. We found that the critical tasks could be "frozen" in their original schedule and that the remaining tasks might be re-scheduled within their individual floats. It might become necessary for critical tasks to be re-scheduled, with a resulting extension of the project.

We needed to be careful to ensure that the original precedence requirements were not violated after some tasks were re-scheduled. It is always more challenging to try to level several resources at once rather than only one.

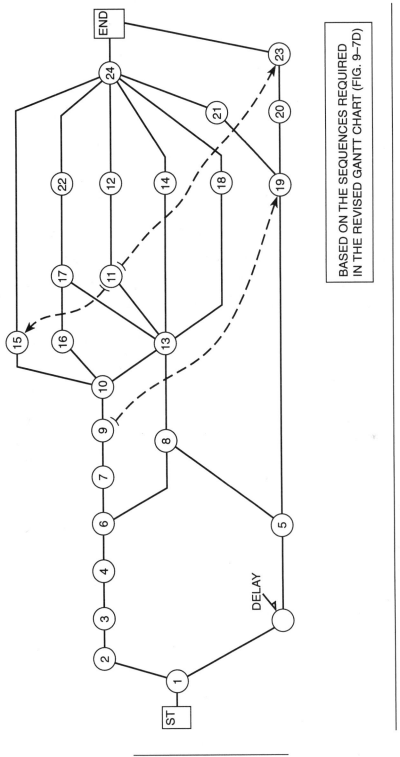

BASED ON THE SEQUENCES REQUIRED
IN THE REVISED GANTT CHART (FIG. 9–7D)

Figure 9-9 The Updated AON Network: New Links.

159

EXERCISES AND PROBLEMS

1. For the small example project of Figure 9–5, smooth the loading for the crew according to the changed manpower requirements below. Draw the histogram for the initial case, determine the total effort (man-days), the average number of workers needed per day, and try to achieve this target number through judicious re-scheduling. As a supplementary problem, stretch several tasks so that the work can be completed with a maximum of 6 workers.

TASK IDENTITY	A	B	C	D	E	F
NO. OF WORKERS	4	3	5	3	3	3

2. The first attempt at leveling the laborer crew is reported in Figure 9–7D. Study this analysis and consider how you might re-schedule some tasks to smooth out the variations near the end of the project, after Day #86. As part of this resolution, you should consider "filling in" the loading between Day #33 and #66 currently with a crew of 3. After making the bookkeeping check, update the AON network to make it consistent with your worksheet. Recalculate the AON to compare the times from the Gantt Chart on the worksheet.

10

REDUCING THE
DURATION OF A PROJECT

LEARNING OBJECTIVE

After completing this chapter, you should be able to:

1. Reduce the duration of a project in two ways:
   a. by subdividing pairs of sequential tasks so that the second one can begin before the first is completely finished; and
   b. by "Crashing" selected tasks; that is, by accelerating the rate of doing the work through an increased supply of resources.

PREPARATION FOR THIS CHAPTER

Every refinement described in earlier chapters tended to increase the duration of the project; this chapter introduces two methods for shortening a project. These techniques for accelerating a project can be applied at any stage during the evolution of a schedule, but it is logical to attempt to shorten a project only after all slow-downs have been considered.

You must be familiar with all the resources needed for each task and the physical layout of the project. Some of the things you may need to consider are that the delivery of resources may be limited by the suppliers, cramped working conditions may prevent a larger crew and more equipment from being accommodated, and storage of extra building materials may be limited by a small site.

INTRODUCTION

In a our private lives, we often take all the time available before we finish a job. In industry, there are many arguments in favor of shortening a project.

1. Money is *borrowed* for a shorter time and the interest to be paid is therefore reduced.
2. Completing *more* projects in a year means that the costs of running the company are shared by more projects, reducing the "overhead" charge against each project.
3. Poor *attitudes* lead to other inefficiencies.

STRATEGIES FOR SHORTENING A PROJECT

Recall that the longest path through a network determines the project's duration, and, therefore, the critical path must be shortened to save time. If another path through the project has only a small amount of float, then it can become the critical path if the original critical one is shortened by more than the amount of the float. We can shorten a task on a critical path by only the amount of the smallest float of all the tasks in the network; then we select other paths to shorten. There are two ways to shorten a critical path: task splitting and "crashing."

Task Splitting

Task splitting is re-organizing the (usually) larger tasks into several smaller components, so that the follower tasks *can begin sooner*, after completion of only *part* of the preceding task. For example, the painting of a multistorey apartment building could be done as each floor is completed, rather than waiting until all the floors are complete. Defining painting as a single task in the initial network would force us to consider splitting as a way of saving time, especially if painting were a critical task.

"Crashing"

Increasing the rate of supply of resources by increasing the size of the crew on the job or adding another crane increases the daily effort applied to a task and shortens its duration. Adding a second shift or working a longer day accomplishes the same thing, but it may be cheaper to add more resources to the day shift. There are rules for selecting the most effective task to crash.

Tasks are split without increasing the flow of their resources, but crashing does increase the flow of resources. We will study the constant resource technique first in this section. Following this we will study two variations on "Crashing" in which the specific objectives have been defined: crashing to minimum project duration OR crashing to minimum *total* cost of the project.

PROBLEMS DUE TO INCREASED COMPLEXITY

The simplest project is the "One-Man-Show," where one person does *all* the work, executing one task after the other. Its Network Chart is very simple: there is one line of tasks from START to END and the total duration is the sum of the individual task durations. Additional new helpers can be applied either to assist the original lonesome worker or execute some of the other tasks in parallel with the original worker, thus producing a second path in the network. The single worker can manage his solitary project all by himself, but the complication of adding several new workers requires monitoring and coordinating—a manager is needed and overhead costs rise.

As more and more workers (and equipment and materials) are added, the network becomes more complex and involved; individual task durations can be shortened, and floats are systematically reduced until a near-panic working environment evolves. At worst, all tasks (and all paths through the network) become critical and any slip-up causes the project to stretch out. Thus, management of the project becomes more difficult, requiring more managers, more coordination, and more meetings. In short, projects can be over-refined to the point that they become almost impossible to manage. Fortunately, this all-critical situation is seldom attained, but parts of all projects can display the tendencies when they are squeezed.

PRINCIPLES FOR SPLITTING TASKS

The method to be described here is restricted to increasing only the number of tasks *without adding any new resources.* Two tasks are subdivided into smaller parts, allowing the second task to start earlier. In practice, resources might be increased as well, but, for this learning exercise, the two tactics are separated. The objective is to subdivide tasks into two (or more) shorter tasks so that a dependent task can be started before the first one is completely finished. Even though a task is subdivided into several shorter tasks, its total duration will not be changed, nor will the total resources required for the task be changed.

To shorten the total duration of a pair of sequential tasks requires that the second task be able to be started while the first (predecessor) task is still being executed. For example, if a room must be fumigated before it can be painted, it would be impossible to begin painting before the fumigation was finished, unless some very special, more expensive precautions were adopted. But as we are not adding any resources (existing or new), we must finish fumigating before starting to paint.

In addition, the pair of tasks to be split cannot use the same resources. If the same crew works on both of the tasks that are to be split, the crew would then have to work on both part-tasks simultaneously after the split. This would not be possible without adding another crew.

DAYS	0	6	14	18	24
TRENCHING	XXXXXX				
GRAVEL BED		XXXXXXXX			
LAY PIPE			XXXX		
BACKFILL				XXXXXX	

Figure 10–1 Simple Pipe Laying Project.

Therefore, in order to split two tasks to shorten the duration of the project, there are three criteria to be observed:

1. Both tasks must be on the critical path.
2. Both tasks must be in sequence.
3. Both tasks must use independent resources.

Consider digging a mile-long ditch (6 days), laying a gravel bed (8 days), laying drain pipe (4 days), and then re-filling the excavation (6 days). Figures 10–1 and 10–2 describe the project; initially it will take 24 days when the tasks are executed in series. The obvious question arises: "Must I wait for 6 days before I can begin laying the gravel bed?" Obviously not.

The simplest first try would be to divide ditching and graveling into two halves: Ditching #1 and #2 (three days each) followed by Graveling #1 and #2 (four days each). The original 14-day total duration for these two is now reduced to 7 days. Similarly, the remaining tasks can be split. The original 24-day project

DAYS	0	3	7	11	16
TRENCHING #1	XXX				
TRENCHING #2		OOO			
GRAVEL BED #1		XXXX			
GRAVEL BED #2			OOOO		
PLACE PIPE #1			XX		
PLACE PIPE #2				··OO	
BACKFILL #1				XXX	
BACKFILL #2					OOO

Figure 10–2 Task Splitting the Pipe Project.

can now be accomplished in 16 days. The duration is not halved, partly because the task durations do not match in length.

Other splitting strategies might be considered in an attempt to save a few more days, possibly splitting tasks in thirds. In an extreme case of splitting, transmission pipelines for natural gas are laid in one continuous process across hundreds of miles. Resources for all tasks are assigned so that each task has the same duration: clearing, trenching, tube welding, and laying occur within sight of one another. Repetitive processes like this one can be planned in a like manner. Scrutiny of your construction project may reveal similar opportunities.

TASK-SPLITTING FOR THE 24-TASK WAREHOUSE

As is our regular practice when explaining new techniques, we will shorten the basic schedule of only the construction tasks. For a real application, you would shorten the network after all the delays are included. The following discussion applies to the basic AON network of Figure 6–15.

For an introductory example, consider the three tasks for building the basic structure of the warehouse: the three major ones (approximately 20 days each) are the Foundations, Walls, and Roof (tasks #7, #9, and #10), as illustrated in Figure 10–3.

If the Foundation work could be split, the block Walls could be started sooner. The complete foundation job is in two parts: 2 days of excavation and 18 days to build forms and pour and cure the concrete. The latter 18 days could be split into two 9-day periods. The block work could then begin nine days earlier than before.

Naturally, you would want to begin building the roof structure when the first part of the wall was completed. As long as the mortar had achieved adequate strength by Day 46, the first steps in the roof work could begin, starting on the morning of Day 47. The 19-day roof construction would then be completed on Project Day 65, 20 days earlier, due solely to the splitting of the tasks. The mortar would be set in time if the building was completed at one end first, with the side walls "growing" at full height toward the other end. Safe working conditions would have to be maintained by the manager when the different crews worked near one another.

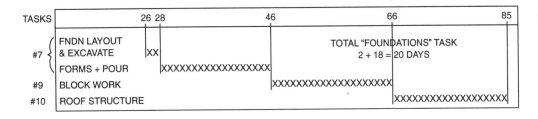

Figure 10–3   A Part of the Warehouse Project.

PROJECT DAY	26 28		36	46	56	65
FNDN LAYOUT & EXCAVATE	X XX					
FORMS + POUR (A)		XXXXXXXXX				
FORMS + POUR (B)			XXXXXXXXXX			
BLOCK WORK (A)			XXXXXXXXXX			
BLOCK WORK (B)				XXXXXXXXXX		
ROOF STRUCTURE					XXXXXXXXXXXXXXXXXXX	

Figure 10–4   Warehouse Project—Splitting Three Tasks.

The Gantt Chart in Figure 10–4 shows the solution. However, before deciding that we have shortened the whole project by 20 days, we must recalculate the new times for all the tasks of the project. It is easy to fall into the trap of stating that the above project has been shortened by 20 days because the critical path has been shortened by 20 days. In many situations this will not be the case.

TASK SPLITTING ON A BUBBLE (AON) DIAGRAM

While Gantt Charts are ideal for visualizing task splitting, it is better to deal directly with the AON network. The network is easily modified by replacing each of the paired tasks with two "half-tasks" linked into a small parallelogram. This four-sided pattern is easy to remember, as shown in Figure 10–5. You might argue that it is unnecessary to split Task "Q" because Q_2 must follow Q_1; but it must also follow P_2, and both tasks must be split.

In the warehouse example (Figure 10–6), two groups of tasks on the critical

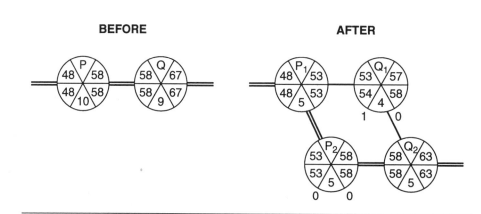

Figure 10–5   Bubble Patterns When Splitting Tasks.

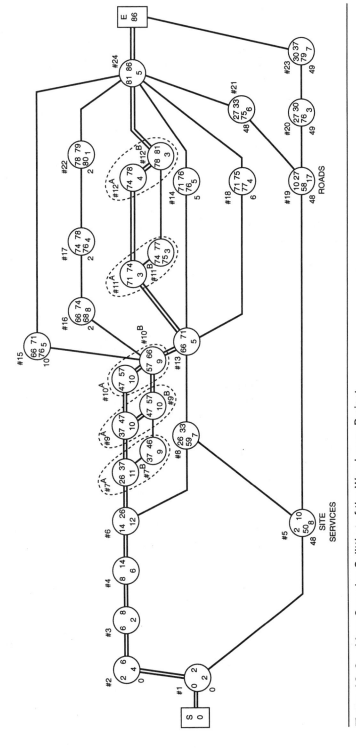

Figure 10–6 More Complex Splitting of the Warehouse Project.

path have been split; Tasks #7, #9, and #10; and #11 and #12. The first set saved 19 days, while the second saved 3 more. These modifications shortened the project by 22 days. Compare this AON network with Figure 6–15 and note the reduction in floats for the non-critical tasks.

The modifications are made more complicated when there are two parallel critical paths; shortening one path will not shorten the project. Therefore *both paths* must be shortened simultaneously by about the same amount. The path shortened the least will still be critical and will determine the time saved. Split a pair of tasks in each critical path by approximately the same amount. Then recalculate the EST, LST, and the TF for all the tasks in the network before considering the next splitting stage.

When selecting the pair of tasks for splitting ensure that there will be no conflict in any of the resources caused by the overlapping task segments. When your modifications are complete, check to ensure that the three rules have not been violated. It might be necessary to construct a revised resource histogram.

CRASHING

The term **crashing** means to speed up an activity by adding more resources over and above the normal levels planned. For example, the "normal" level of manpower planned for a task is based on the "standard" crew selected for the task. Tasks are "crashed" by increasing the crew-effort supplied to the job: that is, by enlarging the size of the "normal" crew.

The commonest resource to add is human effort, but the principle applies to any active resource. Simply supplying more construction materials will not in itself accelerate a task, but adding another complete standard crew will. "Effort" is the key word.

This piling on of resources is not done indiscriminately or irrationally: not all tasks are crashed. Tasks are crashed that minimize the added cost of doing the crashing.

Before looking at the process, we must first consider the idea of a "normal" crew and the penalties in cost and time of using non-normal crews.

NORMAL CREWS AND NORMAL DURATIONS

Most companies record the daily accomplishment of a "normal" crew working on a well-defined task. The output of crews is continually monitored and compared with planned progress so that when unfavorable deviations from the plan arise corrective action can be taken. But there is a second reason for measuring actual work accomplished: the information adds to the basic statistical data for planning new projects. Recall that the duration of a task is estimated by making the following simple calculation:

$$\frac{\text{Task Duration}}{\text{(days)}} = \frac{\text{(Amount of work to be done by Crew "X")}}{\text{(Daily capacity for this work by "Crew X")}}$$

For example, if a standard crew of bricklayers can lay 450 concrete blocks per day, then a Task that involved laying 5000 blocks would be expected to take 11 days. The calculation is quite simple once the crew has been selected and its productivity is known. If you have no personal experience to draw upon, refer to published materials (Means, Dodge, and similar guides), which offer helpful information to start with. Crashing, however, requires further information that is probably available only from experienced foremen in particular trades. What we need to know is the reduction in worker output when the crew size is changed.

PRODUCTIVITY (Output per Worker per Day)

We have just seen that the initial duration is estimated from the QUANTITY of work to be done and the DAILY OUTPUT of the assigned crew. The most effective crew will be selected for the job; that is, the average daily output for each member of the crew will be larger than for any other combination of workers. If there were a more effective crew, it would become the "standard" crew.

$$\frac{\text{The Average Productivity}}{\text{of Each Crew Member}} = \frac{\text{Daily Output of the Crew}}{\text{Size of the Crew}}$$

Because this crew is the most efficient group of workers for this job, any other size of crew will change the efficiency of the crew and the productivity per man will be smaller than for the optimum (best) crew. The total output for the larger crew will increase but the output per worker will decrease. For example, assume that the best masonry crew has three workers and that it can lay 450 blocks/day (150/day *per worker*). Adding one more mason might increase the crew's output to 550/day but the output per worker would be *reduced* to 138/day (550 ÷ 4). One more mason would increase the rate of laying blocks but the laborer could not deliver blocks fast enough and the masons would not be fully employed.

The three-worker crew was considered the "best" crew because it could lay more bricks *per worker* than any other combination of workers and thus could accomplish the work with minimum labor cost. If we could find another combination where the output per worker actually increased, then this new crew would become the "normal" crew! In some companies, the individual crew members have worked together on several jobs and perform well together, which indicates that personalities can also affect output.

These concepts apply to other resources (for example, a crane). For a small site, adding a second crane could complicate the work site and reduce the daily

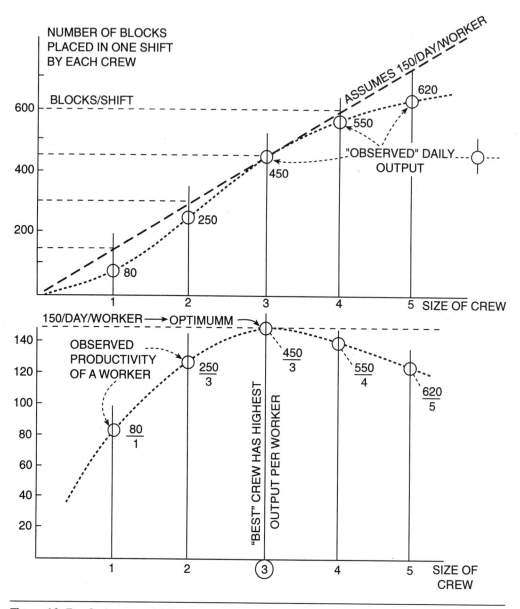

Figure 10–7 Optimum and Off-optimum Crew Sizes.

output for each crane, just as adding one member to the normal crew could reduce the daily output per worker.

Figure 10–7 illustrates this effect. The straight line predicts the theoretical output of a crew—double the size of the crew and the output is doubled. This might be true for a group of gravediggers who are each digging a grave, but it would not be true for a crew that requires a close-knit working arrangement among its members.

The dotted line shows realistic effects. A crew of 3 are expected to lay 450 blocks per day (150 per man) but if one man is removed, the remaining two can lay only 250/day (125/man) not the 300 "expected." Similarly, by adding a fourth man to the crew, the working relationships are disturbed and their individual productivity might fall to 138 (550 ÷ 4). As overcrowding and competition for equipment increases, an individual worker's productivity falls even more, as indicated on the graph. These numbers are used only to represent the principle and the effects of changing the size of the most efficient "normal" crew.

It must be emphasized that deviations from the normal crew depend on how the increase in manpower is achieved. Placing two crews together in the same crowded workspace could easily become counterproductive, whereas assigning each crew to two independent locations might only slightly affect their productivity values. (Competition for common equipment and materials might still occur unless the overlap were provided for by the planner.)

VARIABLE DIRECT COSTS

The previous "data" was presented to illustrate the effect on the direct cost of a task if different-sized crews were used. The table of values in Figure 10–8 is derived from the set of productivity data (above). The task is to lay 7000 concrete blocks and find the variation in cost using different-sized crews.

The calculations are made as follows: We take the daily cost to be $200 per man per day. The "Best" crew of 3 men lays 450/day and takes 15.6 days to do the job (7000 blocks ÷ 450 blocks per day = 15.6 days). The direct cost of laying 7000 blocks therefore is 15.6 days × 3 workers × $200/day = $9,360 and the amount of EFFORT required is 46.8 man-days.

The other results listed in the table are related to the same calculation. As the cost of laying the 7000 blocks increases as the size of the crew increases, we calculate two items: the number of days saved and the increase in cost over the reference crew.

Referring to the table (Figure 10–8), we see that

1. When one worker is added to the three-man crew, 2.9 days are saved (a reduction from 15.6 to 12.7 days), but costs increase by $800 ($10,160 – $9,360). The daily cost penalty is $276 ($800 ÷ 2.9).

CREW SIZE (men) (a)	DAILY OUTPUT (# blocks) (b)	TASK DUR'N (days) (c)	NO. OF MAN-DAYS (d)	TOTAL COST ($) (e)	AVERAGE PENALTY PER DAY SAVED ($/day saved) (f)
1	75	93	93	$18,600	
					$142
2	250	28	56	11,200	
					148
3	450	15.6	46.8	9,360	"Best" Crew
					276
4	550	12.7	50.8	10,160	
					300
5	650	10.8	54	10,800	
					501
6	690	10.1	60.6	12,120	
					715
7	725	9.7	67.9	13,580	

Average $ Penalty per Day Saved relative to the "Best" Crew. A term in Column "f" is found by: "f" = ("e" − 9360) / ("c" − 15.6)

Figure 10–8   Cost Penalties for Off-optimum Crew Sizes.

2. When two workers are added to the basic crew, 4.8 days are saved, the cost rises from $9,360 to $10,800, and the cost penalty per day saved is $300.
3. When three workers are added (doubling the crew), 5.5 days are saved, the costs increase from $9,360 to $12,120, and the cost penalty per day saved is $501.

The graph in Figure 10–9 shows that the cost penalty for each day saved is simply the change in cost divided by the number of days *saved*. This example may appear somewhat academic in nature but it illustrates the concept that crashing to save time costs extra money. Reducing the size of a crew is meaningless for this application because our objective is to shorten a task by adding more resources, not reducing them.

In practice, crashing different tasks incurs different cost penalties, and an estimate of the relative penalties is central to evaluating the merits of different crashing scenarios. The examples given here assume certain penalties; in practice, experienced people provide invaluable input about the potential effects of actual crashing approaches.

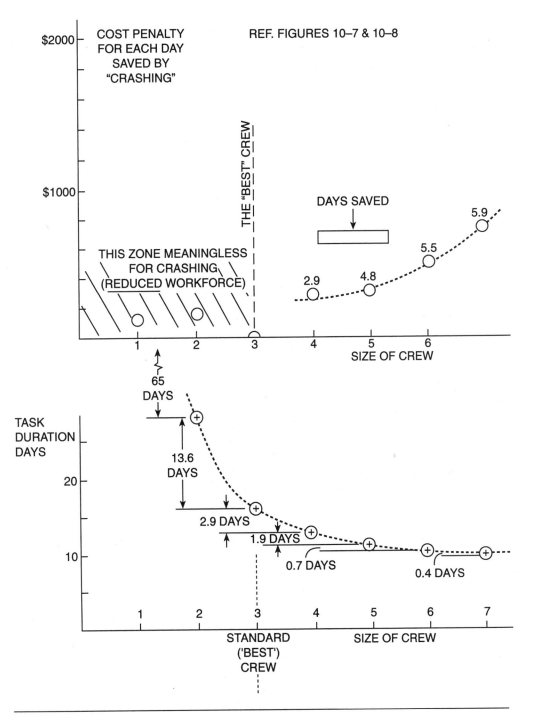

Figure 10–9 Graph of the Direct Cost Penalty.

TOTAL PROJECT COSTS

The above calculations show that any change from the "Best" crew will incur additional expense. So why should we do it? Crashing involves a trade-off between direct and indirect costs and, in many situations, moderate crashing can reduce the *total* cost of the project.

The total cost of a project is made up of the Direct Costs (Materials, Labor, and so forth) plus Overhead/Burden (interest on loans, lease charges, building rental, office costs, and the like). Many of these costs are directly related to the duration of the project. If the above job was being financed by a loan of $1,000,000 at 9%, interest costs are approximately $250 per day and if overhead costs are $150/day, shortening the project by one day would save a total of $400 in overhead cost.

Thus, we can save money by spending more on resources that shorten the project. In the above example, if we add one man to the three-man crew, we save 2.9 days and increase the costs by $800, but we save $1,450 on overhead. On a daily basis, the cost penalty is $276/day but the saving is $500, for a net improvement of $224 for every day saved.

In the example (Figure 10–9) a penalty of $300 is a defensible average value for saving several days. While it is an average value, it is satisfactory for comparison with the penalties of other tasks: $300 identifies a much cheaper penalty than does $800; but there is little choice between $300 and $350. We estimate these values so that we can select the task with the least penalty, even if we are not overly confident about the exact values.

Obviously, no task can be crashed beyond some minimum duration that is based on the physical constraints of the job and the site, irrespective of how much or how many resources are supplied. If a ditch must be dug by hand, you cannot fit laborers with picks and shovels any closer than about five feet apart because of safety considerations. For further shortening of the duration, other methods must be proposed. No task can be completed in zero duration; each task will have its own absolute minimum duration.

TWO OBJECTIVES WHEN CRASHING

It has been shown that total direct costs rise as a task is crashed, but that the total fixed costs fall as days are saved. However, as the schedule "tightens up" because of continued crashing, the cost penalties will increase faster than the savings in the fixed costs. The example plotted in Figure 10–10 shows how the direct and overhead costs change as successive days are saved during a crashing calculation.

Note on the graph that the net change in the cost of the project gently decreases and then starts to rise quite dramatically as days are saved. There is a minimum point at the bottom of the curve. This minimum project cost is reached

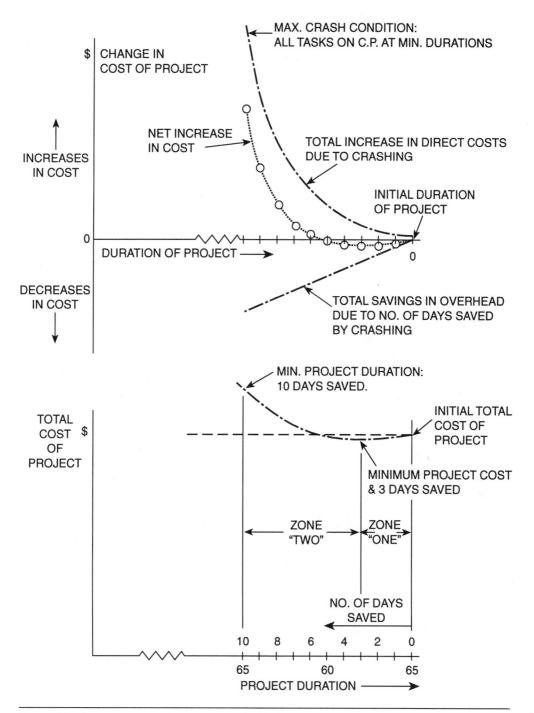

Figure 10–10 Typical Form of Savings and Penalties as a Project Is Shortened.

when the added penalty for shortening a particular task is equal to the added saving; any saving is just canceled out by the penalty.

The crashing can be continued past this point until every task on a critical path has reached its minimum duration and therefore the project has reached its absolute minimum duration. At this point, the total cost penalties will have most likely exceeded the total savings and the total cost of the project will exceed the pre-crashing cost. The building of the Alaska Highway through Canada to Alaska was a "max crash" project in which 1000 miles of highway was built in 14 months in 1942–1943. Apparently limitless resources and 24-hour work days were committed to this project deemed vital to national defense.

ZONES ON THE CRASHING GRAPH

There are two zones to look for on the graph as you shorten the project by one day at a time:

First Zone: The amount saved per day exceeds the penalties incurred from shortening the task(s) by one day.

Second Zone: The penalties for each day saved now exceed the daily saving. The crashing process ends when all the tasks on the critical path have attained their minimum durations.

The minimum total cost of the project occurs for the project duration at the end of Zone 1 and the minimum duration of the project occurs at the end of Zone 2. Thus Crashing can usually proceed toward two objectives:

1. Minimum Total Cost of the Project, then to
2. Minimum Duration of the Project.

Where penalties are very high, there may be no minimum cost condition.

THE TECHNIQUE FOR CRASHING

Particular data is required before embarking on a Crashing analysis of a project:

1. A starting network, showing its critical path based on the initial durations of each task. The Total Float of every task in the project must be recorded.
2. The nominal and minimum durations for every task.
3. A cost penalty for shortening a task by one day.
4. The daily value of the fixed costs for the project.

Steps in the Analysis

1. List the basic data on a Crash Sheet (Figure 10–12).
2. Identify the critical tasks and their critical path.
3. Identify the critical task having the smallest penalty.

4. Reduce its duration by ONE DAY and calculate its revised duration.

5. Reduce ALL FLOATS by one day, noting that zero is the minimum value for any float: that is, (Zero – 1) = Zero. There is an exception: when more paths than one meet at the crashed task, the floats in those paths do not change. Study these cases in detail before blindly reducing float values.

6. Identify all critical paths (new ones will be created).

7. Repeat Step 2 and onward, *but* if there is more than one critical path, then one day must be saved from *EACH CRITICAL PATH* in order to reduce the project's duration by one day. Thus there will be a cost penalty developed from each path in order to save only one day's overhead cost!

8. Determine the cost penalty and fixed cost saved by each cycle of the process (that is, for saving one more day).

9. Determine the project's total cost after any cycle by subtracting the net saving from the previous day's total cost. It is usually adequate to consider only the savings, not the total project cost.

10. Continue the process several cycles past the Minimum Project Cost stage to ensure that penalties are continuing to outpace the savings derived from the fixed costs. If Minimum DURATION is required, continue the process until *one* of the critical paths cannot be shortened further; that is, when all its tasks have been crashed to their minimum duration.

General Comments About the Crashing Process

Monitor the penalty at each stage; it should never be smaller than for the previous step. When this happens, you have made an error in selecting the appropriate tasks to be crashed.

Mark a revised duration that has reached its minimum value to warn you not to crash it further in a later crashing cycle.

A DETAILED EXAMPLE

THE OBJECTIVE IS TO:

1. Find the duration of the MINIMUM COST schedule.
2. Find the duration for the MINIMUM DURATION schedule.
3. Quote the cost saving (or penalty) for each case.
4. Graph the incremental change in cost as the days are saved.
5. Graph the Total Saving (or Penalty) as the days are saved.

STEP 1.   The data for the example project has been recorded in Figure 10–11: the AON Network, the initial and minimum durations, floats, and the daily cost penalty for each task. Some of this data appears on the spreadsheet (Figure 10–12) as the starting conditions for crashing.

TASK NAME	PRECEDERS	TASK DURATIONS		PENALTY $/DAY
		MINIMUM	NOMINAL	
A	START	6	9	$20
B	START	5	8	25
C	START	10	15	30
D	A	3	5	10
E	B	6	10	15
F	C,D,E	1	2	40

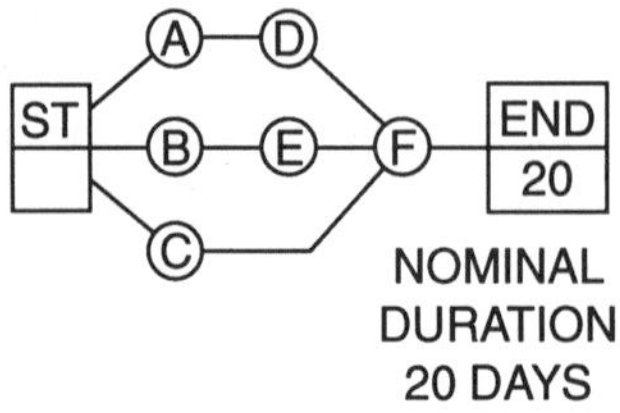

ST — A–D — END 20 / B–E–F / C

NOMINAL DURATION 20 DAYS

Figure 10–11 Data for the Detailed Example: Initial Project Cost is $1000.

STEP 2. The Critical tasks in the basic network are B, E, and F. We will refer to any Critical Path by its critical tasks, in this case: "START-B-E-F-END."

STEP 3. Among tasks B($25), E($15), and F($40) the critical task with the smallest penalty is Task E.

STEP 4. The duration of Task E is now "crashed" by one day, reducing its duration from 10 to 9. It can be done because its absolute minimum duration is 6 days.

STEP 5. Reduce the Floats of the tasks by one day. The floats of A, C, and D are reduced to 3, 2, and 3 days, respectively. The critical tasks (B, E, and F) remain critical (with zero float).

STEP 6. The Critical Path has not been changed after one cycle of crashing.

STEP 7. Returning to Step 2, we note that the situation has not changed and so the above action can be exactly repeated twice more, reducing the duration of E from 9 to 8 to 7, and all non-critical floats are reduced by two more days each. Note that the float of C has become zero by this third crashing of E, producing a second critical path: "START-C-F-END." For Cycle 4, each of the two critical paths must be shortened by one day. Select the cheapest penalty from each path and their sum is the penalty for cutting one day from the project. However, look for a task that is common to both paths and compare its penalty with the penalty from the two tasks. Study task "F."

STEP 8. Cost Penalties: Each time E is shortened by one day, a Cost Penalty of $15 is incurred but $40 in Fixed Costs is saved, producing a net *saving* of $25 for each day cut. These amounts are entered in the appropriate spaces at the bottom of the form.

STEP 9. Revise the total cost of the project after each crashing cycle by subtracting the net saving from the project cost of the previous cycle. In

Figure 10–12 The Spreadsheet for Crashing.

TASK NO.	COST PENALT.	RANK	DUR. NORM.	DUR. MIN.	FLOAT	C1 DAYS CUT	C1 DUR	C1 TF	C2 DAYS CUT	C2 DUR	C2 TF	C3 DAYS CUT	C3 DUR	C3 TF	C4 DAYS CUT	C4 DUR	C4 TF	C5 DAYS CUT	C5 DUR	C5 TF	C6 DAYS CUT	C6 DUR	C6 TF	C7 DAYS CUT	C7 DUR	C7 TF	C8 DAYS CUT	C8 DUR	C8 TF
A	20	3	9	6	6		9	5		9	4		9	3		9	2		9	1		9	0		9	0		9	9
B	25	4	8	5	0		8	0		8	0		8	0		8	0		8	0	−1	7	0	−1	6	0	−1	[5]	0
C	30	5	15	10	3		15	2		15	1		15	0		15	0	−1	14	0	−1	13	0	−1	12	0	−1	11	0
D	10	1	5	3	6		5	5		5	4		5	3		5	2		5	1		5	0	−1	4	0	−1	3	0
E	15	2	10	6	0	−1	9	0	−1	8	0	−1	7	0		7	0	−1	[6]	0		[6]	0		[6]	0		[6]	0
F	40	6	2	1	0		2	0		2	0		2	0	−1	[1]	0		[1]	0		[1]	0		[1]	0		[1]	0

([n] = boxed value / minimum duration reached.)

	CYCLE 1	CYCLE 2	CYCLE 3	CYCLE 4	CYCLE 5	CYCLE 6	CYCLE 7	CYCLE 8
Penalty — This Cycle $	+15	+15	+15	+40	+45	+55	+65	+65
Penalty — Accumulated $	+15	+30	+45	+85	+130	+185	+250	+315
Savings — This Cycle $	−40	−40	−40	−40	−40	−40	−40	−40
Savings — Accumulated $	−40	−80	−120	−160	−200	−240	−280	−320
Change in Project Cost $	−25	−50	−75	−75	−70	−55	−30	+5
Cost of Crashed Project	975	950	925	925	930	945	970	1005

Initial Cost $1000.

179

the example, the revised project cost after three crashing cycles would be $925 ($1000 – $75).

Continue for Three More Cycles

Cycle 4 crashes F to its minimum duration and is so marked.

After Cycle 6, *all three* paths become critical and the "cheapest" task in each path must now be crashed in order to cut one day from the project.

After Cycle 8, path B-E-F cannot be shortened further and even if tasks A and C were crashed, the project would not be shortened; the project has been shortened by 8 days to its minimum duration of 12 days.

Presentation of the Results

The data from the worksheet (Figure 10–12) must be simplified for reporting purposes. A table or a graph condenses the results. Figure 10–13 tabulates this data but when graphed (Figure 10–14), the results are more striking and emphasize important aspects of crashing this project.

Using Graphs of the Results

Graphing numerical results during the calculation can help greatly in getting a "feel" for the progress of sequential and repetitive calculations. "Crashing" calculations are of this type, producing a progression of two interesting numbers: incremental cost penalty (due to crashing one more day) and the total cost reduction

	INCREMENTAL SAVING		INCREMENTAL	TOTAL	TOTAL
DAYS SAVED	COST PENALTY	IN OVERHEAD	CHANGE IN COST	CHANGE IN COST	COST OF PROJECT
0	0	0	0	0	$ 1000
1	+15	–40	–25	–25	975
2	+15	–40	–25	–50	950
3	+15	–40	–25	–75	925
4	+40	–40	0	–75	925
5	+45	–40	+5	–70	930
6	+55	–40	+15	–55	945
7	+65	–40	+25	–30	970
8	+65	–40	+25	+5	1005

Figure 10–13 Tabulated Results of Crashed Costs.

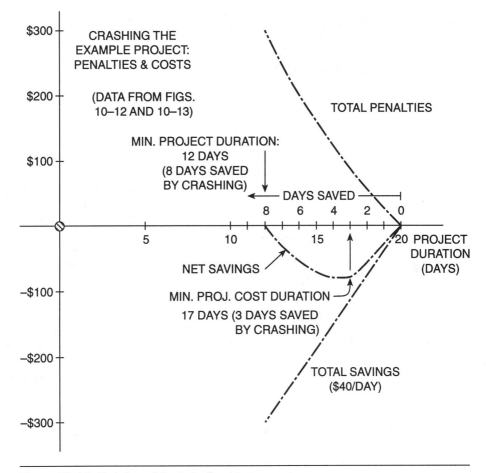

Figure 10–14 Variation of Costs by Crashing.

achieved after each step of the crashing. These results are useful to review, first as a sequence of numerical values and then on a graph.

Figure 10–14 shows how these values change as the project's duration is reduced. The minimum total cost is reached when the daily saving in overhead cost is balanced off by the increased direct costs: cutting four days saves $40 in overhead but penalties from inefficiencies cost $40. In this example, the minimum total project cost is the same for cutting 3 and 4 days.

Maximum Crashing reduces the project's duration by 8 days, increases total project cost by $35, and causes all tasks to be critical, with all tasks but two at their shortest duration—a difficult project to manage but not impossible to achieve. The project cannot be shortened further when all tasks on the critical path are at their minimum attainable durations.

CRASHING THE 24-TASK WAREHOUSE PROJECT

A table of data for crashing the 24-task warehouse project is provided in Figure 10–15. The cost penalties for the tasks have been assumed for this example, but with attention to their relative sizes. Likewise, their minimum durations are estimated relative to the normal durations, with a view to activity levels short of heroic. The first few crashing cycles have been calculated as a base for a later exercise. In this example, the overhead costs are estimated to be approximately $500 per day, so that for each day the project is shortened, $500 is saved. Study the last few lines of the spreadsheet to see the daily costs and the accumulated savings. See Figures 10–15 and 10–16.

You may wish to think of other ways these tasks could be accelerated.

1. The Soils Survey could use an extra borer to obtain soil samples.
2. A second pile driver is expensive, but pile driving goes slowly and would be accelerated by a second driver.
3. The Masonry wall construction could be built simultaneously from both ends if an extra crew were used. There would be some confusion when the two met near the middle, so it is unlikely that the duration would be halved.
4. The Roof Construction could absorb more workers for decking, insulating, and weather-proofing whenever there is room for the additional people to work.
5. Landscaping is labor-intensive, so adding more laborers would shorten the job.

We have assumed that some tasks cannot be accelerated and therefore cannot contribute to shortening the project.

SUMMARY

Two methods have been presented to show how a project can be shortened: Task Splitting and Crashing. The first method is the more obvious one to use. Crashing is done as a last resort because it is more complicated to organize and can directly add to the cost of the project. Task Splitting is relatively easy to organize, but it can be done to extreme detail if it is not governed by a clear overview that weighs the gains in time against the confusion that can result on the job-site.

TASK NO.	STARTING VALUES PENALTY PER DAY $	TASK START	DUR'N MIN.	START FLOAT	PRI	1ST CYCLE DAYS CUT	1ST NEW DUR	1ST NEW TF	2ND CYCLE DAYS CUT	2ND NEW DUR	2ND NEW TF	3RD CYCLE DAYS CUT	3RD NEW DUR	3RD NEW TF	4TH CYCLE DAYS CUT	4TH NEW DUR	4TH NEW TF	5TH CYCLE DAYS CUT	5TH NEW DUR	5TH NEW TF
1	250	2	1	0	2	−1	1*	0		1*	0		1*	0		1*	0		1*	0
2	800	4	3	0	1		4	0		4	0		4	0		4	0		4	0
3	—	2*	2	0			2*	0		2*	0		2*	0		2*	0		2*	0
4	260	6	5	0	3		6	0	−1	5*	0		5*	0		5*	0		5*	0
5	1100	8	6	68	13		8	67		8	66		8	65		8	64		8	63
6	1100	12	10	0	13		12	0		12	0		12	0		12	0		12	0
7	600	20	19	0	9		20	0		20	0		20	0		20	0		20	0
8	400	7	5	52	7		7	51		7	50		7	49		7	48		7	47
9	800	20	19	0	11		20	0		20	0		20	0		20	0		20	0
10	950	19	18	0	12		19	0		19	0		19	0		19	0		19	0
11	300	6	4	0	5		6	0		6	0		6	0	−1	5	0	−1	4*	0
12	450	7	6	0	8		7	0		7	0		7	0		7	0		7	0
13	—	5*	5	0			5*	0		5*	0		5*	0		5*	0		5*	0
14	200	5	4	8	1		5	7		5	6		5	5		5	4		5	3
15	—	5*	5	13			5*	12		5*	11		5*	10		5*	9		5*	8
16	750	8	6	5	10		8	4		8	3		8	2		8	1		8	0
17	—	4*	4	5			4*	4		4*	3		4*	2		4*	1		4*	0
18	280	4	3	9	4		4	8		4	7		4	6		4	5		4	4
19	1600	17	15	70	14		17	69		17	68		17	67		17	66		17	65
20	—	3*	3	71			3*	70		3*	69		3*	68		3*	67		3*	66
21	350	6	4	70	6		6	69		6	68		6	67		6	66		6	65
22	—	1*	1	5			1*	4		1*	3		1*	2		1*	1		1*	0
23	200	7	6	71	1		7	70		7	69		7	68		7	67		7	66
24	280	5	4	0	4		5	0		5	0	−1	4*	0		4*	0		4*	0

OVERHEAD BURDEN IS $500 PER DAY

	1ST	2ND	3RD	4TH	5TH
PENALTY FOR THIS CYCLE	$250	260	280	300	300
SAVING FOR THIS CYCLE	$500	500	500	500	500
NET SAVING (OR COST)	$250	240	220	200	200
ACCUMULATED CHANGE IN TOTAL COST	$250	490	710	910	1110

Figure 10–15 Spreadsheet for Crashing the Warehouse Project.

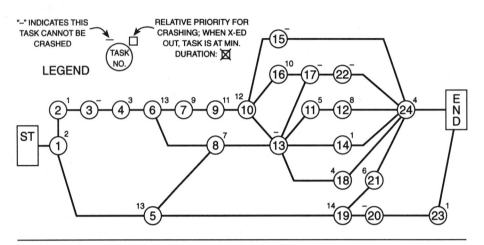

Figure 10–16 AON Network for Warehouse.

EXERCISES AND PROBLEMS

1. Using the AON network for the Warehouse project (Figure 10–6), split tasks 6, 7, 9, and 10 into 3 subtasks each and recalculate the times and floats for the project.

2. Modify the network of Figure 10–6 by adding two dummy tasks before and after Task 19, Road Building. Lag the start of Task 19 by 35 days and lead its ending with a 15-day dummy task, as discussed in Chapter 7. Recalculate the modified network and consider the result. Explain how you would alter the schedule.

3. Using Figures 10–15 and 10–16, continue the crashing of the warehouse project to determine the duration for minimum cost and the minimum duration (full-crash condition) of the project. Draw graphs to illustrate the results as the crashing evolves. Identify the key parts of the graph.

CHAPTER

11

PERT—THE BASIC CONCEPTS

LEARNING OBJECTIVES

After completing this chapter, you should be able to:

- Appreciate the implications of UNCERTAINTY.
- Understand some basic concepts of STATISTICS.
- Calculate expected duration and Standard Deviation (SD) of a single task.
- Determine the duration and SD of any path through the network of a project.
- Determine the probability of completing a project at a stated duration earlier or later than the expected time.

PREPARATION FOR THIS CHAPTER

This chapter may seem like a diversion from the flow of ideas and techniques that evolved through the earlier chapters. Consider it to be a refinement of Chapter 5 and the duration of activities. The PERT system traditionally uses the AOA system for its networks, so you should feel comfortable with arrow diagrams and the associated calculations. The concepts of statistics require you to think in terms of groups of data rather than individual pieces of data. A few formulas are introduced rather than proven which you should be able to apply without much difficulty.

INTRODUCTION

Much of the work of the earlier chapters concentrated on the analysis of Bubble Diagrams in which the durations were accepted as true data. However, forecasts of durations are seldom realized in real-world circumstances. Consider your feelings of uncertainty when you promise to complete an important job in a very specific time. This chapter investigates a method of dealing with the uncertainty of estimating task durations and of the useful results that can be developed by accepting the realities of not being sure. Your goal is always to develop realistic schedules, but in this chapter you are urged to include uncertainty as a real-life phenomenon when you are doing your planning.

UNCERTAINTY   "The only things certain are Death and Taxes."

"Uncertainty" is the opposite condition of "certainty." We have all met people who are (or act) absolutely certain about things: dates, politics, ideas, numbers, . . . "Certain" means being 100 percent sure of some piece of information. But in real life, seldom is anything that certain, especially our estimates of task durations. In our minds, we rate the uncertainty of our ideas according to some form of grading system. We consider our friends to be 99.99 percent loyal and true to us but we view a used-car dealer with a much lower degree of certainty.

It would be useful to have a scheduling method that accepts the uncertainty of each estimated task duration and produces the degree of uncertainty of the duration of the whole project. Fortunately, such an application has existed for almost 30 years; it is called **PERT**, the acronym for *Program Evaluation and Review Technique*. The system was developed as a management tool for reporting and coordinating the efforts of many sub-contractors on the Polaris missile and submarine project during the 1960s. Since then, many computerized variations have become available commercially, and proprietary scheduling programs include applications of probability imbedded in them. There are differing opinions about the value of PERT for construction applications, but its concepts are introduced here to help readers decide for themselves.

Many builders want a schedule only to guide their activities; they consider the schedule as a challenge to be met, and beaten. This aggressive mood is necessary for a competitive contractor, but refinements like PERT can identify areas of potential trouble (having high degrees of uncertainty) that can be given special attention before crisis conditions arise. Work areas with excellent chances of success require less of the manager's time and attention.

To obtain a rudimentary appreciation of the terms and basic applications of PERT, we must study the basic concepts of statistics. The following few pages attempt to define the basic *ideas* of statistics without obscuring them with too much "math." The concepts are important to gaining an appreciation of how PERT works.

SOME BASIC CONCEPTS OF STATISTICS

Statistics deals with "POPULATIONS" of things more than just with large groups of *people*. In general, any large group of related items constitutes a "population" for statistical purposes: 10,000 bolts, a forest of fir trees, the leaves on a maple tree, all the students in a college, the bricks on the walls, and the marbles in a bag. Aspects of populations can be measured (like the daily variations in your travel time) and the group of all such measurements can be described using a few "statistical terms."

Think about something you do repetitively, like driving from home to work or to school. You are used to leaving at the same time every day, but you arrive there at different times. You are used to an average travel time and you quote it to others. If you wrote down these durations for a whole year, you would have collected 200 or so numbers that could be used for a statistical analysis.

If someone wanted to know more about your travel experience, you could say that your average travel time was 35 minutes and that over 68 percent of your recorded times were within 7 minutes of that average, that is, between 28 and 42 minutes. The number 7 describes the "spread" of your collection of data. A friend's travel route may be through quite variable traffic conditions, with a resulting higher average travel time of 50 minutes and a wider "spread" of 20 minutes (between 30 and 70 minutes). Now, if you and your friend estimate how long your trips would take *tomorrow*, your estimate would be considered more certain than hers because of the narrower spread.

We can display the measured travel times for each person on separate graphs so that we can compare them; we can "see" the average values and decide which one has the larger average deviation. Figure 11–1 shows two graphs typical of the two commuters. Such graphs are called **Frequency Distributions** because we graph the number of occurrences (a frequency) of a specific travel time. For your collection of 200 trips, you might have taken 38 minutes on 17 occasions: 17 is the frequency of occurrence of 38-minute trips. Note that your frequency distribution is narrower than your friend's: the average width of these distributions is called the **Standard Deviation** (SD).

STATISTICS AND CONSTRUCTION

Recall that when we estimated the duration of a particular task, we used a "best" value (from published data) and confidently used it for our own application. The published data usually does not include a measure of the spread (SD) of the measured values. For example, if 500 bricks/day is the average productivity of a masonry crew in North America, we do not know whether all the individual measurements were between 450 and 550/day or between 300 and 700/day. This "spread" would be useful to know. The bigger the "spread," the lower is our

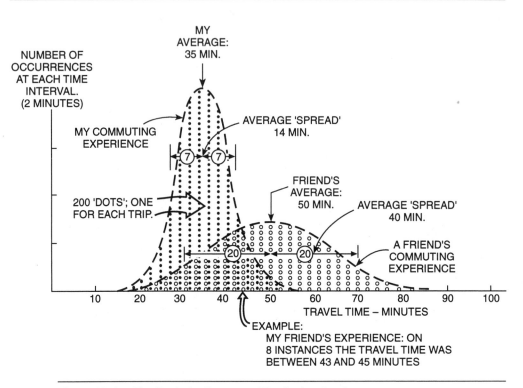

Figure 11–1   The Basis for Frequency Distribution Graphs.

confidence in using the data. The Standard Deviation of the basic data would provide a measure of this "spread."

Statistical Terms

Common statistical terms are introduced via an analysis of the construction of the Suez Canal in the nineteenth century.

We have made some assumptions about the history of that project: 104 builders were each given a contract to build *simultaneously* one mile of the canal, each was given 10 years to complete their one-mile section. After completion, the quickest contractor finished in 8.6 years while the slowest took 11.2 years, with the remaining 102 contractors somewhere in between these extremes.

We arranged these 104 durations in increasing order and counted the number of durations in each 0.2-year period. This list of number of occurrences was the basis for drawing a frequency distribution of the 104 durations. Also, from the list of 104 durations, we calculated two numbers that describe those results in statistical terms: the mean (average) and the Standard Deviation, the average amount the 104 durations deviated from the mean.

The Addendum at the end of this chapter explains how these calculations are made and you should become familiar with the significance of these calculations and the two statistical numbers that result. As the explanation for PERT uses these terms, become familiar with them before proceeding. The Suez example illustrates the uncertainty of estimates and the useful tools of statistics.

A PROJECT'S PERT NETWORK

Traditionally, PERT uses the arrow diagram for its particular analyses, but computer programs may use (or appear to use) both AON and AOA types. We shall use Arrow diagrams for our manual calculations because they provide more space (along the task arrows) for recording data.

Three Time Estimates for PERT

Now that you have an understanding of the statistical background, we can apply it to the warehouse project. PERT requires three time estimates to incorporate statistical aspects into a schedule. As single time estimates have an unconscious time cushion built in by a contractor, three estimates should have smaller cushions because a range of durations allow for uncertainty in the estimates. The three estimates (a, m, and b) will be in response to the following questions:

- **a:** "What is the shortest duration for this task, when everything is perfect for your work?"
- **m:** "How long do you think it will really take?"
- **b:** "If most of your worries materialize, how long will the task take under those conditions?"

A sub-contractor or journeyman making these estimates should be satisfied if the job is completed by duration **m**, the most likely duration, even though there is only a 50 percent chance that it will be achieved. The duration, **m**, should be shorter than the single (cushioned) estimate made by the journeyman.

Time Calculations

The time calculations for a PERT network are the same as those made using single-estimate durations: Early Start, Early Finish, LS, and LF are made the same way as before. The difference now is that the duration of each task is t_e, and every task now has a Standard Deviation, a measure of the uncertainty of its expected duration, t_e; $t_e = 1/6 \cdot (a + 4m + b)$ and $SD = 1/6 \cdot (b - a)$.

We can calculate the Slack at each event or milestone, the total floats of all tasks, and identify the critical path just as before. However, we can now learn more about our project. Using the Standard Deviation of each task along the critical path, we can calculate the SD of the duration of the project. This can help us estimate the chance of finishing the project a few days earlier or later than the indicated value, which is very useful for discussions with the owner. Moreover, we can obtain the SD of other, nearly non-critical paths to identify any dangers that might change them to critical.

The SD of the project duration is readily calculated by squaring the SD's of each of these tasks *along the critical path*, finding the average of their squares, and then taking the square root of this average. This is commonly known as the ROOT MEAN SQUARE (RMS) value. Consider the following example:

> If the tasks on a short critical path through a project have SD's of 2.5, 1.0, 3.1, and 5.0 days, the sum of their squares is 41.86; its average is 41.86 ÷ 4 = 10.46; and the square root is 3.2 days. This is the SD of the critical path.

AN EXAMPLE PROJECT

A simple network was studied as an AON diagram in Chapter 5. We will re-use this network for a PERT example by assuming values for **a**, **m**, and **b** (that are reasonably consistent with the single duration used before), calculate the new durations (t_e), and use them for the time calculations. The bubble diagram and the table of values are shown in Figure 11–2.

The critical tasks are A, C, D, F, and G, all of which are marked with an asterisk (*).

An option for calculating the SD of each path is to tabulate the square of the SD's of each path in its own column. The SD of each path is the square root of the total in the last row for each column. *Note:* "Variance" is often used by mathematicians instead of "the Square of the SD." Statisticians like to invent new names for long familiar names!

USING STATISTICAL THEORY

We studied the Suez Canal Project to explain some of the concepts of statistics. The frequency distribution and "S-Curves" (Cumulative Probability graphs) described that specific project. In order to study other projects, we need general graphs that have universal application. Statisticians have developed standard shapes for these curves based on the mathematical formula for the Standard Normal Distribution. The standard "S-Curve" based on this theory is included in Figure 11–3. A long discourse on the subject is not necessary here because there are many good texts that give extensive explanations. (See, for example, Anderson et al., *Quantitative Methods for Business*, West Publishing, San Francisco.)

TASK IDENT		a	m	b	te	SD	(SD)²	
AOA	AON						PATH 1	PATH 2
1,2	A*	2	3	4	3.0	.33	0.11	0.11
2,3	B	2	3	8	3.7	1.00		1.0
2,4	C*	3	4	5	4.0	.33	0.11	
4,6	D*	2	6	7	5.5	.83	0.69	
3,5	E	3	5	17	6.7	2.33		5.43
6,7	F*	1	2	5	2.3	.67	0.44	
7,8	G*	2	3	8	3.7	1.00	1.0	1.0
5,7	(DUMMY)	Variance of each Path (SD2) . . .					2.35	7.54
		SD of each Path					1.53	2.75

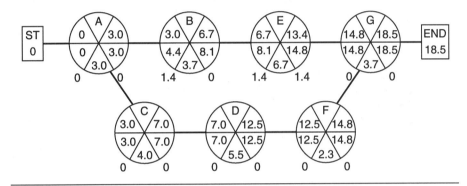

Figure 11–2   Details of the Example Project.

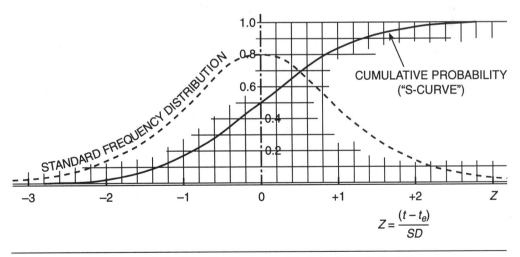

$$Z = \frac{(t - t_e)}{SD}$$

Figure 11–3   The Normal Probability Distribution and Its Cumulative Probability.

PROBABILITY OF FINISHING EARLY OR LATE

The Standard Deviation of the Critical Path and the Cumulative Probability curve can help us forecast our chance for finishing earlier or later than the expected duration of the project. The standard Cumulative Probability graph can be applied to any project with a known SD. Only three steps are needed:

1. Determine the deviation of your target duration from the project's expected duration: $D = (T_T - T_e)$.
2. Convert this deviation into the number of SD's: $Z = D \div (SD)$. Z is measured from the center of the S-Curve, plus is to the right, and negative to the left of the its centerline.
3. Read the probability from the cumulative probability graph, the "S-Curve."

For the Example Project

Consider the Critical Path first: The expected duration of the project is 18.5 days and the SD of the Critical Path is 1.53 days (last row of the table). Statistical theory tells us that t_e durations have a 50 percent chance of being realized; this also applies to the length of any path through the network, when t_e's are used. Therefore, there is a 50 percent chance of the project being finished in the Expected Time of 18.5 days.

Referring to the Cumulative Probability graph (Figure 11–3), if we wanted to complete the project one SD (1.53 days) sooner than the expected duration (18.5 – 1.53 = 17.0 days), there is only a 16 percent chance of doing it. Alternatively, there is an 84 percent chance of finishing in 20.0 days, one SD later than 18.5 days.

Limits to the Duration of the Project

Consider the upper and lower limits of the project's duration: If the optimistic durations ("a" durations) for all the tasks were achieved, the project duration would be 10 days, but there is zero chance of doing the project any faster. Alternatively, if every task took its pessimistic time (b), the duration of the project would be 29 days. Under the rules of PERT, the project is limited to these two extreme durations of 10 and 29 days. In the real world, Murphy's Law applies and anything can happen. Compare these project durations in Figure 11–4.

Now consider the Non-Critical Path: The duration and SD of the other path (A, B, E, G) are 17.1 and 2.8 days, respectively. This path has a TF of only 1.4 days (18.5 – 17.1) and a slightly larger SD, indicating a lower chance of success.

To contrive a more extreme comparison, consider the effect on the project if the second path had a SD of 5.0 days and a TF of only 0.5 days; it is almost critical. The critical path has a 50 percent chance of finishing in 18.5 days, and for the

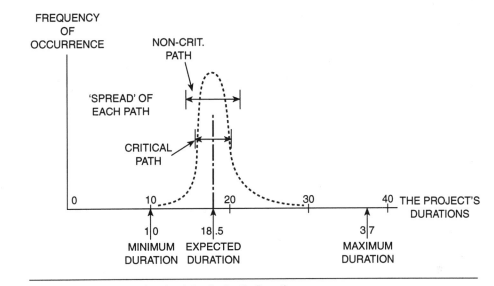

Figure 11–4   A Line Graph of the Project's Durations.

other path, 50 percent in 18.0 days. The chances of these two paths finishing in 20 days raises a challenging situation:

For the CP: SD = 1.5 days. Its chance of finishing 1.5 days late is 84 percent.

For the Other Path: SD = 5.0 days. Its chance of finishing 2.0 days late is only 66 percent.

In this more extreme case, there is less chance of the non-critical path being completed in 20 days than for the critical path. The large SD could likely obliterate the small float of the off-critical path.

This analysis points out that the float in a non-critical path may be effectively obliterated by its large SD. The chances are higher for the tasks on such a path to have unpredictable durations. A manager, knowing this sensitivity, can pay close attention to these more uncertain tasks and be ready to act to keep them on track.

DOCUMENTATION ON "ARROW" NETWORKS

Because of its familiarity, we have used a Bubble Diagram for making the time calculations for the above example, but PERT typically uses the Arrow diagramming method. Chapters 3 and 6 explain the use of Arrow Diagrams for networking and doing the calculations. We shall expand on those studies to include the information for PERT. See Figure 11–5.

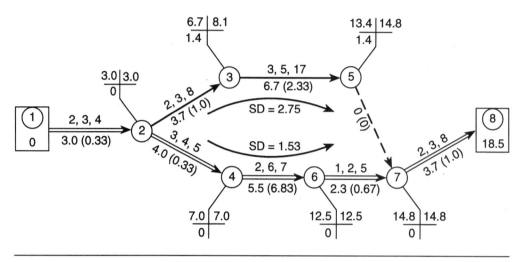

Figure 11–5   PERT Notations on AOA Networks.

We will use the small example to display this information. The three time estimates can be written (a, m, b) along the task arrow; the MOST LIKELY TIME and the SD appear on the other side of the line. In large networks, record only the calculated duration and the SD for reference in calculating the ET and LT of the events and comparing SD's in paths. Recall that the "tree" on each event is for recording the Early and Late Times, and the Slack of each event.

SUMMARY

We have investigated the effect of uncertainty in estimating task durations and the advantages gained by incorporating the uncertainties into the schedules. We found that PERT can identify paths that have unpredictable natures that can disturb a seemingly good schedule. Alert managers can use PERT to identify these unstable areas and then apply extra care in their management.

EXERCISES AND PROBLEMS

1. Three time estimates have been obtained from a sub-contractor for building the roads and parking for the warehouse project (Task #19 in the network). Originally he was confident that 8 days was more than adequate, but when the task was scheduled into mid-summer and the manager asked for three

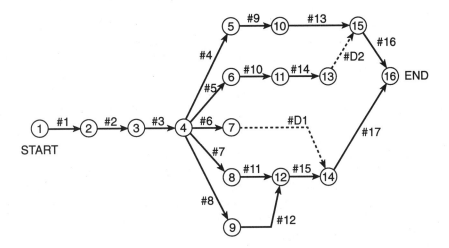

estimates for a PERT analysis, he responded with: a = 4, m = 7, and b = 13. Find t_e and the SD for Task #19, and consider whether the sub-contractor's confidence has improved since he made the original estimate.

2. The AOA network describes a construction project and the table provides the three PERT time estimates for its tasks. The problem is to calculate the expected duration and Standard Deviation of the 17 tasks, find the Early and Late Times for the events and the duration of the project. Identify the critical path and find its standard deviation. Also find the SD of the other four main paths through the network. Determine the probability of completing the Project two days late and the probability of completing a non-critical path (the one having the lowest Slack) two days late. How many days late must the CP be to be 90 percent sure of completion? Find the absolutely shortest duration of this project based on the "a" durations and identify its critical path by naming its events.

AOA NETWORK:

TASK	1	2	3	4	5	6	7	8	9	10	11	12	13	14	15	16	17
a	2	1	1	13	3	3	1	7	2	9	3	6	6	6	2	1	4
m	3	2	2	14	4	6	2	9	3	10	4	8	7	10	3	2	5
b	6	5	3	16	6	7	3	13	5	21	17	15	12	30	12	4	13

ADDENDUM TO CHAPTER 11

STATISTICAL STUDY OF THE CONSTRUCTION OF THE SUEZ CANAL

A realistic example helps to introduce and define the few formal terms we need to understand PERT. In the 1860s it took just over 11 years to complete the project. Imagine that you researched the records for digging the 104-mile-long canal and you found that there were 104 contractors, each of which won a contract to build a one-mile segment of the canal. The imaginary "data" listed in the Figure 11A–1 gives the "actual" durations for digging each one-mile segment by the 104 contractors.

To reduce the amount of data to be listed, we have already grouped the data into small ranges (of 2/10ths of a year) and counted the number of contractor's durations that fell within each short period. For example, there were 5 contractors who completed each of their 1-mile projects between 8.9 and 9.1 years—their individual durations might have been 8.94, 9.0, 9.02, 9.05 and 9.09 years.

The numerical information just described is more conveniently displayed in graphical form (a FREQUENCY DISTRIBUTION) because it displays the number of occurrences of values lying within each narrow range over the extent of the data. The RANGE of the data is between 8.5 and 11.3 years (no data exists outside this range) and each narrow band is 0.2 years wide. Tabulated data has an official appearance, but a graph provides a "feel" for the distribution from the shape of the graph. See Figure 11A–2.

DURATION RANGE	NUMBER OF OCCURRENCES	DURATION RANGE	NUMBER OF OCCURRENCES
8.5		10.1	
	1		13
8.7		10.3	
	1		11
8.9		10.5	
	5		6
9.1		10.7	
	8		3
9.3		10.9	
	11		2
9.5		11.1	
	13		1
9.7		11.3	———
	14		104 values
9.9			
	15		

Figure 11A–1 Durations of 104 Contracts.

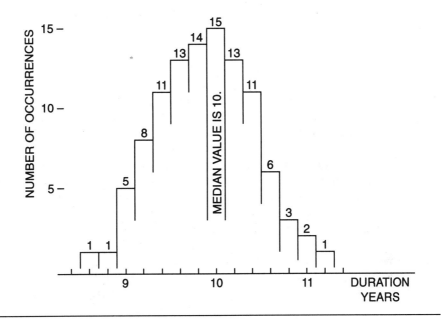

Figure 11A–2 Frequency Distribution Graph.

THE STATISTICAL TERMS DEFINED

Mean

The Mean is the simple average value of the 104 durations recorded. It is found by summing the 104 values and dividing by 104 (the number of values recorded): [8.6 + 8.8 + 9.0 + 9.0 + 9.0 + 9.0 + 9.0 + 9.2 (8 times) + ... + 11.2], divided by 104. The five 9.0's emphasize that there are five values between 8.9 and 9.1 and could have been replaced by (5 × 9.0) as was the case with the next set (8 × 9.2). The average value then is: 1036.4 ÷ 104 = 9.88 years.

Median

The most frequently occurring duration was 10 years. There were 15 durations counted between 9.9 and 10.1 years, thus 10 is the Median value. The Median value is usually near the middle; there are as many occurrences above the average value as below it.

Standard Deviation (SD)

The SD of a set of data is a measure of the shape of the frequency distribution: a small value means that the curve is tall and thin; a large value, that the curve is short and fat. Numerically, it measures the average spread of all the data around the mean value. A band two SD's wide down the middle of the frequency distribution will enclose about 70 percent of all the data collected. Thus a small value for the SD means most of the collected data has values not too different from the mean. See Figure 11A–3.

The SD is found by calculating the difference between a value and the mean, squaring it and summing these squares for all the data collected, dividing this sum by the number of values (that is, finding their average) and, finally, finding the square root of this average. This odd kind of average is based on a theoretical concept, but it has wide application in the real world, including construction. For the Suez Canal, its SD calculation is: $(SD)^2 = [1x(8.6 - 9.88)^2 + 1x(8.8 - 9.88)^2 + 5x(9.0 - 9.88)^2 + 8x(9.2 - 9.88)^2 + etc. ... + 2(11.0 - 9.88)^2 + 1(11.2 - 9.88)^2]$, all divided by 104.

The square root of this result is the Standard Deviation: it is 0.52 years. This value measures the average spread of all the 104 durations; that is, about 70 percent of the contractors completed their contracts between 9.36 and 10.40 years $(9.88 - 0.52)$ and $(9.88 + 0.52)$. Therefore, if one of the contractors estimated 10 years for doing his one-mile section, the project manager could assume there was a better than 50 percent chance of him doing it.

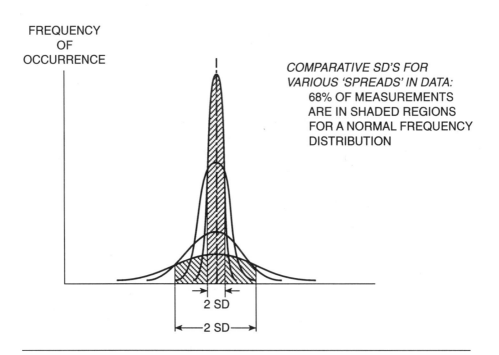

Figure 11A–3 Comparing Standard Deviations.

PERT

In the real world of construction scheduling, we are not going to build another Suez Canal, and even if we did, we would not repeat the old methods. So the details of this historical data may not be of much use to us. The specific numbers are not, but the **shape** of its frequency distribution and only three of its "numbers" can help make PERT useful in modern projects. The three numbers are the minimum and maximum durations taken to build the canal and the median of the 104 durations: the most frequent duration (the 15 contractors who took between 9.9 and 10.1 years).

Modern-day managers have devised a formula that would have given a measure of the uncertainty (SD) of the 104 contractors that built the Suez Canal. Each contractor is asked to provide *three* time estimates for a job: an optimistic duration (**a**), a most likely duration (**m**), and a pessimistic duration (**b**). The formulas are:

The EXPECTED TIME, $t_e = 1/6 \times (a + 4m + b)$ (this calculation is called a "weighted" average)

The STANDARD DEVIATION, $SD = 1/6 \times (b - a)$

We can find those three values for the Suez Canal in the table of recorded data or its graphed frequency distribution (Figure 11A–2). We can find these three durations (the shortest, longest, and "most likely" durations) to be: 8.6, 11.2, and 10.0, which are **a**, **b**, and **m** for the data. The most likely time (**m**) is the tallest bar of the graph (the Median value); it is not the calculated Mean but will be close to it if the frequency distribution is fairly symmetrical.

For our Suez Canal example, these calculations give: the Expected Time is $t_e = 9.97$ years and the Standard Deviation is $SD = 0.43$ years

We calculated the actual values using all 104 values of the data as 9.88 and 0.52 years. The comparison illustrates that a simple approximation can provide credible results. This works well when the actual Frequency Distribution curve is smooth and approximates the theoretical curve used by statisticians.

To interpret these PERT numbers further, we have a 50 percent chance of completing our contract in 9.97 years (the Expected Time), 100 percent chance in 11.2 years, but zero chance in less than 8.6 years (the limits to the recorded durations). There is also a 68 percent chance of completing the work between 9.54 and 10.4 years (in the middle band of the population). In other words, there is a 16 percent chance of completing in 9.54 years (50% – 34%), 50 percent by 9.97 years, and rising to 84 percent (50% + 34%) by 10.4 years; 34 percent on each side of the average is 68 percent total. These probabilities may be more easily seen using the graph of Cumulative Probability (see Figure 11A–5).

CUMULATIVE PROBABILITY

The final argument above can be more easily visualized by determining the number of contractors who have completed their contracts as time goes on. After 8.5 years

TIME	NUMBER COMPLETED	PERCENT OF TOTAL
0–8.5	0	0
8.7	1	0.97
8.9	2	1.9
9.1	7	6.7
9.3	15	14.4
9.5	26	25.0
9.7	39	37.5
9.9	53	51.0
10.1	68	65.4
10.3	81	77.9
10.5	92	88.5
10.7	98	94.2
10.9	101	97.1
11.1	103	99.0
11.3	104	100.0

AVERAGE:
9.88 yrs ———→ (9.9)

Figure 11A–4 Cumulative Probability Data.

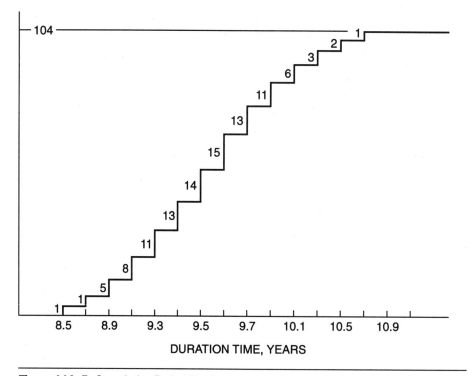

DURATION TIME, YEARS

Figure 11A–5 Cumulative Probability Graph.

into the work, all 104 contractors will have started but only one is almost finished and will be finished by 8.7 years into the contract. The table in Figure 11A–4 adds on the number of completing contractors as each time slot is passed. When expressed as a percent, this graph gives the Cumulative Probability of a contractor being finished at a certain duration. After 11.3 years all contractors (100 percent) will have finished.

Note: The blank rows enclose the data approximately one SD on either side of the Mean duration. The percentages in the last column show that 73.8 percent of the contractors (88.5 – 14.4) finished in that band two SD's wide; the theoretical value from PERT is 68.8 percent. The table (or its graph) can divulge other information: there is a 97.1 percent chance of completing a one-mile segment of canal in 10.9 years.

The graph of this information presents the familiar "S" curve displayed by most growing things. See Figure 11A–5. There is slow early growth, followed by rapid growth in mid-life, and then declining growth before it ends. The growth of total funds expended over the life of a typical project follows the same "S-Curve" growth pattern.

Compare the theoretical curves of Figure 11–3 with the Suez Canal data of Figures 11A–3 and 11A–5.

12

SOME COMPUTER APPLICATIONS

LEARNING OBJECTIVES

After completing this chapter, you should be able to:

- Discuss the advantages (and perhaps some disadvantages) in applying computer programs to scheduling.
- Replace certain manual calculations with a spreadsheet software program.
- Input formulas to spreadsheet programs.
- Begin using a commercial software program.

PREPARATION FOR THIS CHAPTER

Because this chapter repeats the manual work covered in the other chapters of this book, it is imperative that you feel reasonably secure about the concepts, methods, and techniques presented there. In the main, we shall replace most of the manual techniques with specific application software. A computerized spreadsheet replaces tabular calculation sheets. Project management programs can draw networks, make time calculations, and do other complex scheduling calculations with relative ease.

INTRODUCTION

The argument for including this chapter on computers responds to the question: "Why are manual methods provided at all in this book?" An introduction to the methods and techniques of scheduling projects must start with the basic concepts before advancing to those labor-saving devices that make our lives easier. We learn a lot about traffic rules and driving courtesy by riding a bike before we drive our first car and not many of us ever graduate to driving high-powered Formula I racing cars. So it is with computer-assisted analysis. We must know what the computer is trying to do in order to understand the results and decide whether the computer has done what we expected it to do. Beginning schedulers should know the basics of scheduling before being turned loose on a computer.

Software programs are becoming more "user friendly" as new versions and completely new programs enter the market, but most exhibit idiosyncrasies that can cause near madness in the operator. This is not meant to discourage anyone from craving the experience of "playing" with a new program to see what it will do. The demonstration disk accompanying most software can do this without causing undue stress.

Like most books, this book was confronted with the problem of scope. Once the introductory level of scheduling was accepted as the goal of its presentation, there was little room left for discussing advanced methods. Even this short chapter on computerized scheduling cannot go into the details and intricacies of how to use specific software, nor can it introduce you to the basics of computer operation. These are left to the many excellent manuals, periodicals, and books available from software suppliers and computer sections in bookstores.

Manual and Software Methods

When we studied the manual calculation methods, we moved from one calculation to another, making subjective decisions and modifying data where required. But casual meandering through a series of calculations is not the way of computer programs that must have pre-defined steps written into their software commands. The basis for programming is the Flow Chart, which shows the disciplined flow of information. We use flow charts to illustrate data flow by defining the input information needed to develop the next batch of data. This chapter attempts to show how the results from one software program can become the input for the next program. These Flow Charts may also be used by advanced computer users for automating these calculations by using the unique languages ("macros") for simplifying many repetitive calculations.

REVIEW OF THE SCHEDULING PROCESS

The first flow chart (Figure 12–1) shows the development sequences for producing a schedule, starting with the basic information provided in the drawings, specifications, and contract documents. The arrows that lead into a window show the sources of information for producing the contents of that window. For example, to determine the Start Times (and so forth) for all the tasks, we require a network of tasks, the durations of the tasks, and the Start Date from the contract. The "oil"

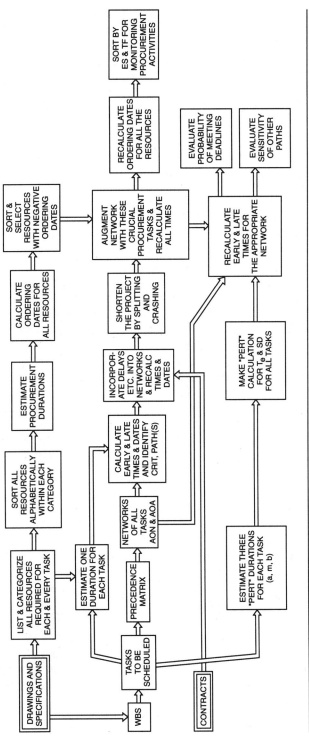

Figure 12-1 Flow Chart of the Complete Process.

to lubricate the unfolding of this new information is the knowledge and experience of the person managing the process.

We manually worked through each step of this process in the earlier chapters, producing the packages of data noted in each window of this flow chart. Now we must consider which of these data transformations can be more easily done using the computer, describe how to go about it, and provide an example.

THE WORK BREAKDOWN STRUCTURE

Most projects begin with thinking about how to organize the whole job, with much scribbling on pieces of notepaper. Constructing the WBS is no exception. The objective is to get a list of the tasks comprising the project by building the WBS. Certain Project Management software programs help by defining a sub-project as the group of sub-tasks that define the details of another more general task. Earlier we studied the "Roof Construction" general task which was composed of sub-tasks such as Trusses, Sheathing, Insulating, Moisture-Proofing, Weather Surface, Eaves, and Overhang. See Figure 12–2.

In this way, the tasks in one level are the components of a sub-project having the name of the task in the level above. In Chapter 2 we constructed the WBS this way, down to the desired level of detail through layers of sub-projects. Very large projects are computer-organized this way, scheduled separately, and then merged with the other sub-projects to give the master schedule.

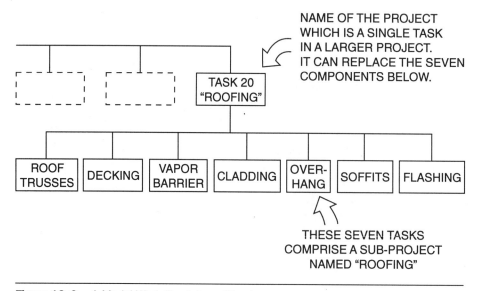

Figure 12–2 A Model Work Breakdown Structure.

Most up-scale scheduling programs accommodate the use of sub-projects in building super-projects. Several software programs will display and print the WBS when tasks are grouped into super-tasks. These super-project to sub-project relationships can relate all the tasks in the project to the Goal of the project, just as we developed (and drew) it manually. When the network for a group of tasks is entered into the computer, it must be named so that it can be saved; this name then appears in the next higher level of the WBS.

PRECEDENCE INFORMATION AND THE PRECEDENCE GRID

Most scheduling programs accept task names and their precedence links to other tasks as its basic input through the keyboard of the computer, but you must have already decided on the order and logic of the network elsewhere. Of course, you can begin by typing data directly into the program without much pre-thinking, but a precedence matrix can save much confusion later on, when you try to unravel the confusion on the screen.

The Precedence Grid (P-G) we developed in Chapter 3 was initially laid out manually on squared paper, but it could just as well have been laid out on the cells of a spreadsheet program. Some advantages of using the spreadsheet are that

- rows (and columns) can be rearranged easily
- redundant relationships can be identified
- loops (errors) can be identified

Consider the P-G for the trip from San Francisco (Appendix D); it is repeated below in Figure 12–3.

PRECEDING TASKS	THESE ARE FOLLOWERS									
	A	B	C	D	E	F	G	H	I	END
START	X		X			X		X		
A	O	X								
B		O			X					
C			O	X						
D				O					X	
E				X	O					
F						O	X			
G					X		O			
H			X					O		
I									O	X
END										O

Figure 12–3 Basic Precedence Grid for the Trip.

Assigning symbols to tasks is seldom done in their sequence of construction and so the first draft of the P-G usually has X's all over the grid, below and above its diagonal. This matrix would be easier to understand if the rows and columns were rearranged (in the same order) so that all linkages (X's) were above the diagonal. This rearrangement would allow the plotting to be done in order of appearance in the revised task order, rather than jumping around looking for the next best task to plot. The resulting network will be much better behaved this way. Using a popular spreadsheet program makes the work almost effortless. The P-G has been rearranged: relocate row H to follow B, then repeat with column H. The example P-G is simplified by revising the order to A-B-H-C-F-G-E-D-I, as shown in Figure 12–4. Note that all X-links are now above the diagonal.

LOOPS

Now Figure 12–4 has a redundancy but no loops. To illustrate loops, we will add two extra links (*) to the P-G for this example only: at cell E-B and D-B.

In Figure 12–5 one of the links B-E or E-B is wrong, because two tasks cannot both follow each other; this is a direct loop. You can identify this type when you cannot rearrange the rows and columns to remove an X-link from below the diagonal, but indirect loops can be harder to identify. Consider the following case: D follows E, E follows B, and B now is reported to follow D (this last link has been added to the P-G for this example). The pattern points out the error. Any X-link remaining below the diagonal indicates that a loop will occur when you draw the network. There is no way to rearrange the rows and columns to correct this.

Note that the order of the *names* of the tasks must be the same in the left

PRECEDING TASKS	THESE ARE FOLLOWER TASKS									
	A	B	H	C	F	G	E	D	I	END
START	X		X	X	X					
A	O	X								
B		O					X			
H			O	X						
C				O				X		
F					O	X				
G						O	X			
E							O	X		
D								O	X	
I									O	X
END										

Figure 12–4   Rearranged Precedence Grid for the Trip.

| PRECEDING | THESE ARE FOLLOWERS | | | | | | | | | |
TASKS	A	B	H	C	F	G	E	D	I	END
START	X		X	X	X					
A	O	X								
B		O					X			
H			O	X						
C				O				X		
F					O	X				
G						O	X			
E		(*)					O	X		
D		(*)						O	X	
I									O	X

New Links Marked (*)

Figure 12–5   Travel P-G with Modified Precedences Identifying Loops.

column and the top row: if you moved the complete row C above row H, then you must also place column C to the left of column H. If your diagonal (A-A, B-B, and so forth) is not straight, then your rearrangement is wrong. This why you mark the diagonal ("o") in your P-G as a check; its straight pattern ensures that the row and column order is identical.

The popular spreadsheet programs allow effortless rearranging of rows (or columns): you select Move, name the row to be moved and its destination, and confirm the commands. The rearranged data is displayed.

REDUNDANT LINKS

Checking for redundant links may not be as straightforward as in the above checks. In the latest P-G (Figure 12–5), D follows C, C follows H, and H follows START; also, the matrix shows that C follows START. This last link (C-START) is unnecessary because C follows start in the C-H-START route. This can be found (by eye) by looking for a row and a column, each containing more than one X that intersects with one of the X's (common to both the row and the column). This pattern *may* indicate an unnecessary link that should be checked. If it is not redundant, then this link must be drawn as a dummy task in an AOA (Arrow or PERT) network.

There may be several ways of commanding the computer to look for such patterns and to report them for your action. One strategy is for it to check every X (in turn) by checking the row and column it identifies, by counting the number of X's in the row (and in the column), and reporting back when the sums are greater than one in both row and column. In the above P-G, only row START and column

C satisfy the rule, with counts of 4 and 2, respectively; columns B, F, E, and D also contain more than one X but no multiple-X rows cross it.

An automated checking macro program would only identify potential problems because the links may indicate only that dummy tasks need to be created for the AOA network. Another macro program of commands might be written to list each route back to START from each X and compare them all for internal duplications. A macro is a sequence of commands that the computer "remembers"; it can be activated by calling up its name. Macros save time on the keyboard.

LISTING OF THE CHIEF RESOURCES FOR EACH TASK

The Estimator produces a Quantity-Take-Off to estimate the cost of the project. A typical item might be 750 lineal feet of 8-foot drywall partitions. The spreadsheet listing from the Estimator will also include the estimated cost of materials and labor. It may include the estimated duration of the component.

The value of assembling this data on an electronic spreadsheet lies in the ease of accepting data from someone else, removing unwanted columns of data, adding more rows, re-arranging the order of the rows, and adding more columns required for our unique application to scheduling.

Working directly from this basic data from the Estimator, we have removed unnecessary columns from Figure 12–6, assigned each resource to one of our construction tasks, and sorted the rows in order of our task numbers. This collects together all materials needed for each task. Several items common to the same task, such as the two types of cement blocks, were added together (using the program) and recorded as the total for that task. The results were saved with a new file name onto a specially named computer disk: "Tasks and Resources." This new spreadsheet (Figure 12–7A) was then printed out, ready for checking and inclusion in a scheduling report.

CREWS AND TASK DURATIONS

This modified spreadsheet (Figure 12–7A) can be further developed to estimate task durations based on the chief resource. We added new columns (5, 6, and 7) to name the crews assigned to the tasks, together with their daily work output, taken from catalogues such as *Means Building Construction Cost Data*. The durations were easily calculated by the program by dividing the work to be done by the crew's productivity. Once the simple formula is entered and copied down the column, the program computes the durations and displays all of them almost instantaneously. The most time-consuming part of this work is selecting the appropriate crew for each job, but the drudgery of writing and copying names and data and doing the calculations is eliminated. In addition, final "hard copy" is immediately available for the final report. The resulting data sheet is shown in Figure 12–7B.

PORTION OF A QUANTITY TAKE-OFF LIST

CODE	DESCRIPTION	COMMENTS	QUANTITY	UNITS	RATE	LBR COST	RATE	MTL COST	RATE	TRAD CST	TTL COST
201	BLDG. EXCAV	ALLOW									1000
203	SERVICE TRENCH		160	CY			5	800			800
205	SERV TRNCH B'FILL		160	CY	2	320	5	800			1120
207	B/F UNDER BLDG		740	CY	2	1480	5	3700			5180
207	ROADWAYS—EXCAV		398	CY		0	7	2786			2786
207	ROADWAYS—B/F		398	CY	3	1194	15	5970			7164
207	ROADWAYS—COMPACT		7170	SF	.25	1792.5		0			1792.5
211	SITE GRADING		1900	SF	.25	475		0			475
223	ON-SITE UTIL CB Bal	CB BAL INC PBG	3	NO.	66.7	200.1	200	600			800.1
227	OFF-SITE UTIL—CROSS'G		1	NO.		0		3000			3000
227	OFF-SITE UTIL—WATER	1 INCH	1	NO.		0		600			600
227	OFF-SITE UTIL—STORM	8 INCH	1	NO.		0		675			675
227	OFF-SITE UTIL—SANIT'Y	4 INCH	1	NO.		0		0			780
227	OFF-SITE UTIL—ELEC					0		0			4000
231	ASPHALT PAVING		796	Sq Yd		0	12	9552			9552
233	CURBS & GUTTER		170	LFt		0	6	1020			1020
237	CONC WALKS—POURING		2	Cu Yd	50	100	100	200			300
237	CONC WALKS—FINISHING		144	SF	.25	36		0			36
241	FENCE—GARBAGE FLOOR	CONCRETE	2	CY	50	100	100	200			300
241	FENCE—GARBAGE FLOOR	CONCRETE	80	SF	.25	20		0			20
241	FENCE—GARB ENCL		26	LF	8	208	8	208			416
243	PC WHEEL STOPS	?????	17	NO.	5	85	35	595			680
	LANDSCAPING		1367	SF		0		0		10936	10936
	PILING		64	NO.		0		0		28800	28800
	CONC. GRADE BEAMS	SUPPLY/PLACE	127	CY	5	635	50	6350			6985
	CONC. SLAB-ON-GRADE	SUPPLY/PLACE	164	CY	5	820	50	8200			9020
	CONC. SLAB-ON-GRADE	FINISHING	6650	SF	.25	1662.5		0			1662.5
	CONC.—PUMPING		305	CY		0	7	2135			2135
	FORMWORK		4970	SF	1	4970	.5	2485			7455
	FRMW'K NAILS, TIES,..		4970	SF		0	.1	497			497
	REBAR/CY	291cyX180#/CY	52380	LBS		0	.45	23571			23571
	MASONRY WEST WALL	STANDARD	4180	SF		0		0			0
	MASONRY—S. WALL	RIBBED	770	SF		0		0			0
	MASONRY—NORTH WALL	RIBBED	378	SF		0		0			0
	MASONRY—NORTH WALL	STANDARD	152	SF		0		0			0
	MASONRY—EAST WALL	STANDARD	1204.5	SF		0		0			0
	MASONRY—EAST WALL	RIBBED	581.5	SF		0		0			0
	MASONRY—TOTAL		7229	SF		0		0		44000	44000
512	STR.ST COLUMNS		1	NO.		0	150	150			150
521	STEEL JOISTS		30	NO.		0	175	5250			5250
531	METAL ROOF DECK		6650	SF		0	1.17	7780.5			7780.5
558	MISC. METALS	ALLOW				0		0			500
560	CHAIN LINK	FOR GAS METER	1	NO.		0	200	200			200
610	OVERHANG WD. BRACKETS	2 × 4	1577	BM	.6	946.2	.25	394.25			1340.45
611	OVERHANG WD. BRACKETS	1/2"PLY	69	SHTS	5	345	10	690			1035
610	OVERHANG WD. BRACKETS	NAILS & H'WARE	2177	BM		0	.05	108.85			108.85
610	OVERHANG WD. BRACKETS	NAILS & H'WARE	69	SHTS		0	2	138			138

Figure 12–6   Typical Materials Take-off Data.

In practice, Figures 12–7A and 7B are the same spreadsheet. Before printing or saving as a file we select certain columns and move them to the left side of the spreadsheet and output only those columns. Figure 12–7B is simply a different selection of columns that is appropriate to the need for segregated data. Most spreadsheet programs allow for several hundred columns and over 1000 rows.

TASK NO. (1)	MATERIAL NAME (2)	QUANTITY (3)	UNITS (4)
1	(Sub)		
2	(Sub)		
3	Bulk Excav	800	CY
4	Fill & Compact	800	CY
5	Bulk Trench	160	CY
6	(Sub)		
7	(Sub)		
8	Fill Trench	160	CY
9	Bulk Excav	325	CY
10	(Sub)		
11	Formwork	4970	SF
12	Reinf. Steel	2000	LF
13	Concrete	127	CY
14	Moist Proof	2000	SF
15	Trenching	40	CY
16	(Sub)		
17	(Sub)		
18	Fill U/Slab	130	LF
19	Masonry Walls	7229	SF
20	Roofing SubProj		
21	Doors & Windows	11	NO.
22	Paint (Sub)		
23	Vapor Barrier	6650	SF
24	Steel Mesh	6650	SF
25	Concrete	6650	SF
26	Plumbing Sub		
27	Storm Drains		
28	Elect		
29	HVAC		
30	Communications		
31	Roads & Parking		
32	Conc Walkways	600	SF
33	Area Lighting		
34	Fencing		
35	Landscaping		
36	Clean-Up		

Figure 12–7A Task and Crew Spreadsheet.

TASK NO. (1)	MATERIAL NAME (2)	QUANTITY (3)	UNITS (4)	CREW NO. (5)	PRODUC-TIVITY (6)	UNITS (7)	DURATIONS CALC (8)	DURATIONS QUOTED
1	(Sub)							2
2	(Sub)							4
3	Bulk Excav	800	CY	B-12C	600	CY	1.333	
4	Fill & Compact	800	CY	B-15	600	CY	1.333	
5	Bulk Trench	160	CY	B-53	550	LF	.2909	
6	(Sub)				1		0	2
7	(Sub)				1		0	5
8	Fill Trench	160	CY	A-1	270	LF	.5926	
9	Bulk Excav	325	CY	B-11C	170	CY	1.912	
10	(Sub)				1		0	12
11	Formwork	4970	SF	C-1	440	SFCA	11.30	
12	Reinf. Steel	2000	LF	4 RODM'N	2	T	1000	
13	Concrete	127	CY	C-17B	30	CY	4.233	
14	Moist Proof	2000	SF	2 Rofc	665	SF	3.008	
15	Trenching	40	CY	B-53	550	CY	.0727	
16	(Sub)				1		0	2
17	(Sub)				1		0	4
18	Fill U/Slab	130	LF	A-1	270	LF	.4815	
19	Masonry Walls	7229	SF	D-3	365	SF	19.81	
20	Roofing SubProj				1		0	19
21	Doors & Windows	11	NO.	F-2	2	NO.	5.5	
22	Paint (Sub)				1		0	4
23	Vapor Barrier	6650	SF	1 Rofc	665	SF	10	
24	Steel Mesh	6650	SF	2 Rodm	35	CSF	190	
25	Concrete	6650	SF	C-8	2025	SF	3.284	
26	Plumbing Sub				1		0	5
27	Storm Drains				1		0	2
28	Elect				1		0	5
29	HVAC				1		0	4
30	Communications				1		0	1
31	Roads & Parking				1		0	6
32	Conc Walkways	600	SF	B-26	2000	SF	.3	
33	Area Lighting				1		0	2
34	Fencing				1		0	1
35	Landscaping				1		0	7
36	Clean-Up				1		0	2

NOTE: In column #5, the 1's prevent an automatic division by zero by the formula: the 1's do not affect any of the results.

Figure 12–7B Spreadsheet for Crews and Task Durations.

INPUTTING TASK DATA TO THE SCHEDULING PROGRAM

We are using a mid-range program that runs on a PC with 640kb of memory. There are other more powerful programs costing five times as much that include costing and other valuable components, but the simpler ones are good to learn on.

Fundamental task data is input manually from the keyboard into "forms" on the screen. Two such forms are reproduced in Figure 12–8. Scheduling programs that can input files from spreadsheet programs save time and reduce keyboard input errors.

There are at least two ways of typing in task data:

1. by entering data directly to an on-screen form called the Task Data Screen (Figure 12–8), typing in the task's Name, Duration, its precedence information and its Resources; or
2. by linking each new task box on a PERT (AON) network (as you would do with pencil and paper) and typing in its name and duration, shown in Figure 12–9.

The precedence information is obtained from the P-G chart for the project. The PERT task boxes must first be created, named, and linked to their predecessors by two key strokes. The program locates the box in the "best" place, but the operator can relocate the box anywhere on the extended screen. Inputting to the on-screen form is the easier method. When one field is entered, the program skips to the next field and the screen for the next field pops up with one keystroke. The task screen can accept more information than the PERT box. The program can rearrange the PERT chart to simplify the placement of task boxes, but it can be a relatively time-consuming operation.

Once all tasks are input to the computer's memory, the program can display the project as a PERT network or as a Gantt Chart, by the touch of a button. Because only a part of a large network can be displayed on the screen, the network can be reduced in size in order to scrutinize the sequences and the layout. Refer to Figure 12–9A and B. Eight other displays are similarly available that list the project data, such as Task Gantt Charts, Resource Gantt Charts, work calendars, resource data, general project data, and so forth.

Unlike manual development of the network, which is followed by the durations and time calculations, the computer program does it all at once when the durations are input along with the definitions and precedence logic. The drudgery of making the time calculations manually has now been eliminated. If any duration needs to be corrected or updated, new data is simply typed over the old data into the appropriate form and the new times are immediately updated.

Most programs compute the calendar dates directly for the Early and Late Start and Finish times. The Total Floats and the Critical Path are also given. But

ID:	P1							
Name: Proj-1.pj								

				——— Start ———	——— Finish ———	——— Totals ———
Duration: 0				Schd:	04-23-93	Hrs: 0
					Priority:	Ovr: 0

Resource	Hrs	Allc	Un	Predecessors	Successors

Name:Proj-1.pj
ID:P1   Directory:C:\ANALYSIS\SCHEDULE\

				——— Defaults ———	——— Totals ———
Author:		Leader:		Hours: 40	
WBSMask: 11.22.33.44.???? Freeze:Yes No					
Created: 04-23-93 Revised:04-23-93 # 0					
Start: 04-23-93				Rate Mult: 1.00	
Finish: 04-23-93		Dur: 0 0h		Duration: 5	Hours: 0 Ovr: 0
Late: 04-23-93				Allc: dayx Pr: 50	Tasks: 0 Rsrc: 0

Workday	Start	Finish	Hrs	121 2 3 4 5 6a7 8 9 1011121 2 3 4 5 6p7 8 9 1011
Sunday	8:00a	8:00a	0	------------bb--------------------bb--------------------bb--------
Monday	8:00a	5:00p	8	------------bb--------------------bb--------------------bb--------
Tuesday	8:00a	5:00p	8	------------bb--------------------bb--------------------bb--------
Wednesday	8:00a	5:00p	8	------------bb--------------------bb--------------------bb--------
Thursday	8:00a	5:00p	8	------------bb--------------------bb--------------------bb--------
Friday	8:00a	5:00p	8	------------bb--------------------bb--------------------bb--------
Saturday	8:00a	8:00a	0	------------bb--------------------bb--------------------bb--------

Figure 12–8   Representative Task Data Input Screens   (Courtesy Computer Associates).

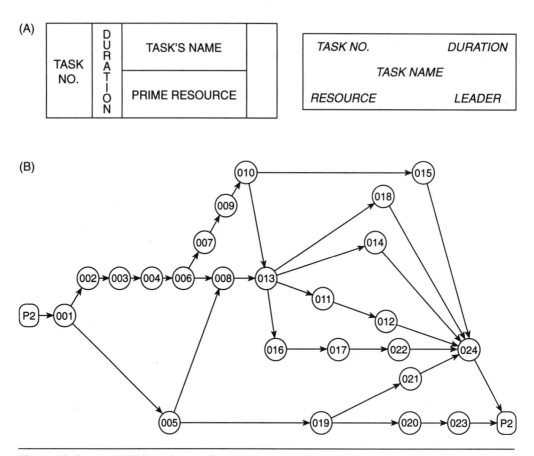

Figure 12–9   (A) PERT Task Boxes; (B) AON Network   (Courtesy Computer Associates).

converting dates to the number of project days from the start usually requires a manual calculation.

INCORPORATING DELAYS AND OTHER CONSTRAINTS

Once the durations of the weather-delay dummy tasks are found they are easily incorporated into the network and the revised schedule is immediately produced. We manually tabulated our delay calculations when we analyzed Leads and Lags and Weather effects. We can now automate some of these calculations on a computer spreadsheet. These spreadsheet tables of data can be printed out ready to be incorporated into reports, whereas hand-written notes need to be neatly copied or typed. The computer deals immediately with changes. The formulas in the spreadsheets recalculate the complete table in an instant and updating is no longer a chore.

WEATHER DELAY CALCULATIONS ON A SPREADSHEET

This spreadsheet helps to mechanize weather delay calculations. Much of the data can be selected from the scheduling program and output directly as files readable by a spreadsheet program. Tasks may be sorted in order of TF to aid in selecting the ones requiring more analysis.

Figure 12–10 shows two print-outs of the same data. The lower one shows the

A "SCREENPRINT"

	C	D	E	F	G	H	I	J	K	L
1	CAUSED BY MULTIPLE WEATHER CONDITIONS									
2										
3										
4	DUR'N	SCHED	MID-DATE		PROBABILITY OF BAD			TOTAL	TOTAL	WEATHER
5					CONDITIONS			FACTOR	DELAY	WINDOW
6		EST	OF TASK	RAIN	WIND	TEMP	OTHER	("P")		
7										
8	2	66	Jan 8		.15		.3	.60504	1	3
9	7	69	Jan 14		.15	.2		.42647	3	10
10	2	76	Jan 20	.65	.15			2.0336	4	6
11	2	79	Jan 22	.65				1.8571	4	6
12	4	76	Jan 21					0	0	4
13	4	80	Jan 26					0	0	4
14	6	83	Feb 3		.18	.2		.46951	3	9
15										
16								THIS FORMULA FOR "P"		
17								IS "BEHIND" EVERY CELL		
18								IN THIS COLUMN.		
19										
20										

WEATHER!J10   Form = $F10/(1-F10)+G10/(1-G10)+H10/(1-H10)+I10/(1$

Width: 7 Memory: 164 Last Col/Row: L31

1>

READY F1:Help F3:Names Ctrl-Backspace:Undo Ctrl-Break:Cancel CAPS

FORMAL PRINT-OUT OF DATA ONLY

DELAYS CAUSED BY MULTIPLE WEATHER CONDITIONS

TASK	IDENTITY	DUR'N	SCHED	MID-DATE		PROBABILITY OF BAD			TOTAL	TOTAL	WEATHER
						CONDITIONS			FACTOR	DELAY	WINDOW
NO.	NAME		EST	OF TASK	RAIN	WIND	TEMP	OTHER			
Ⓐ	Ⓑ	Ⓒ	Ⓓ	Ⓔ	Ⓕ	Ⓖ	Ⓗ	Ⓘ	Ⓙ	Ⓚ	Ⓛ
1	TRUSSES	2	66	Jan 8		.15		.3	.60504	1	3
2	DECKING	7	69	Jan 14		.15	.2		.42647	3	10
3	INSULATIO	2	76	Jan 20	.65	.15			2.0336	4	6
4	CLADDING	2	79	Jan 22	.65				1.8571	4	6
5	OVERHANG	4	76	Jan 21					0	0	4
6	SOFFITS	4	80	Jan 26					0	0	4
7	FLASHING	6	83	Feb 3		.18	.2		.46951	3	9

Figure 12–10 Spreadsheet for Weather Delays.

complete table of data while the upper one shows part of the table as seen on the screen. The formula the computer uses for calculating the value in cell J10 is displayed on the "screen-print."

Data for columns A, B, C, and D can be read from an output file from the scheduling program. The data in columns E to I are decided by you based on a subjective evaluation of the mid-date for the task and the chances of bad weather. The formula for calculating the delay factor and the weather window is "hidden" in columns J and K, respectively, which the program executes immediately as values are input. The weather window is also calculated immediately by adding C to K. Although integer values are displayed, the computer uses full decimal values in its calculations.

Formulas are hidden "behind" the appropriate cells of the spreadsheet to allow automatic calculation when values are inserted in the data cells. The program recognizes the differences between data and formulas and stores them appropriately. For example, when you are calculating the total delay (F × D) for the data in Row 6 of the spreadsheet, store the formula (J6*C6) in cell **K6**. The computer reads the values from cells C6 and J6, multiplies them together, and displays the result in cell **K6**. The formula for F is more cumbersome, but almost any size formula will fit "behind" a cell.

Inserting a delay (or window) into the network is simply adding a dummy task with the correct links to existing tasks. The time recalculations are made in several seconds and the modifications are done.

Because such refinements are so easily made, the schedule should be updated for weather based on actual forecasts rather that relying on the long-term statistical data. Short-term forecasts should be more reliable than those that are long term. Because cumulative delays can re-schedule tasks into extreme weather periods, long-range predictions are questionable. Make long-range schedules only when necessary, perhaps for resource procurement or when the politics of a situation require you to make "promises."

A Sequence of Steps for Weather Calculations

STEP 1   Fill out columns A, B, C, and D, noting that the dates in columns D and E may be changed later.

STEP 2   Sort the tasks in order of column D, so that the earlier tasks appear at the top of the table.

STEP 3   Estimate the date of mid-task for the tasks starting in the first month of the project.

STEP 4   For those tasks starting in the first month, estimate the "bad" probabilities for columns F, G, H, and I.

STEP 5   Calculate the values for columns H, I, and J (the program will do this automatically). The formula for the delay factor is copied from

Chapter 7: $F = \{p/(1 - p)_{rain}\} + \{p/(1 - p)_{wind}\} + \{p/(1 - p)_{temp}\} + \{p/(1 - p)_{other}\}$; column J = the result of the above calculation by the computer. The Total Delay is $F \times$ task's duration, DELAY = $F \times D$; that is, column K = column J $\times$ column C.

The Weather Window's Duration (column L) is the sum of the values in column C and column K; $L = C + K$. When you change any value in a cell, numerical results immediately appear in the appropriate cells. Changing a rain probability (p) causes P to be recalculated, then the total delay (column K) and the Window, (column L). Spreadsheet calculations make updating very simple.

STEP 6 Insert the appropriate dummy weather tasks into the network and recalculate all the dates.

STEP 7 Insert the revised ES dates into the table and then be ready to return to Step 2 and deal with ES dates for "next" month.

This may seem overly detailed, but the work can actually move quite quickly because the computer does the hard work. The revised dates will affect only those tasks downstream from the latest weather delays. Because you will be adjusting only the next month's schedule, only those tasks starting or in-work in that month need be reviewed. Without the computer to do most of the work, this would be a very time-consuming job. If your computer can run several programs at once (called "multi-tasking"), then the scheduling program can output Start Dates in a spreadsheet format for direct input to the weather calculation table, whose results can be fed back into the scheduler to modify the network and durations for the next cycle of calculations.

MECHANIZING PROCUREMENT CALCULATIONS (CHAPTER 8)

Chapter 8 provided explanations of the techniques for scheduling procurement of resources. In discussing the subject, Figures 8–6 to 8–13 were produced. The discussion in that chapter centered around manual calculations, but the illustrations were produced via a computer spreadsheet program. The data was collected from several sources.

The many simple calculations (subtracting a duration from a project day) was a help, but the real value of the program lies in its ability to rearrange the rows of data into more useful orders. The reasons for the sorting were given in Chapter 8.

To monitor the progress of the procurement, mark up a printout of the tickler sheet as dates are successfully met, or blank out the information in the row that no longer matters. This will indicate clearly the current status. When any new durations are promised or negotiated, enter them into the computer and print out a revised tickler sheet. Every new sheet should be saved with a new and unique file name.

To help the expediter, add several new columns near the resource name for the supplier's name, contact person, and phone number. If your computer set-up has a modem, the computer can remind you when to phone the supplier, dial the supplier, or send a FAX.

UNCERTAINTY AND TASK DURATIONS

Many mid-level software programs for scheduling can accept uncertainty into its task durations. Data can be entered in two ways: the three PERT time estimates (a, m, b), or the expected duration plus the Standard Deviation (t_e and SD). The program accepts (or computes) t_e, then calculates the schedule and the SD for the project. It is very straightforward in application, for when the statistical option is selected, the data input forms are changed to accommodate the PERT input data. It calculates the chances of finishing earlier or later than the expected time.

RESOURCE BALANCING

Leveling (or balancing) resources using paper and pencil requires careful attention to detail and correct arithmetic, as well as a clear overview of the effects of the re-scheduling on the whole project. You can use a computer in two ways to level resources. One method is to use the techniques already covered in Chapter 9, but on a computer spreadsheet. The other method is to use a formal scheduling program, where pressing one key can start the process but there is a feeling of being out of control after that key is pressed.

When you command the program to balance resources, it needs to know the relative importance of every task in the project. When two tasks clash over the same resource, the higher-priority task is scheduled first, removing that clash. The application is especially clear when workers or equipment are involved and when one is required by two tasks at the same time. The masses of data are stored in the computer's memory for ready access during its programmed step-by-step balancing process. Most users treat computer programs as elegant tools for solving problems; some industrial users get curious about how the program actually solves a problem; and only occasionally does a "computer hacker" take an illegal interest in the actual commands stored on the program disks. The set of rules the computer programmer follows to write the detailed commands is called an **algorithm.**

We are curious about how the algorithm will go about balancing *multiple* resources. Ignorance of the algorithm prevents us from anticipating the form of the results; hence we must carefully review the overall effect on the schedule by the automatic leveling procedure. Task priorities must be checked to ensure that a casually made priority rating has not caused a critical modification to the schedule.

The human mind needs to evaluate the computer's actions every step of the way. Never assume that "The Computer is Always Right" unless you have checked its results on a simple example.

REPORTING OF RESULTS

Computer programs are powerful tools for analysis because they produce graphs, tables, and charts of consistent numerical results when they are applied to complicated problems, many of which would remain unsolved were it not for the computer. As an extra bonus, these raw pages of output data can be enhanced with titles and so forth and become the core pages of technical reports (see Chapter 13). Many of the illustrations in this book were direct computer printouts, only slightly refined for publishing purposes.

All the data about a schedule is stored in a large database managed by the computer. Selected packages of information can be defined for the computer, which then sorts out the selected material, displays it on-screen, and prints it, customized to the needs of the report. Using these computer-generated illustrations, an author can tailor consistent data to the targeted reader. The next chapter focuses on the types of reports needed by various readers and how standard forms can make the task easier.

EXERCISES AND PROBLEMS

For computer novices: Take a course in the basic operation of a computer, including exposure to spreadsheet and word processing programs. Get to feel at ease with a computer.

For learned post-novices: Take a spreadsheet program and re-calculate some of the spreadsheets in this book. Concentrate on inputting simple formulas and rearranging the column order and sorting by rows. Take one of the precedence grids and "move" all the X-links above the diagonal. Add a few links at random and try another rearrangement.

For "hackers": Gain access to a scheduling program and input the 24-task warehouse model, view the network and Gantt Chart, review several resource Gantts, include a weather delay and a window, and so forth.

13

COMMUNICATING YOUR PLANNING INFORMATION

LEARNING OBJECTIVES

After completing this chapter, you should be able to:

- Recognize the major differences between the various types of documents presented and appreciate their applications.
- Lay out the formats for each type of document.
- Construct a Mind Map.
- Assemble a Topic Outline from a written text.

PREPARATION FOR THIS CHAPTER

The earlier chapters in this book have explained how to develop a schedule from fundamental information about your project. The results of your labor will be tables, graphs, flow charts, and many rough worksheets. You will have lived and breathed the details of your project intensely over a considerable period of time and you will have a unique understanding of the project. This accumulation of sheets of paper, both rough and neat, must be organized and edited before you should even consider writing about what it contains.

First of all, your original worksheets (tables, graphs, and basic data) should be arranged in the order that they were developed and headed by a table of contents. Each group of related worksheets should be preceded by a short example showing how each one was developed from earlier data. The whole package becomes a brief but complete record of your work. Your descriptions and examples describe the flow of your thinking and the depth of your work. They remind you how you did the work in the first place, particularly when you deviated from the usual method. It should be sufficient for you to repeat the analysis, and adequate for someone else to repeat your calculations to verify any part of the work.

Your notes must be in such a state that you could write a progress report at any time during your analysis, and especially so when the technical work is done and a final report is expected. Even if such formal reports are not required by your organization, always have your work available for your own checking, for further development, or even as legal evidence in court challenges. This may seem like an ultra-conservative attitude, but one challenge makes it all worthwhile. Be prepared.

INTRODUCTION

This final chapter provides a framework for presenting your thoughts to others. You have learned how to produce scheduling information and you should feel comfortable with the meaning and significance of the graphs and tables of data. Your co-workers, even though they may have a need-to-know, may not understand this bare technical data and will require your explanations, opinions, and recommendations so that they can use the information knowledgeably.

You are responsible for communicating your findings in a manner appropriate to your readers' particular levels of authority and responsibility. Not only must you describe and discuss your technical findings but since all communications (a memo, a letter, or a report) are addressed to someone, you must know your targeted reader. Does your reader understand technical illustrations, is jargon acceptable and is an average vocabulary level all right, is he/she open-minded on the topic, and so forth? There are many books that can advise you how to become an accomplished writer, and although it is not the intention of this section to offer a course in writing, this section can help you organize your thoughts, select the appropriate type of document, consider the breadth and depth of its content, and remind you to write in a *clear, concise, complete, correct,* and *courteous* manner. You should consult the writing section of your local library and study several references because each book emphasizes different aspects of writing. Writing is an acquired skill and requires continual practice.

Before embarking on a system for preparing complete documents, consider the types of records that a planner must write: records of phone messages, minutes of meetings, memos to all levels of the organization, notes for verbal presentations, and preliminary and final reports and letters to external organizations. Each of these contain one common element: a **body** of **text**. The amount, depth, and breadth of information in each record will vary according to the need, from a single component in a phone record to masses of data and results in a formal report.

PLANNING THE BODY OF TEXT

The text will contain information that you need to communicate to a specific person; you may be responding to a request or initiating it yourself. Most important, how you view this person will color the way you form the communication. With this in mind, you should answer the following questions to help plan the text of the communication.

The Guiding Questions

What is the purpose of the document?

What are the relevant characteristics of your reader?

When must it be submitted to the reader?

What type of document is appropriate?

What will be the breadth/depth (scope) of its contents?

What style and tone are appropriate for this reader?

Purpose

You must know clearly *why* you are writing and *what* you expect to achieve. You must write down a statement to unequivocally define this purpose for yourself. This is really the *goal statement* for your writing project.

Typical action phrases for *why* you are writing might be:

Company policy requires . . .

To request . . .

To provide . . .

To convince . . .

To correct . . .

In response to . . .

What you expect to achieve through your communication depends on whether the writing is informational or diagnostic. Most letters and memos tend to be informational, such as those that respond to a request from your superior for certain information or provide periodic progress reports. Minutes of meetings and lecture notes tend to be informational as well.

Diagnostic writing results from analysis and comparison of alternatives for solving problems, followed by recommendations and conclusions for the best solution. A review of recent magazine articles for selecting a new computer or an analysis of the effect of a new tax policy on the development plans for a shopping plaza would be diagnostic in nature.

Your Reader

A successful communication must speak directly to your targeted reader, who is a real person with likes and dislikes, who has a known amount of authority and responsibility in the organization, who may prefer charts to lengthy written descriptions, who may have a specific need and use for ideas and information but who may know very little about the details of your work, who may be a specialist in another field entirely, and so forth.

A good writer is like a good salesperson. As a writer you should know your client's needs, wants, abilities, and weaknesses and make your response consistent with your view of your reader. Make a list of the strong and weak characteristics of your reader.

Your Timeline

Memos, phone calls, and letters can be prepared on a same-day schedule, but major letters and reports require more time to prepare. Even when all your data is available, your thoughts must be organized, the presentation must be thought through and written down, and more than one draft text must be written. Computers can record information as fast as the writer can enter it, but they cannot speed up the writer's thought processes.

When you are required to respond "by tomorrow," you must tailor the response to the time available. An opinion can be given over the phone and written in a memo in a few minutes, but a full analysis, with conclusions and recommendations, may take a week or more of day-and-night hard work.

What Type of Document?

This is likely the easiest question for you to answer, but you should always strive to respond with the shortest and least time-consuming method of reporting. If you write a memo when a phone call would suffice, you are making work for yourself. If your client requires a final report when the work is done, ensure that your time was budgeted for in the bid.

The Scope of Your Document

The breadth of topics and the depth of detail are determined by the needs of your reader. Your personal goals may tell you to engage in overkill when dealing with either or both of these items to show how much you know about the subject, but by doing so you may lose your reader before he finds what he was asking for. Conversely, you may be too brief, and thereby frustrate your reader and lose some credibility in the rest of the organization. You must have a clear understanding of the needs of your reader and then carefully write *to* those needs.

Writing Style

"Style, traditionally defined, is 'The arrangement of words in a manner which at once expresses the individuality of the author and the idea and intent in his mind.' " (Keithly, p. 14). A good writing style is often defined by what you should *not* do with your words.

1. *Avoid trite, hackneyed language.* Overused expressions that are common in conversation have no place in formal, technical reporting: such as, "cold as ice . . . ," "light as a feather . . . ," "so near and yet so far . . .".

2. Vigorously edit your writing to *reduce wordiness*: for example, replace "At the present time" with "now," and so forth. Complex verbs can be edited to single words without losing meaning: "tools *that have been* lost through carelessness" becomes "tools *lost* through carelessness."

3. Refrain from using words with *indistinct meanings* or connotations. Be explicit: Instead of "far" or "distant," say "50 miles" (the exact distance).

4. Do not put seemingly unimportant words in the *wrong place*: "I *only* like you" when you mean "I like *only* you." The former statement really implies the second half of the thought, . . . "but I do not love you."

5. Do not use long and involved sentences. Consider several shorter ones, or replace "and" and "but" with a semicolon if you want the thoughts more closely connected.

ORGANIZING YOUR THOUGHTS

There are as many ways of "getting organized" as there are authors of books on writing. This author has several ways, none of which are perfect or universally useful. However, there are fundamental practices that prepare you to write. You have noted all the points you want to cover to achieve your stated goal, and then you organized them in the best order to achieve your objectives:

1. List the topics, and
2. Put them in sequence.

Listing the Topics

A final list develops slowly as you search your mind, first for all topics remotely related to the subject and, second, when you relegate the less-important ones to the bottom of the list. File cards have been used for years because they make sorting easier. They are particularly useful for research papers in which reference material is collected from many publications.

Then there is the "Topic Outline," which is a Work Breakdown Structure for a writing project. It presupposes which topics are subordinate to others and is

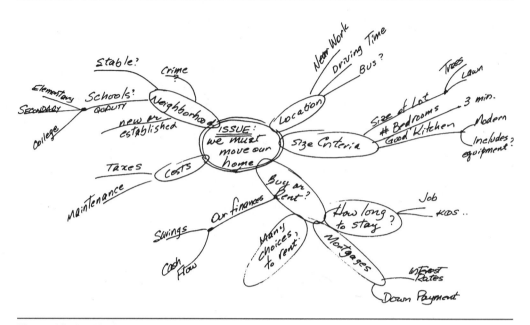

Figure 13–1   Note-taking Technique by "Mind-Mapping" or "Thinking Pictures."

valuable for putting the topics in a sequence. But it is not the way to brainstorm a writing project.

This book emphasizes graphical displays for the development of schedules. This section, too, has a particular graphical method for developing and recording ideas: it is called Mind Mapping (Buzan, 1974, page 86). In contrast to the rigid Topic Outline, a Mind Map begins with the Subject to be pursued written in a closed shape (a "cloud") at the center of a blank sheet; related concepts are added in other "clouds" and connected to related clouds. When a line of thought dries up, pursue another avenue, and record each one as before. The method may be reminiscent of building a draft Bubble Diagram, but the linkages here define your thought connections, not sequence.

Sorting the Topics into a Desired Sequence

As you study and edit your Mind Map, you will see that some topics are very important and others are not; some will even seem irrelevant to the central purpose of your communication. Emphasize the prime topics by double-circling their phrases. Cross out the irrelevant ones, but darken the very strong linkage between topics. Consider which major topic should be presented first in your document and mark it as #1. Then continue to identify the remaining major points.

A Topic Outline is a linear, top-to-bottom arrangement of ideas but it does not

GOAL: To Move Our Place of Residence

New Neighborhood
    Quality of Schools
    Stability of Population
    Crime Statistics
Residence Criteria
    Number of Bedrooms
    Quality of Kitchen
    Size of Property
How to Acquire
    Duration of Stay
    Our Financial Situation
        Savings
        Cash Flow
            Current
            Forecast
General Financial Picture
    Interest Rates
    Down Payment Required
    Taxes
    Moving Costs

Figure 13–2   Topic Outline from the Mind Map.

represent how the brain functions. In the brain, words can trigger several other ideas almost simultaneously and they need to be quickly recorded without considering sequences. The Mind Map is the interface between the brain and the written word.

The Topic Outline should be easy to construct now that the Mind Map has transformed the topics from your mind to paper. When you start to write the text of your document, these written thoughts must physically follow one after the other down the page. The Topic Outline provides this linear order for you to follow.

For organizing your topics prior to expanding them into the text of your document, your topic outline must be complete down to the deepest level (like a WBS). Each paragraph is an expansion of a topic in the deepest level of the topic outline. The leading sentence in any paragraph (the "topic sentence") flows directly from one of these deepest topics. In some paragraphs where much of the important detail will be presented, you may need to list these details by adding them in one deeper level in the outline.

Writing the Text

The style of your writing will reflect your command of the rules of grammar, your vocabulary, and your skill in connecting the thoughts between sentences. Do not stray from the topic at hand. Ensure that every sentence in a paragraph expands on the subject of the topic sentence; if it does not, then re-work it or remove it. Strive for clarity by reading your work aloud, listening for any ambiguity or double-talk. Be careful not to use long words when commonly understood ones will do. Check the logic of your sentences by considering whether the literal meaning of the words you used conveys the meaning you intend. Shun long, complicated sentences by using a semicolon instead of a conjunction or split it into several shorter, cleaner sentences. Stay away from double negatives, which are often the favorite constructions of politicians who wish to be non-committal: "I do not believe that I shall not ignore my opponent."

There are many books devoted to explaining the art and skills of writing that you should peruse before tackling a challenging writing assignment. Such reading can give you confidence that there is a technique for writing that can be learned and that good writers are seldom born pre-programmed with writing skills that have been plugged in like a piece of software.

COMPUTERS ARE HELPERS

Computer programs can help tremendously. Most word processing programs contain an outlining utility that helps with the layout:

- Grammar-checkers and spell-checkers can monitor your creations and an on-line Thesaurus can provide alternative words when your mind keeps re-using the same word.
- Blocks of text can easily be relocated to a better place after you have typed an especially good sample as an afterthought.
- Items can be marked for inclusion in the Contents or the Index.
- Depending on the electronic sophistication of your workplace, you can send your communications instantaneously to your reader by E-Mail or Fax or by direct connection to another computer via a Local Area Network (a LAN).
- You may find that you can contribute your portion of a large report through the LAN system to the general editor.
- You can search your files-on-disk for specific words (subjects, reader's name, dates, etc.) and thereby retrieve particular information very quickly.

New applications of computer systems for the preparation and distribution of ideas arrive on the magazine racks monthly and you should try to keep up to date to apply what you can where you can.

FORMATS FOR DOCUMENTS

We have focused on preparing the body of text but have delayed describing how it should be packaged for the reader. This section illustrates the format of these packages into which the body of text can be inserted. The Standard Formats presented here should be regarded as guides that can be modified to suit the needs of your organization. Once adopted, a standard format prepares the reader to receive a particular type of information and may suggest the type of response expected.

PHONE/DIARY ENTRY

DATE: <u>YY/MM/DD</u>;   TIME: <u>HH/MM</u>;   DURATION: <u>(minutes)</u>
BY: <u>(Initiator's Name & Position)</u>   TO: <u>(Receiver's Name, Position)</u>

    PURPOSE:

    ISSUES: 1
           2
           .
           .

    CONCLUSIONS:

    FOLLOW-UP:

EXAMPLE OF PURPOSE
"Invitation to special meeting (Planning Committee); to discuss proposed project; March 21, 10:15 am, Room 12."

Figure 13–3   Record of a Diary Entry or a Phone Conversation.

MINUTES OF MEETINGS

MINUTES
OF SPECIAL MEETING OF PLANNING COMMITTEE
of March 25, 1994
10:00 am to 12:30 pm in Company Board Room

PRESENT (Identify who was in the Chair and who was Record Keeper)

ABSENT

VISITORS

Agenda
Item

Call to Order at (__time__)

Approval of Agenda:

The Agenda was APPROVED with the following additions:

(Enumerate and State the Titles clearly & concisely).

Approval of Previous Minutes:

The Minutes of the Meeting of February 10, 1994 were APPROVED with the following corrections:

(Correct the wording but it is not necessary to re-quote the complete statement unless directed by the meeting.)

THE BODY OF THE MINUTES APPEAR HERE IN THE ORDER COVERED BY THE MEETING.

ADD THE INITIALS OF PERSONS ASSIGNED TO TAKE ACTION AS DIRECTED BY THE MEETING.

EXAMPLE OF TEXT

. . . .

Item #4 - *"Bill Smith moved "That the Estimating Group prepare a preliminary overview of the Multi-Tenant Warehouse Project, including Direct Construction Costs, its likely Duration and forecast of special issues affecting it; and to report back by April 2."*

The Motion was ADOPTED, unanimously . . . . BY HN

. . . .

Final
Item   The meeting was adjourned at 12:15 pm

Figure 13–4   Minutes of Formal Meetings.

MEMOS

M E M O R A N D U M
(Name of Department)

TO: (Name_____and Position:_____)   DATE: (YY/MM/DD)
FROM: (Name_____and Position_____)
SUBJECT: (Clear and Concise Title, often preceded by "RE:")

Introductory remarks provide continuity and state the problem or reason for sending the memo.

The body of the discussion, information, data, etc.

Promises or requests for follow-up action along with a target date for action or a response.

EXAMPLE OF TEXT

"In response to request of Meeting of March 21:
The estimates for construction of tenant space (Phase 2) is separate from the basic structural and site work, known as Phase 1.

Phase 1: $750,000 over a 10-month construction period.
Phase 2: $35,000 per unit over a 6-week period.

POTENTIAL PROBLEM AREAS:

- Soil conditions, as the site has been backfilled.
- Weather, as the potential start is in November.
- Skilled trades people, as the industry is projected to be in a building boom for this period.
- Fabricated steel, due to the building boom. . . . .cont'd

These quick estimates are based on current building data for our area and should be within 15% of actual depending on resolution of the issues listed above. I will be pleased to enlarge on these points at your next meeting."

Initials (Typist or. . . .)
Enclosures Listed:
Copies Sent To: (often C/C:. . . . . .)

Figure 13–5   Internal Memorandums.

PRESENTATIONS

PAGE 1   Title Page with Author's Name and Presentation Date, Target Audience, and Name of Contact Person

PAGE 2   Explanation of Purpose of Presentation and Use to be made of it by the Meeting

PAGE 3   An exact copy of the Visuals to be Shown along with the "Talking Points" in point form for each one; including such information as: source of information, purpose of the visual, implications of the information for the members of the audience, etc.

LAST PAGE   Resume and Wrap-Up of information presented. Notes and One Visual

EXAMPLE OF TEXT

. . . . (Typical speaking notes for each Flip Chart, Overhead Transparency, Video Display, photographic slide, etc.)

SLIDE #1.   *Area Map and The site* at Wharf/Bay Streets
N/S Orientation, truck and railroad access
Contours: old and proposed
Zoning Boundaries
Actual developments New & Proposed

SLIDE #2.   . . . .

Figure 13–6   Formal Presentation to a Meeting.

INTERNAL REPORTS

A RECORD OF COMPLETED WORK
(*Informal* Report For Filing)

PAGE 1   THE TITLE
          AUTHOR
          DATE

PAGE 2   *The executive summary* on less than half-a-page:
          Reason for doing the work
          Important source of information
          Important findings and conclusions
          Recommendations

PAGE 3   *Contents:* Title of each segment of the work.

PAGE 4   *Introduction:*
and on-   Problem Statement of Purpose
wards   Specific Objectives
          Scope: (what it does not do)

          Body of the Report:
          Each section of work opens with the source information, an example of the work done and an example of the results. The complete results for each section (computer print-outs, graphs, tables, etc.) can follow immediately or be in an Appendix when large amounts of materal must be saved.

EXAMPLE OF TEXT
"LIST OF TASKS

The Quantity Take-Off material (computer file name: PROJ_9406.QTO, Disk No. 7) was sorted by material type, collapsed into a single item and renamed. Sub-contracted work was introduced as one Task (to start with). The total amount of material (from the Take-Off) was listed with each task but Sub-contract tasks were marked as 'SUB'."

          Appendices:

Figure 13–7   For an Internal Report.

BUSINESS LETTER

LETTER-HEAD
(Generally includes the complete address and phone/fax numbers, either here or across the bottom of the first page)

(DATE:)
(COMPLETE ADDRESS as it would appear on the envelope)

REF: (Optional to include reference to subject matter and file number of previous correspondence)

Dear Mr. (Ms.),

> *EXAMPLE OF TEXT* (Letter to City Planner)
>
> "We are planning to build a multi-tenant warehouse on the vacant parcel of land at the corner of Wharf and Bay Streets in the City (Parcel #200087). We are unsure if the current zoning in that area (Heavy Industrial) is consistent with our proposed development.
>
> We would like to meet with you to determine the city's position regarding our proposal and to begin planning the next steps. Might we meet with you during the week of October 12 at your convenience?"
>
> > Yours truly,
> >
> > (Space for your signature)
> >
> > Type your name and position

(Reference Initials)
Enclosures:

Figure 13–8   The Business Letter (For External Communications).

Components of the Formal Report

The PREFACE explains the purpose of the document, the methods used, and thanks those who helped in the work.

The FOREWORD is similar in function to the preface but it normally is written by a well-known authority in the same field to support the work reported in the document.

The ABSTRACT or EXECUTIVE SUMMARY is a brief account of the highlights of the report. It often is called the Executive Summary because busy executives can obtain the gist of the report without studying all its details.

The INTRODUCTION prepares the reader for main ideas of the text: background material, statement of the fundamental reason for writing the report, and the breadth and depth of its contents.

FORMAL REPORTS

	A Cover (to Protect the document) Show Title & Author
	Several Fly Pages: a Title sheet & several blanks
	Title Page: Full Title of the Report
	BY: (Author's Name & Position)
	FOR: (Recipient's Name & Position)
	(Date Submitted)
	Copies of Letters that:
FRONT	Authorized the Work
MATTER	Accepted the Assignment
	Accompanied the Report
	Preface or Foreword & Acknowledgments
	Table of Contents
	List of Illustrations and Tables
	Abstract or Executive Summary
	Introduction
TEXT	Main Text of the Report
	Conclusions and Recommendations

EXAMPLE OF TEXT

".....................

6.4 PROBABILITY OF COMPLETING "ON SCHEDULE"

The initial schedule based on the single time estimates from the trades indicated a completion date of December 16 but the durations using the three (PERT) time estimates indicated a completion date of November 10. Implicit in the PERT date is the proviso that there is only a 50% chance of that date being realized; the December 16 date implied that IF all task durations were realized in practice, then the project would be completed then. There was 100% certainty.

The PERT date allows some judgement to be exercised: if the PERT analysis showed that the path of critical tasks had a Standard Deviation of 12 days, then there was an 86% chance of being finished 12 days later and a 98% chance another 12 days later. Perhaps the owner would appreciate knowing the degree of uncertainty and the construction manager could measure his own chances of saving time. . . . ."

	Endnotes
BACK	Bibliography
MATTER	Appendix
	Index

Figure 13–9   The Formal Report.

ENDNOTES is the assembly of many of the footnotes into one section of the report; they should be arranged in the same order as the major sections of the report.

The BIBLIOGRAPHY lists the sources of information referred to in the text. An example of the format is: Keithly, Erwin M., Marie E. Flatly, and Philip J. Schreiner, *Manual of Style for Business Letters, Memos & Reports*, U.C.L.A., Southwestern Publishing Co., 1989.

EXERCISES AND PROBLEMS

1. Select a magazine article covering several pages and construct its topic outline using the title, its sub-headings and paragraph topic sentences.

2. You have just completed the first draft of a schedule from construction information you collected from persons in your company. You want feedback from them. What form of communication would you use and what major topics would you address in it? You should consider drawing a mind map to record your ideas as you ponder the subject. Write all related thoughts, rejecting later all those that do not apply.

3. After you incorporated the responses from your colleagues and updated the schedule, you were informed that the General Manager wants a status report by tomorrow morning. What form do you select for this?

4. Because you know more about the details of a forthcoming project to build a warehouse in a neighborhood bordering a residential area, you have been selected by your boss to describe the construction program at a neighborhood meeting. Sketch out a mind map of the issues you think you will have to address.

Design Data for the Warehouse

The warehouse was planned to be built on a small parcel of land near a deep-sea terminal where there is a market for small warehousing space for trans-shipment of goods. The site had been extensively filled at some time in the past when this coastal area was originally developed. The municipal building code required that foundations had to be based on undisturbed soil, and the old fill therefore had to be removed and replaced with acceptable material. The upgraded fill had to be compacted to provide sufficient soil strength.

The rectangular lot is 220 feet by 66 feet. It is to be developed with 17 parking spaces, six loading bays, space for a garbage container, access paving, curbs, and landscaping with shrubs and grass. The footprint of the building is 190 feet by 35 feet and covers an area of 6650 square feet; its height is 18 feet, allowing for two floors of office space. The long structure is expected to be subdivided into five small warehouses, with offices provided later to suit individual tenants.

The conventional structural shell is built of concrete blocks on a poured foundation with an interior floating slab. Each unit has a large shipping door, windows, doors, and roughed-in plumbing services; adequate electrical power is connected to each unit. There are no internal transverse bearing walls, so tenants can lease adjoining units to form double units. The steel-decked roof structure is supported by prefabricated open-web-steel joists that cross the 35-foot span. Non-structural awnings improve the proportions of the building, making it blend in better with the mixed-use area of the city.

There are to be four identically sized units (at 1283 sq ft) and one larger unit

(1518 sq ft) at the prominent end of the building. Four alternate floor plans are provided for each of the two types on one- or two-floor layouts, thus giving prospective tenants a good selection.

Instead of including a complete set of working drawings suitable for material estimates, we have included the quantity of materials prepared by an estimator. The basic geometry of the building is described in the enclosed drawings (Figure A–1, "a" through "e"); they are not scale.

The materials listing describes the types of materials used in this building; it is reproduced from the estimator's computerized quantity take-off spreadsheet. See Figure A–2.

PROPOSED WAREHOUSE

Figure A–1a Warehouse Drawings: Perspective of the Building. (Courtesy Costex Management Inc.)

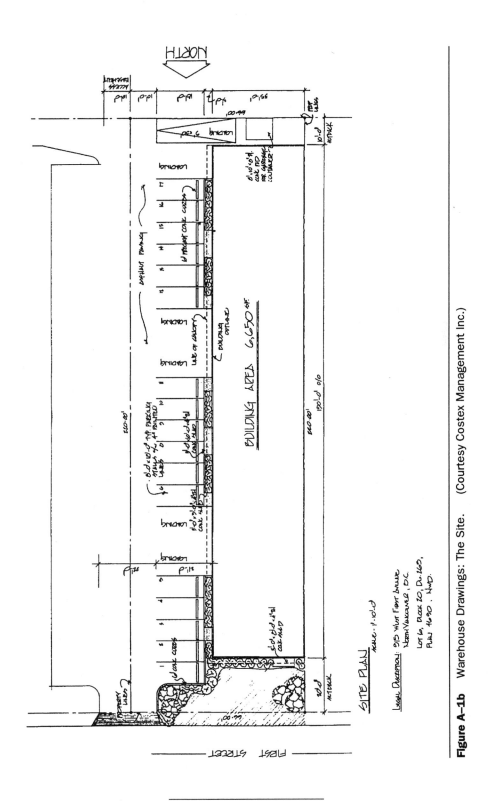

Figure A–1b Warehouse Drawings: The Site. (Courtesy Costex Management Inc.)

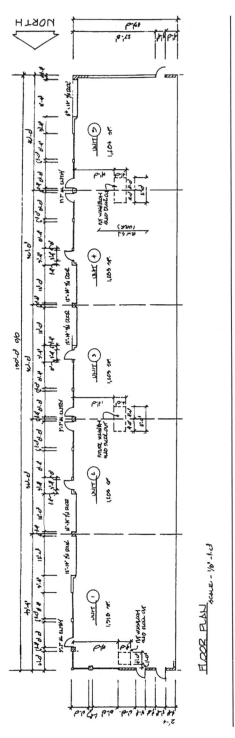

Figure A-1c Warehouse Drawings: Floor Plan of the Building. (Courtesy Costex Management Inc.)

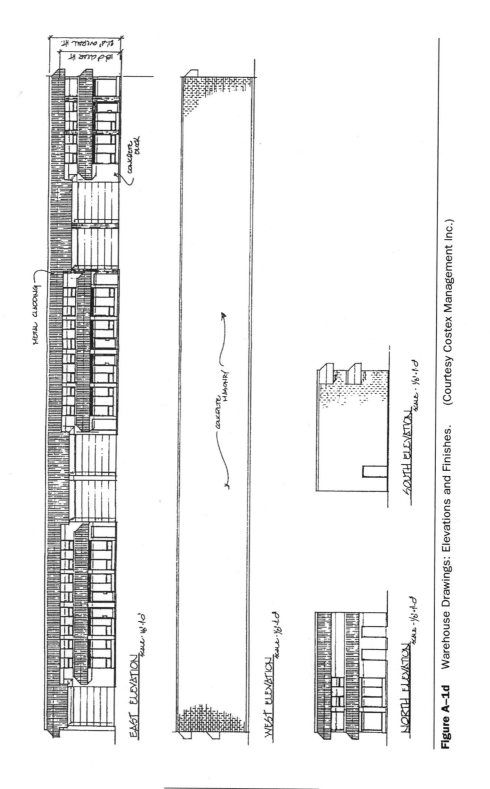

Figure A–1d Warehouse Drawings: Elevations and Finishes.   (Courtesy Costex Management Inc.)

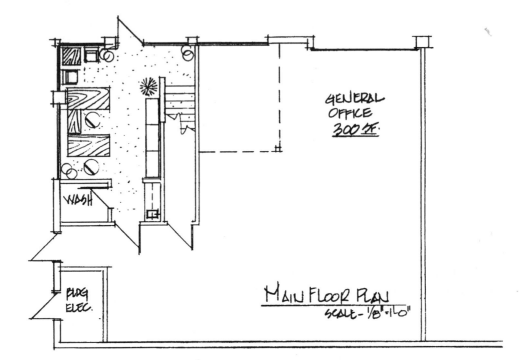

GENERAL
OFFICE
300 SF.

MAIN FLOOR PLAN
SCALE - 1/8" = 1'-0"

WASH

BLDG
ELEC.

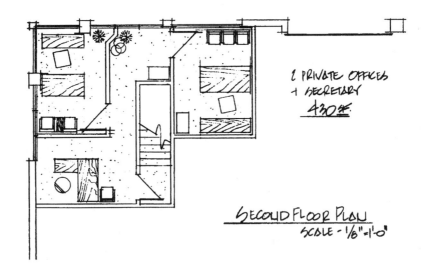

2 PRIVATE OFFICES
+ SECRETARY
430 SF.

SECOND FLOOR PLAN
SCALE - 1/8" = 1'-0"

Figure A–1e Warehouse Drawings: Office Floor Plans—Unit A. (Courtesy Costex Management Inc.)

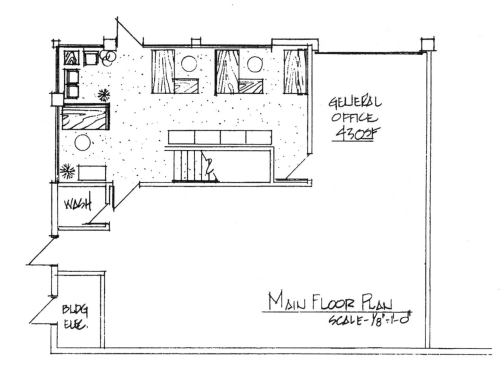

GENERAL
OFFICE
430 SF

MAIN FLOOR PLAN
SCALE - 1/8" = 1'-0"

WASH

BLDG
ELEC.

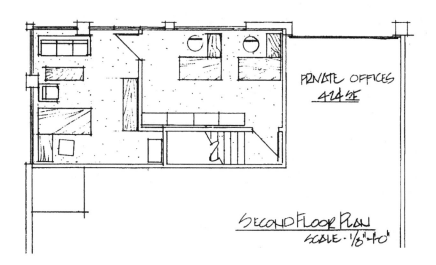

PRIVATE OFFICES
424 SF

SECOND FLOOR PLAN
SCALE - 1/8" = 1'-0"

Figure A–1e   Warehouse Drawings: Office Floor Plans—Unit B.   (Courtesy Costex Management Inc.)

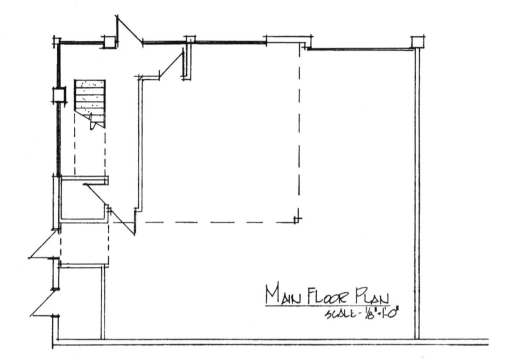

MAIN FLOOR PLAN
SCALE - 1/8" = 1'-0"

GENERAL OFFICE
+ 2 PRIVATE OFFICES
(10'x12' EACH)
560 SF

SECOND FLOOR PLAN
SCALE - 1/8" = 1'-0"

Figure A–1e Warehouse Drawings: Office Floor Plans—Unit C. (Courtesy Costex Management Inc.)

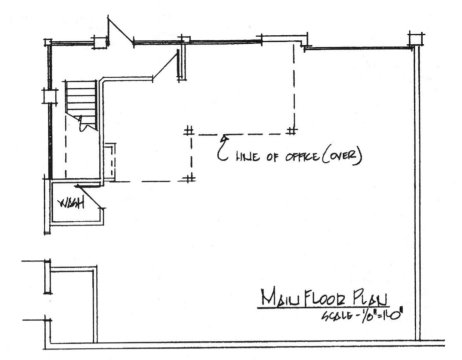

LINE OF OFFICE (OVER)

WASH

MAIN FLOOR PLAN
SCALE - 1/8"=1'0"

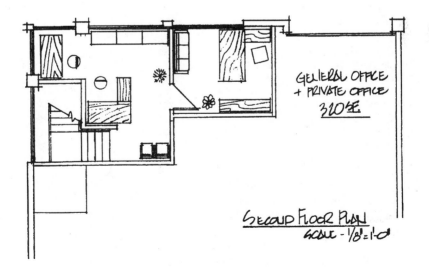

GENERAL OFFICE
+ PRIVATE OFFICE
320 S.F.

SECOND FLOOR PLAN
SCALE - 1/8"=1'-0"

Figure A–1e   Warehouse Drawings: Office Floor Plans—Unit D.   (Courtesy Costex Management Inc.)

CODE	DESCRIPTION	COMMENTS	QUANTITY	UNITS	TRAD CST	TTL COST
201	BLDG. EXCAV					1000
203	SERVICE TRENCH		160	CY		800
205	SERV TRNCH B'FILL		160	CY		1120
207	B/F UNDER BLDG		740	CY		5180
207	ROADWAYS—EXCAV		398	CY		2786
207	ROADWAYS—B/F		398	CY		7164
207	ROADWAYS—COMPACT		7170	SF		1792.5
211	SITE GRADING		1900	SF		475
223	ON-SITE UTIL CB Bal	CB BAL INC PBG	3	NO.		800.1
227	OFF-SITE UTIL—CROSS'G		1	NO.		3000
227	OFF-SITE UTIL—WATER	1 INCH	1	NO.		600
227	OFF-SITE UTIL—STORM	8 INCH	1	NO.		675
227	OFF-SITE UTIL—SANIT'Y	4 INCH	1	NO.		780
227	OFF-SITE UTIL—ELEC					4000
231	ASPHALT PAVING		796	Sq Yd		9552
233	CURBS & GUTTER		170	Lin Ft		1020
237	CONC WALKS—POURING		2	Cu Yd		300
237	CONC WALKS—FINISHING		144	SF		36
241	FENCE—GARBAGE FLOOR	CONCRETE	2	CY		300
241	FENCE—GARBAGE FLOOR	CONCRETE	80	SF		20
241	FENCE—BARB ENCL		26	LF		416
243	PC WHEEL STOPS		17	NO.		680
275	LANDSCAPING		1367	SF	10936	10936
240	PILING		64	NO.	28800	28800
341.2	CONC. GRADE BEAMS	SUPPLY/PLACE	127	CY		6985
341.2	CONC. SLAB-ON-GRADE	SUPPLY/PLACE	164	CY		9020
330.3	CONC. SLAB-ON-GRADE	FINISHING	6650	SF		1662.5
330.4	CONC.—PUMPING		305	CY		2135
305.4	FORMWORK		4970	SF		7455
305.3	FRMW'K NAILS, TIES,..		4970	SF		497
	BAR STOCK	291cyX180#	52380	LBS		23571
412	MASONRY WEST WALL	STANDARD	4180	SF		0
412	MASONRY—S. WALL	RIBBED	770	SF		0
412	MASONRY—NORTH WALL	RIBBED	378	SF		0
412	MASONRY—NORTH WALL	STANDARD	152	SF		0
412	MASONRY—EAST WALL	STANDARD	1204.5	SF		0
412	MASONRY—EAST WALL	RIBBED	581.5	SF		0
412	MASONRY—TOTAL		7229	SF	44000	44000
512	STR.ST COLUMNS		1	NO.		150
521	STEEL JOISTS		30	NO.		5250
531	METAL ROOF DECK		6650	SF		7780.5
558	MISC. METALS	ALLOW				500
560	CHAIN LINK	FOR GAS METER	1	NO.		200
610	OVERHANG WOOD BRACKETS	2 × 4	1577	BM		1340.45
611	OVERHANG	1/2" PLY	69	SHTS		1035
610	OVERHANG	NAILS & H'WARE	2177	BM		108.85

610	OVERHANG	NAILS & H'WARE	69	SHTS		138
701	WATERPROOF MASONRY		7229	SF		2168.7
710	VAPOR BARRIER	6 mil	6650	SF		332.5
720	INSULATION—ROOF	(in roof est)	6650	SF		0
720	INSULATION—DEMISIDE WALLS		2940	SF		1323
720	INSUL'N—PERIMETER		900	SF		1890
733	METAL ROOF CLADDING		2172	SF		6516
733	METAL SOFFITS		802	SF		1684.2
750	METAL ROOFING		6650	SF		13965
751	FLASHING	COLORED				400
790	SEALANTS					100
801	METAL DOORS & FRAMES		6	NO.		1350
830	OVERHEAD DOORS				7592	7592
840	ENTRY DOORS—STOREFRONT		5	NO.		2500
850	WINDOWS					0
901	STEEL STUDS		2800	SF		1400
902	DRYWALL	5/8" type "X"	5600	SF		4760
990	PAINTING		5600	SF		2240
1020	LOUVERS & VENTS					0
1050	IDENTIFYING DEVICES		5	NO.		1000
1501	PLMBG (INCL STORM,NIC W'SHRM)				10476	10476
1530	HEATING				6098	6098
?	GAS SERVICES				1000	1000
1601	ELECTRICAL				22127	22127

Figure A–2   Materials List (with Quantities).

B

THE WAREHOUSE: SUPPLEMENTARY PLANNING DATA

The tasks are listed below in outline form; they name most of the work to be done in preparing the warehouse for its tenants. The outline is more condensed than the usual layered Work Breakdown Structure and some may find it easier to work with. However, the WBS clearly shows the families of tasks and the names of their super-tasks. Each level of the WBS is given in Figure B–2. There are advantages to each mode of display: the WBS clearly shows each "family" of tasks that could be scheduled while the outline breaks down each portion of the project into all its components.

In the outline (Figure B–1), the project is named in the largest type, the stages of the project are in large type, and the main segments of each are in **bold**. Each indentation identifies a lower level of detail of the task area immediately above.

The arrangement of all the tasks by Level is straightforward: each family of tasks in one level covers a complete description of the project at that level. A schedule could be developed using only the tasks in one level. This is quite different from the outline arrangement of all tasks.

TO BUILD THE MULTI-TENANT WAREHOUSE

STAGE ONE: BUILDING THE STRUCTURE

TO PREPARE THE SITE

1 Perform a Legal Survey of the Site
2 Perform a Soils Analysis
  Rough Excavate the Building Area
3   Excavate out the Old Fill
4   Remove the Material
  Provide a Solid Soil Base
5   Import Quality Fill
6   Level and Compact

TO INSTALL SITE SERVICES

(Water, Storm, Sanitary, Electrical, Natural Gas)
7 Trench & Bed
8 Install Conduit
9 Connect to Municipal Services
10 Backfill and Compact

TO INSTALL FOUNDATIONS

11 Excavate and Level
12 Drive Piles
  Build and Place Formwork
13   . . For Perimeter Footings
14   . . For Grade Beams
15   . . For Column Footing
16 Place Steel Reinforcement
17 Pour (and Cure) Concrete
18 Moisture-Proof below grade

TO INSTALL UNDER-SLAB SERVICES

(Water, Storm, Sanitary, Electrical, Natural Gas)
19 Trench and Bed
20 Install Conduits & Risers
21 Connect to Site Services
22 Backfill and Compact

TO BUILD THE STRUCTURE

  Construct External Block Walls
23   Mortar Blocks
24   Place Reinforcement
25   Moisture-Proof Walls
26   Structural Steel Column

  Erect Roof Structure
27   Place and Secure Roof Trusses
28   Install Roof Deck
29   Install Vapor Barrier
30   Lay Roof Cladding
31   Construct Overhang
32   Install Soffits
33   Install Flashing
34 Install Doors and Windows
35 Paint

TO LAY CONCRETE SLABS (Building Floor & Garbage Area)

36 Lay Vapor Barrier
37 Place Reinforcement
38 Pour & Finish Floor Surface

TO INSTALL BUILDING SERVICES

  Sanitary Plumbing
39   Install and Connect Water Pipe
40   Install and Connect Sanitary Drains
41   Install Fixtures
  Storm Drains
42   Install Downspouts
43   Install / Backfill Foundation Drains
  Electrical
44   Install Conduits
45   Pull Wires
46   Install Boxes
47   Install Main Panel
48   Install Fixtures
49   Connect to Power and Ring-Out
  Heating and Ventilating
50   Install Natural Gas System
51   Connect to Main Supply
52   Install Equipment and Venting
  Install Communication System
53   Install Devices

TO FINISH STAGE ONE

  Site Work
    Roadways and Parking
54   Excavate

55	Prepare Bed		Area Lighting
56	Pour Curbs	62	Pour Foundations
57	Lay Paving	63	Erect Light Standards & Connect
	Install Walkways	64	Erect Fencing for Gas Meter
58	Excavate		Landscaping
59	Prepare Bed	65	Import Topsoil
60	Forms	66	Finish Grading
61	Pour and Finish Concrete	67	Plant Shrubs & Sod

STAGE TWO: MODEL DISPLAY OFFICE

	Framing		Electrical & Mechanical
68	Erect Steel studs	71	Install Services
69	Construct Floor structure	72	Install & Connect Fixtures
70	Lay Floor covering	73	Install and Joint Drywall
		74	Paint and Decorate Office

STAGE THREE—OFFICES TO SUIT TENANTS

(Repeat the above seven tasks for each tenant.)

Figure B–1   Warehouse Project: Outline Arrangement of Tasks.

WORK AREA OF LEVEL I

THE PROJECT: THE MULTI-TENANT WAREHOUSE

WORK AREAS OF LEVEL II

STAGE ONE: THE PRIMARY CONSTRUCTION (Substantial Completion)
STAGE TWO: MODEL DISPLAY OFFICE
STAGE THREE: OFFICES TO SUIT TENANTS

WORK AREAS OF LEVEL III—(for STAGE ONE ONLY)

1	TO PREPARE THE SITE	5	TO BUILD THE STRUCTURE
2	TO INSTALL SITE SERVICES	6	TO LAY CONCRETE SLABS
3	TO INSTALL FOUNDATIONS	7	TO INSTALL BUILDING SERVICES
4	TO INSTALL UNDER-SLAB SERVICES	8	TO FINISH SITE WORK

WORK AREAS OF LEVEL IV (Thirty-Six Tasks)

1	Legal Survey of the Site	19	Construct External Block Walls
2	Perform a Soils Analysis	20	Erect Roof Structure
3	Rough Excavate the Building Area	21	Install Doors and Windows
4	Provide a Solid Soil Base	22	Painting
5	Trench & Bed for All Site Services	23	Lay Vapor Barrier for Slabs
6	Install Conduit	24	Place Reinforcement
7	Connect to Munic. Services	25	Pour & Finish Floor Surface
8	Backfill	26	Sanitary Plumbing in Building
9	Excavate and Level for Foundations	27	Storm Drains
10	Drive Piles	28	Electrical
11	Build and Place Formwork	29	Heating and Ventilating
12	Place Steel Reinforcement	30	Install Communication System
13	Pour (and Cure) Concrete	31	Roadways & Parking
14	Moisture-Proof below grade	32	Walkways
15	Trench and Bed for Under-Slab Services	33	Area Lighting
16	Install Conduits	34	Fencing
17	Connect to Site Services	35	Landscaping
18	Backfill and Compact	36	Clean-Up

TASKS OF LEVEL V

Building Excavation
    Excavate out the Old Fill
    Remove the material
    Import Quality Fill
    Level and Compact

Install Reinforcement: (Foundations)
    For Perimeter Footings
    For Grade Beams
    For Column Footing

Walls
    Mortar Masonry Blocks
    Place Reinforcement
    Moisture-Proof Walls
    Erect Structural Steel Column

Roof
    Place and Secure Roof Trusses
    Install Roof Deck
    Lay Vapor Barrier

Install Roof Cladding
Construct Overhang
Attach Soffits
Install Flashing

Sanitary Plumbing
Install Water Supply Piping
Install Sanitary Drains
Install Fixtures

Storm Drains
Install Downspouts
Lay Foundation Drains

Electrical
Install Conduits
Pull Wires
Install Boxes
Install Main Panel
Install Fixtures
Connect to Power

Mechanical
To Install Natural Gas System

Connect to Main Supply
Install Equipment incl venting
Install Identifying Devices

Roadways
Excavate for Roads
Prepare Bed
Curbs
Paving

Walkways
Excavate for Walkways
Prepare Bed
Forms
Pour and Finish Concrete

Area Lights
Foundations for Light Standards
Erect Light Standards

Landscaping
Import Topsoil
Finish Grading
Planting (Shrubs & Seed)

Figure B–2   Warehouse Project: Tasks by Level of the WBS.

FOR LOWER LEVELS

Further breakdown of these Level V tasks into more detail would require detailed knowledge of the processes of each task, which is the realm of the local foreman. This added detail would not improve the overall schedule of the project unless fine coordination with other such tasks was necessary. In this case, a schedule for a sub-project should satisfy these needs.

C

A TECHNIQUE FOR DECISION MAKING

PROCESS OF SELECTION

As an aid to making good, defensible decisions, there is a business process that charts progress through certain specific steps in choosing "best" solutions. This process applies to making decisions on very simple "projects" (such as selecting the most appropriate restaurant) and to much more complex and expensive ones (such as selecting the "best" site for a new college campus). The steps are the same for both but become more extensive and involve greater risks for increasingly larger and more complex projects.

The process is quite simple to apply, but you must make value judgments as to the relative strengths and weaknesses of the several factors that influence the decision. You must take an "arm's length" view of your own ideas to do this, otherwise you will invariably conclude that the idea you prefer will automatically be judged the "best" by your analysis. Remember that the values you assign to each option will likely have to be defended in discussion with your colleagues and critics.

The accompanying table in Figure C–1 shows how the method works in selecting the "best" method of "getting to town." *Note:* The winning score of 680 for the BUS option is found by calculating:

$(50 \times 8) + (20 \times 5) + (30 \times 6) =$
$400 + 100 + 180 = 680$ points

Only the relative values of the ratings matter. For example, there is not much difference between traveling by car or by bus, but a taxi ride is the least desirable.

A PROCESS FOR MAKING THE "BEST" SELECTION

YOUR ACTION	AN EXAMPLE
1. Study the Objective	"TO GET TO TOWN"
2. Investigate alternate ways for achieving this objective	My Car, the Bus, Taxi, Bicycle
3. Determine all the resources necessary for each one	Gas & Parking, Bus Fare, Taxi Fare, Time
4. Establish criteria for evaluating/ comparing each of the alternatives	Low Expenditure Short Time Out of the Rain
5. Give relative ratings for each criterion	Cheapest: 50 Shortest Time: 20 Being Dry: 30

	Cheap	Short	Dry	Score
Car	4	10	8	640
Bus	8	5	6	680
Taxi	1	8	10	510
Bike	10	1	1	550

6. Rate each method by resources needed and factor each by the ratings from #5

7. Decide on the Best Method   The BUS rates highest.

Figure C–1   The Options Evaluation Table.

The values you assign to each option represent their *relative* value to you. "Cheapest" is rated 2.5 times as important as being "dry"; perhaps this is too extreme and you might have chosen a different value. Ensure that all values in a set honestly reflect your opinion.

This common method is useful when enough is known about the alternative ways of accomplishing an objective. Problems arise when rare or novel alternatives are considered; these are often rejected out of ignorance, whereas a little research and analysis, such as was done in the example above, could make such creative ideas practical and your project more successful.

This common method applies to personal as well as corporate decision making. It provides a rational approach that can be defended when the decision maker is asked: "Why is that the best way?"

D

CONSTRUCTING PRECEDENCE GRIDS

A Precedence Grid (P-G) was introduced in Chapter 3. A P-G can be constructed from the unedited precedence information you obtained from all your knowledgeable sources. The project will already have a Work Breakdown Structure listing all the tasks, so your consultants could comment on the order of doing the work. They probably assisted in identifying many of the tasks.

Starting with these written opinions from your consultants and having augmented them with your own opinions, you are ready to condense all this data on one sheet (possibly a large one) by following the procedures outlined below.

Other than clarifying conflicts inadvertently presented by your consultants, the P-G can also be a tool for refining the data by removing redundant precedence information, identifying dummy tasks for AOA Networks, and finding loops in the logic.

We shall develop a P-G for the trip across the continent that was introduced in Chapter 3. The precedence information is reproduced here (from Figure 3–6):

LOGIC STATEMENTS FOR THE TRANSCONTINENTAL TRIP

"MUST PRECEDE" STATEMENTS			"MUST FOLLOW" STATEMENTS		
START	precedes	A	A,C,F & H	follow	START
A	precedes	B	B	follows	A
START	precedes	C	C	follows	START & H
START	precedes	F	D	follows	E & C
F	precedes	G	E	follows	B & G
B & G	precede	E	F	follows	START
START	precedes	H	G	follows	F
H	precedes	C	H	follows	START
E & C	precede	D	I	follows	D
D	precedes	I	END	follows	I
I	precedes	END			

PROCEDURE FOR DEVELOPING A PRECEDENCE GRID

Lay Out the Grid

On a piece of squared paper, name the columns and rows of the grid with the letter symbols (or abbreviations) of all the tasks in the WBS, and include a START as the first Preceder and an END as the last Follower. The order of tasks must be the same order in the row and column. You do not need a START as the first follower (top row) or an END as the last preceder (last entry in the first column) because nothing can precede START and nothing can follow END. The empty grid is shown in Figure D–1. The "O's" identify the diagonal (where no "X" entries can appear) to help you navigate around the grid.

Enter "X's" in the START Row

The precedence table states that tasks **A, C, F,** and **H** all follow **START**; this can be graphically displayed very concisely in the first row:

	A	B	C	D	E	F	G	H	I	END
START	X		X			X		X		

Similarly, for the next two rows, we can show "B follows A" and "E follows B."

	A	B	C	D	E	F	G	H	I	END
A		X								
B					X					

We follow all the precedence statements, translating each condition into an X in the appropriate cell in the grid until we have dealt with all the precedence statements. We must check that all rows and columns contain at least one X; if a blank

	A	B	C	D	E	F	G	H	I	END
START	·	·	·	·	·	·	·	·	·	·
A	O	·	·	·	·	·	·	·	·	·
B	·	O	·	·	·	·	·	·	·	·
C	·	·	O	·	·	·	·	·	·	·
D	·	·	·	O	·	·	·	·	·	·
E	·	·	·	·	O	·	·	·	·	·
F	·	·	·	·	·	O	·	·	·	·
G	·	·	·	·	·	·	O	·	·	·
H	·	·	·	·	·	·	·	O	·	·
I	·	·	·	·	·	·	·	·	O	·

Figure D–1   The Blank Precedence Grid for the Trip.

row or column is found, then the precedence logic is incomplete and more information is needed. An exception must be checked: if a task has no follower task stated, the END milestone may be the correct follower "task." If a task has multiple preceder or follower tasks, the P-G will not find missing ones; each X should be checked against the original data to search for errors and omissions.

The Precedence Grid is a simple way of displaying all the precedence information in unambiguous terms. It condenses all of the written statements onto one simple figure that can be inspected to uncover conflicts in the logic. The completed Grid is displayed in Figure D–2.

Carefully note certain important aspects of this Grid:

1. The "O's" mark the diagonal, helping you to orient yourself in the grid: there is an "O" in cells A-A, B-B, C-C, and so forth.
2. The X's in a **row** show which tasks *follow* the task naming the row; the **X** in position E-D (row E and column D) means that D must follow task E.

	A	B	C	D	E	F	G	H	I	END
START	X	·	X	·	·	X	·	X	·	·
A	O	X	·	·	·	·	·	·	·	·
B	·	O	·	·	X	·	·	·	·	·
C	·	·	O	X	·	·	·	·	·	·
D	·	·	·	O	·	·	·	·	X	·
E	·	·	·	X	O	·	·	·	·	·
F	·	·	·	·	·	O	X	·	·	·
G	·	·	·	·	X	·	O	·	·	·
H	·	·	X	·	·	·	·	O	·	·
I	·	·	·	·	·	·	·	·	O	X

Figure D–2   Complete Precedence Grid for the Trip.

3. The X's in a **column** show which tasks must *precede* the task naming the column; the X's in column **E** mean that **B** and **G** must precede **E**.
4. There is no need to include a **START** column or an **END** row because there can be no X's in them.
5. Where space permits, place the names of the Tasks in the left column next to their symbols. Alternatively, the names can be placed above the row of symbols. The names help in checking the work.

In recording the task logic in this Grid, you fill in a row at a time by noting the tasks that *follow* the task naming that row: for example, A, C, F, and H are "X-ed" in row "START." Or you can fill in a column by noting which tasks must *precede* the task naming that column: that is, C and E are "X-ed" in column D because D follows both C and E.

USES FOR THE PRECEDENCE GRID

Other uses can be made of the Grid: it is a simpler way of identifying duplicated precedence relationships. Clearly, every task must begin after the START but only a few begin *immediately* after. In the alphabet, for example, all the other letters come after "A," but only "B" comes *immediately* after. In the above Grid, Tasks **H** and **C** are required to follow **START**, but in row "H," **C** is also required to follow **H**. This latter requirement also means that **C** must follow **START**, because **H** also follows **START**, in row START. It refines the requirement that **C** is to start after the START milestone, but not immediately after it. The X in cell START-C is redundant and unnecessary.

The Grid can identify potential redundant logic statements in the basic precedence information. For example, look for a row *and* a column having multiple "X's" in them that share a common "X" at their intersection. Figure D–3 shows a row and a column separated out from the full Grid.

In this case, when three X's form the corners of a **square** (row H and Column H), the X at the intersection of the row and column is unnecessary and could be removed without losing any logic. It would simplify drawing the network because

```
                  · · · · ·  C  · · · · ·  H  · · · · ·
        START     · · · · ·  X  · · · · ·  X  · · · · ·
          ·       · · · · ·  ·  · · · · ·  ·  · · · · ·
          ·       · · · · ·  ·  · · · · ·  ·  · · · · ·
          ·       · · · · ·  ·  · · · · ·  ·  · · · · ·
          H       · · · · ·  X  · · · · ·  ·  · · · · ·
```

Figure D–3   Segment of the Precedence Grid to Illustrate Redundant Data.

	A	B	C	D	E	F	G	H	I	M	END
START	X	·	X	·	·	X	·	X	·	·	·
A	O	X	·	·	·	·	·	·	·	·	·
B	·	O	·	·	X	·	·	·	·	·	·
C	·	·	O	X	·	·	·	·	·	·	·
D	·	·	·	O	·	·	·	·	X	·	·
E	·	·	·	X	O	·	·	·	·	·	·
F	·	·	·	·	·	O	X	·	·	·	·
G	·	·	·	·	X	·	O	·	·	X	·
H	·	·	X	·	·	·	·	O	·	·	·
I	·	·	·	·	·	·	·	·	O	·	X
M	·	·	·	·	·	·	·	·	X	O	·

Figure D–4   Augmented Grid to Exhibit Potential Dummy Tasks.

one less link would need to be drawn and it would remove the resulting confusion from the drawing problem.

In another case that looks similar, duplication of the logic may be present but you must study it closely to understand what it means. Here, if a new Task **M** were added to represent Bill's mother's bus trip from Fresno to meet the group at Reno, then the Precedence Grid would expand as shown in Figure D–4. New precedence links occur at **M-I** and at **G-M**. Note that **START-C** and **G-D** indicate possibilities for redundancies or dummy tasks (in AOA networks).

If we separate out (Figure D–5) row "G" and column "E," each of which have multiple "X's" and intersect at cell G-E, it looks like a redundancy but it actually signifies a need for a dummy task in the AOA network. It is not a redundancy

	A	B	C	D	E	F	G	H	I	M	END
START					·					·	
A					·					·	
B					X					·	
C					·					·	
D					·					·	
E					O					·	
F					·					·	
G	·	·	·	·	X	·	O	·	·	X	·
H					·					·	
I					·					·	
M					·					·	

Figure D–5   Portion of a Grid to Exhibit Need for a Dummy Task.

		(Followers)		
		JACK	SALLY	JIM
	JACK	O	X	X*
(Preceders)	SALLY		O	X
	JIM	X*		O

Figure D–6   A Precedence Grid for Identifying Loops.

because the X's are not symmetrical about the diagonal. A redundancy would exist if there were an X in cell **I-M**. When a dummy is identified in the P-G, mark it by circling the X to remind you to take it into account when you are drawing the AOA network.

Loops in Network Logic

The Grid can discover logic loops in a network. A complex chain of precedence relationships can produce a loop. A simple one is "Jack is older than Sally, Sally is older than Jim, and Jim is older than Jack." This contains an error in logic because it says that Jack is both older *and* younger than Jim—we are unsure of Sally's age. These relationships are displayed in Figure D–6:

    The plain "X's" are uncontested, but the relationships marked with the "X*"s are in mutual conflict. Here, the conflict is in cells **JIM/JACK** and **JACK/JIM**; they state that Jack and Jim are each older than the other! When there are X's in symmetrical locations in the Grid, there is an error in the logic. The P-G does not give any clue about which statement is incorrect; they cannot both be correct and one must be removed. If we find that Jack is younger than Jim, then the correct order becomes:

    JACK >>> SALLY >>> JIM

and the X* must be removed from the **JIM/JACK** cell.

    This is *not* a redundancy situation because the off-diagonal cells are symmetrical (i/j and j/i). However, there is a redundant X remaining that is indicated by the 2 X's in row "JACK" and 2 X's in column "JIM": the X* in cell **JACK/JIM** is superfluous. Figure D–7 shows the Grid with the loops and the redundant X* removed.

		(Followers)		
		JACK	SALLY	JIM
	JACK	O	X	
(Preceders)	SALLY		O	X
	JIM			O

Figure D–7   Loops and a Redundancy Removed.

E

DRAWING NETWORKS FROM PRECEDENCE DATA FOR THE WAREHOUSE PROJECT

Sketching out the first draft of your developing network requires a large piece of substantial paper, a soft pencil (for easy erasure), an eraser, and patience. Using a ball-point will strain your patience and add to the amount of paper you will consume. A chalkboard is a perfect medium for your early networks and, after much easy editing, you can make your first paper copy with increased confidence.

Much time and effort can be saved by referring directly to the Precedence Grid rather than working from your original written record of precedence information. Use the final copy of the P-G after you have refined and edited out the redundancies and errors in logic from the original. Even if some were missed, the network diagram should make them more visible.

DRAWING THE BUBBLE (AON) DIAGRAM

Every network diagram (AON and AOA) must begin and end with the milestones **START** and **END.** The diagrams can be drafted out, beginning at the START and working forward through the diagram, or beginning at the END and working backward through the diagram. Often you may do both, depending on the complexity of the relationships among the tasks.

When you are placing a new bubble on your growing diagram and preparing to link it, ask yourself these questions, depending on whether you are developing the network forward from the START or backward from the END:

"Forward" Development: "Before I can place and link the next task bubble, which tasks must be completed?" (They are the X's in the column of the task you want to place.)

or

"Now that I have placed and linked this task bubble, which bubbles can I now place that depend on its completion?" (These are the X's in the row of the bubble just completed.)

Figure E–1 illustrates "forward" development of bubble diagrams.

"Backward" Development: "Now that the current task bubble is placed, which tasks must immediately precede it, so I can place their bubbles?" (X's in the column of the bubble just completed.) This question may help to resolve some issues but most schedulers begin drawing at the beginning, not the end of the project. Figure E–2 illustrates "backward" development of bubble diagrams.

As you ask yourself these questions while you sketch out the network for the first time, read the names of the tasks and consider whether the order makes sense; it is another check on the details of the Precedence Grid. Never assume something is correct just because you developed it. It is a safe practice to slightly distrust your own work just as you would distrust someone else's. Overconfidence leads to errors. A sure check on your network is to make up a Precedence Grid or a Precedence List based solely on your new network, without reference to the original data. When completed, compare the new P-G with the original. P-G's are better than lists because you can lay one P-G over the other to make the comparison.

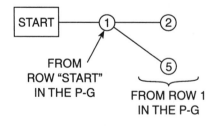

Figure E–1   "Forward" Development of Bubble Diagrams.

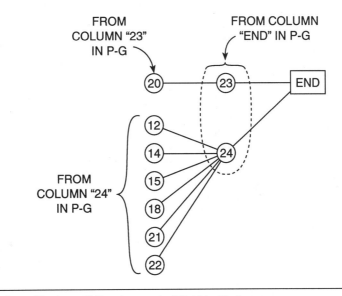

FROM
COLUMN "23"
IN P-G

FROM COLUMN
"END" IN P-G

FROM
COLUMN "24"
IN P-G

Figure E–2   "Backward" Development of Bubble Diagrams.

FIRST DRAFT BUBBLE (AON) NETWORK FOR THE 24-TASK MODEL

The Precedence Grid for this model of the project is reproduced here from Chapter 4 (Figure 4–11). It is the basis for drawing the AON and AOA networks. See Figure E–3.

During sketching of the draft Bubble Diagram, we discovered two oddities when we were placing the followers of task #13: tasks #11 and #17 also were followers of task #10. The first two sketches in Figure E–4 show the followers of #10 and #13 separately, while the last one shows how the two can be combined.

The problem arose because two redundant links were not removed from the P-G diagram: links (10/11) and (10/17) were links common to their rows having multiple "X's." Redundant links are readily found during the drawing stage, when such task placement problems appear. The complete first (rough) draft appears in Figure E–5.

The completed second draft of the AON diagram appears in Figure 4–12 in Chapter 4. The final form of the AON diagram (Draft #3) appears as Figure 4–13. These refinements adjust the layout and the neatness of the diagram to increase clarity and balance. Try to satisfy the following rules when clarifying the diagram.

1. Ensure that all links "move" with time to the right.
2. Use no arrowheads; time always moves to the right.
3. Place the tasks in a pattern that helps in locating them in the diagram.

PRECEDENCE GRID FOR 24-TASK MODEL—(for Stage One only)

		Units										+10									+20					END
		1	2	3	4	5	6	7	8	9	0	1	2	3	4	5	6	7	8	9	0	1	2	3	4	END
START		X	·	·	·	·	·	·	·	·	·	·	·	·	·	·	·	·	·	·	·	·	·	·	·	·
Survey	1	O	X	·	·	X	·	·	·	·	·	·	·	·	·	·	·	·	·	·	·	·	·	·	·	·
Soils	2	·	O	X	·	·	·	·	·	·	·	·	·	·	·	·	·	·	·	·	·	·	·	·	·	·
Excav	3	·	·	O	X	·	·	·	·	·	·	·	·	·	·	·	·	·	·	·	·	·	·	·	·	·
Base	4	·	·	·	O	·	X	·	·	·	·	·	·	·	·	·	·	·	·	·	·	·	·	·	·	·
Serv.	5	·	·	·	·	O	·	·	X	·	·	·	·	·	·	·	·	X	·	·	·	·	·	·	·	·
Piles	6	·	·	·	·	·	O	X	X	·	·	·	·	·	·	·	·	·	·	·	·	·	·	·	·	·
Found	7	·	·	·	·	·	·	O	·	X	·	·	·	·	X	·	·	·	·	·	·	·	·	·	·	·
USlab	8	·	·	·	·	·	·	·	O	·	·	·	·	X	·	·	·	·	·	·	·	·	·	·	·	·
Walls	9	·	·	·	·	·	·	·	·	O	X	·	·	·	·	·	·	·	·	·	·	·	·	·	·	·
Roof	10	·	·	·	·	·	·	·	·	·	O	X	·	X	·	X	X	X	·	·	·	·	·	·	·	·
Doors	11	·	·	·	·	·	·	·	·	·	·	O	X	·	·	·	·	·	·	·	·	·	·	·	·	·
Paint	12	·	·	·	·	·	·	·	·	·	·	·	O	·	·	·	·	·	·	·	·	·	·	X	·	·
Conc	13	·	·	·	·	·	·	·	·	·	·	X	·	O	X	·	·	X	X	·	·	·	·	·	·	·
Plumb	14	·	·	·	·	·	·	·	·	·	·	·	·	·	O	·	·	·	·	·	·	·	·	X	·	·
Drains	15	·	·	·	·	·	·	·	·	·	·	·	·	·	·	O	·	·	·	·	·	·	·	X	·	·
Elect	16	·	·	·	·	·	·	·	·	·	·	·	·	·	·	·	O	X	·	·	·	·	·	·	·	·
HVAC	17	·	·	·	·	·	·	·	·	·	·	·	·	·	·	·	·	O	·	·	·	·	X	·	·	·
Commun	18	·	·	·	·	·	·	·	·	·	·	·	·	·	·	·	·	·	O	·	·	·	·	X	·	·
Roads	19	·	·	·	·	·	·	·	·	·	·	·	·	·	·	·	·	·	·	O	X	X	·	·	·	·
Walks	20	·	·	·	·	·	·	·	·	·	·	·	·	·	·	·	·	·	·	·	O	·	·	X	·	·
Lites	21	·	·	·	·	·	·	·	·	·	·	·	·	·	·	·	·	·	·	·	·	O	·	·	X	·
Fences	22	·	·	·	·	·	·	·	·	·	·	·	·	·	·	·	·	·	·	·	·	·	O	·	X	·
Landsc	23	·	·	·	·	·	·	·	·	·	·	·	·	·	·	·	·	·	·	·	·	·	·	O	·	X
Clean	24	·	·	·	·	·	·	·	·	·	·	·	·	·	·	·	·	·	·	·	·	·	·	·	O	X
END		·	·	·	·	·	·	·	·	·	·	·	·	·	·	·	·	·	·	·	·	·	·	·	·	·

Figure E–3   The 24-task Precedence Grid for the Warehouse.

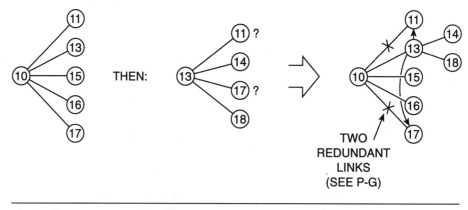

Figure E–4   Odd Linkages in Bubble Diagrams.

268

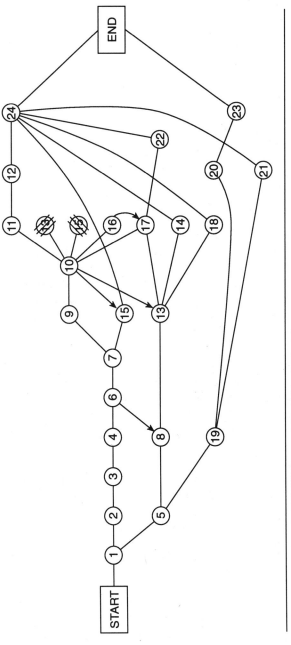

Figure E-5   First Draft AON Diagram for 24-task Model.

4. Minimize the cross-overs by repositioning task bubbles.
5. Look for redundant and inconsistent links that were missed during analysis of the P-G, and remove them.
6. It is useful to add a few task names to the network to maintain realism about the network. You can often assign a general name to a group of related tasks.

DRAWING ARROW (AOA) NETWORKS

Arrow (AOA) diagrams are different from Bubble diagrams and you should *never* try to draw an Arrow network by referring to its Bubble diagram because its graphical building blocks will confuse your understanding of the links. Also, because errors in one diagram can be transmitted to the new network, always refer to the original Precedence Grid for the fundamental linking information.

The process is the same as for AON diagramming: begin with the START milestone and draw an **arrow** from it for each task that follows it from the START row of the P-G. Place a small circle at the end of the arrowhead and identify the task with a name or its number from the P-G. Task arrows #2 and #5 emanate from the end event of task #1. The start of the AOA network appears in Figure E–6. Try to have all arrows "move" to the right; arrows do not have to be straight or always move to the right for the draft, but wandering lines are difficult for the eye to follow and can lead to confusion and errors.

This first draft of the network (Figure E–7) shows all links appearing on the P-G plus quite a few broken lines that appear to be dummy tasks: only a few of them are. Most of them are broken lines drawn to extend "floating" task arrows to their proper end event which was not there when the arrow was first drawn. Recall that, when a task arrow is drawn, we seldom know where its end event will be placed. As other arrows are drawn, these "hanging" events from earlier tasks can be connected to the real end event with a temporary dummy task. In the next draft these extensions become solid lines unless they are real "dummies." Task #15 exhibits this. See Figure E–8.

Note the similarity of the AOA to the AON diagram near the START, but also notice the differences for the tasks after task #10: three dummy tasks are needed. Two were noted on the P-G (10-13 and 13-17). The dummies are necessary when

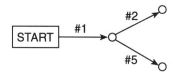

Figure E–6   Beginning the AOA Network.

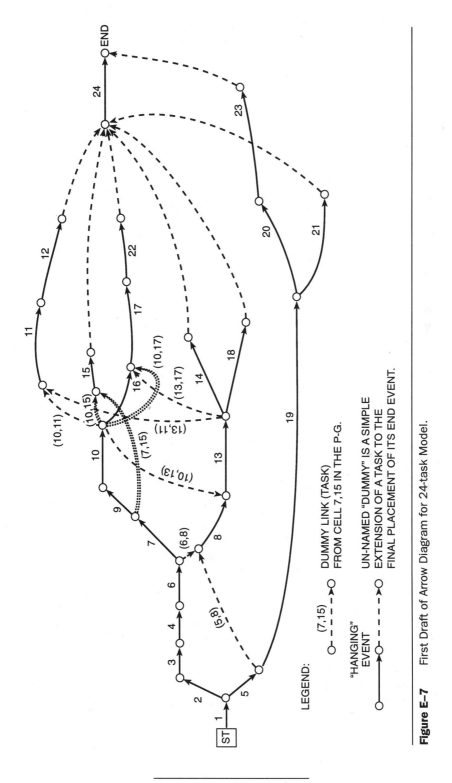

Figure E–7 First Draft of Arrow Diagram for 24-task Model.

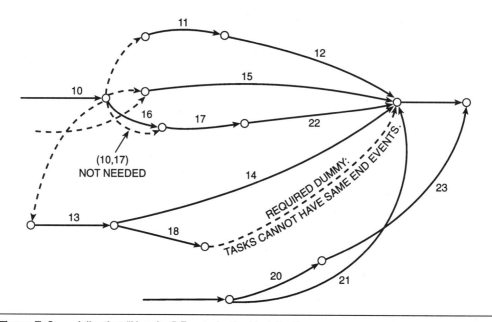

Figure E–8 Adjusting "Hanging" Events in the Next Draft.

a task follows more than one other task; a Task Arrow can start at only one event. Because Task #13 follows tasks 8 **and** 10, one of the links must be a dummy. The same applies for task #17, which follows #16 and #13.

The third dummy must be there because tasks #14 and #18 both start and end at the same events. This is *not* allowed for AOA networks because tasks are code-named by their start and end events. These two tasks would be identically named unless we introduced the dummy event and then linked it to the original end event of task 18. The need for this dummy cannot be predicted from the P-G network. Figure E–9 displays the final Arrow diagram for the 24-task model.

NUMBERING OF EVENTS ON ARROW DIAGRAMS

For consistency with some calculation methods on Arrow diagrams, the events must be properly numbered. The ending event (at the arrowhead) of every task must have a larger number than its starting event. In AOA systems, the tasks are named by their terminating events: for example, the task arrow starting at event #38 and terminating at event #43 is called "TASK (38,43)." These numbers do not have to be in numerical sequence as long as the "bigger-at-the-arrow-end" rule is followed. In cases where more tasks might be added to the network later, the initial numbering scheme could anticipate this by naming the events as 10, 20, 30,

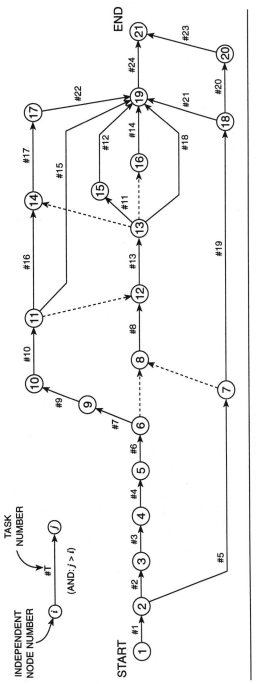

Figure E-9 Final Arrow Diagram: 24-task Model.

273

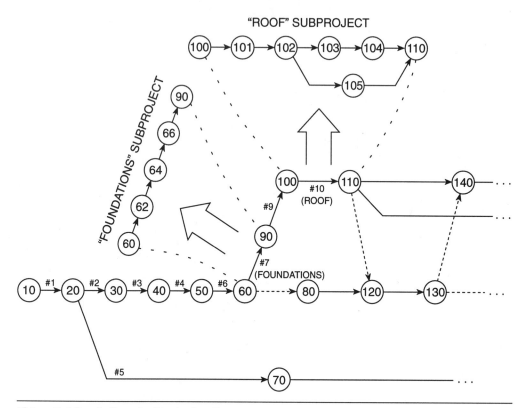

Figure E–10   Options for Numbering Events.

40, etc., or even 100, 200, etc. Using these large numbers allows interjection of intermediate tasks without any renumbering of the existing set and still satisfies the numbering rule. Figure E–10 shows how these added tasks could be included without renumbering any events of the network.

GLOSSARY

ACTIVITY: an action that consumes resources and requires time to accomplish its objective.

AUTHORITY: "The right to command and to enforce obedience; the right to act, decide, etc." Authority should be assigned simultaneously along with responsibility, because responsibility is useless without an appropriate amount of authority. For example, you may be given the responsibility for arranging a party for 500 people, but if you do not have the authority to place orders and write checks to pay the bills, it will not be much of a party.

AVERAGES: The **Simple Average** of a set of numbers is their sum divided by the number of items in the set. The **Weighted Average** (as in PERT time calculations) requires knowing an "importance" factor for each item in the set of numbers: in PERT the middle number of the three durations (a, b, and c) is considered to be four times as important as the other two in calculating their weighted average value: Weighted Average = (1/6) of [1 × "a" + 4 × "b" + 1 × "c"]. The divisor of **6** is the sum of (1 + 4 + 1). Other weighted averages could be calculated in the same way for other applications, when the relative importance of each member of the set to be averaged is known.

FORWARD AND BACKWARD *TIME CALCULATIONS*: The FORWARD calculation for the Earliest Start Times of every task begins at the START milestone (usually set at Time Zero or a specific calendar date) and calculates the times through the network to the END milestone. The BACKWARD calculation begins at the END milestone (usually using its Early Time or a selected calendar date), and works in the reverse direction through the network, thereby determining the Latest Start Time of every task.

CALENDAR DAYS: See "DAYS"

CONSTRAINTS: "The use of force; coercion. Confinement or restriction." In the context of scheduling, a constraint places a restriction on our freedom to schedule a particular task or group of tasks. "BAD" weather constrains our activities; "The Senator will be formally opening the building on June 16" are restrictions on our direct construction activities.

CONTINGENCIES: Unfavorable things are expected to occur during a project; some can be named and others cannot, but experience tells you to make an allowance for them. These allowances are called contingencies, that is, the need for them is contingent on the "thing" happening. The form of the allowance can be money, a resource and, in this context, time.

CONTRACTOR: A person (or company) who signs a contract to perform certain duties for an owner or another contractor with the intention of achieving well-defined objectives.

CRASHING: A technique for speeding up the work to reduce the duration of a project by increasing the flow of resources to certain tasks on the critical path.

CRITICAL PATH: The Critical Path is marked by the sequence of tasks through the network having zero total float. There will be at least one continuous path from the START milestone to the END milestone based on the times from the simple Forward and Backward calculations.

(STANDARD) *CREW*:   The typically "best" crew for the job at hand. It is not necessarily the fastest crew but it is the crew producing the most output per worker.

DAY "ZERO":   Projects are assumed to begin at the end of the (imaginary) shift preceding the first shift of the project. That is, the first day of work is taken to begin at 5:00 P.M. of the previous day, the instant when that "day" ends. There is no break in the flow of time; the work-days are assumed to be tied together end-to-end: 5:00 P.M. on Tuesday is identical to 8:00 A.M. on Wednesday, when the shift ends and the next one begins, because there is no overnight construction activity.

"DAYS" (PROJECT DAYS AND CALENDAR DAYS):   Project Days are the number of working days since the beginning of a project whereas Calendar Days are the number of days counted on a calendar, including holidays, weekends, and so forth. Calendar Days determine interest owed whereas Project Days are a measure of time spent working on the project.

TO DECIDE: Literally, the word means "to cut away." Hence, when you decide something, you select one option from among a group of alternate choices, according to some stated or accepted criteria. In effect, you are removing options (and reducing complexity) when you make a DECISION.

DURATION and TIME: Duration is the elapsed working time between the start and completion of a task. Time is an instant in the passage of time, marked by some event. For example: "The excavator began at 0800 hrs on August 13 ("time") and completed the job at 1600 hrs on August 16 ("time")—the duration was 4 working days.

NOMINAL DURATION: The time required for the STANDARD CREW to complete a well-defined work assignment.

MINIMUM DURATION: The absolute shortest time for a crew to complete a work assignment under **full crash** conditions.

AN "EVENT":   can be considered to be the opposite of a task. An event has no action, no duration, and no consumption of resources. It is a POINT IN TIME and signals only that an objective has been reached. A *MILESTONE* is a special event, such as START OF PROJECT or PHASE ONE COMPLETE.

EXPEDITE: To take action expressly to speed up a process, especially the acquisition of the resources necessary for a construction task. It is a major activity to ensure that suppliers are making progress toward the manufacture and delivery of materials that may not be needed for weeks or months.

EXPEDITERS: Persons assigned the responsibility of carrying out the continuing chores of expediting.

FAX: Facsimile of a page transmitted (electronically) over telephone "lines."

FLOAT: FREE FLOAT is the amount of time a task (i) can be delayed without affecting the Start Time of any task (j) following it, $(EST_j - EST_i)$.
   TOTAL FLOAT of a task is simply the difference between its Earliest and Latest Start Times $(LST_i - EST_i)$.

FREQUENCY DISTRIBUTION: A graph used in statistics to show the number of times a certain value has occurred: for example, in a class of 240 students, 25 were aged 20, 120 were 21, 60 were 22, and 35 were 23. The numbers 25, 120, 60, and 35 would be plotted against their respective age values to produce a Frequency Distribution of Student Ages.

GANTT CHART: Another name for a BAR Chart, where each bar represents a single task. The LENGTH of each bar represents the duration of the task. The ends of a bar mark the START and END events of the task. Generally, successive bars are shown below a preceding bar. Henry L. Gantt was an early innovator in the United States in the practice of Scheduling.

GOAL: "Something (stated in *general* terms) toward which effort is directed that describes a desired end." An example is, "(My Goal is) . . . TO BUILD A GARAGE ON MY LOT. . . ." The GOAL statement is another way of assigning a name to a PROJECT. OBJECTIVES are more specific in nature and "flesh-out" the Goal Statement. An objective usually includes a target date.

HISTOGRAM: A graph showing how the value of something changes with time. In scheduling, a common histogram shows the number of workers on the site from day-to-day over the duration of the project: this would be called a "Manpower Loading Histogram."

LOOP: A loop is an error in the logic of precedence statements and is not possible for real systems; an example is "A follows B, B follows C, and C must also follow A."

MARSHALLING: The action of arranging all the resources so they are ready to be deployed to a task. Placing an order at the union hall for 13 carpenters to be on the job on Monday (and ensuring they will be there) is one act of marshalling a resource.

MILESTONE: A special event, such as START OF PROJECT or PHASE ONE COMPLETE.

MONITORING: "To advise, caution or WARN." It is necessary to watch progress of actual work accomplishment and compare it to what was planned; any deviation from the plan must be observed, noted, and evaluated as to its effect on achieving the GOAL of the project. If the effect is negative, then corrective action must be applied by the manager. Monitoring employs observation, measurement, comparison, and communication skills.

NETWORK: Any graphical array of points interconnected by lines is a network. When the points are symbols for tasks, such a network becomes an Activity-on-Node Network (AON); when the points are events and the links are task arrows, the network is called an Activity-on-Arrow Network (AOA).

NUMERICAL PRECISION: The preciseness of a number is known by the number of digits used to quote the number: 6.6 means the actual number lies between 6.55 and 6.65 but we are not sure where in that range. 6.62 indicates that the actual number lies between 6.615 and 6.625. We must be confident in the last digit quoted.

AN OBJECTIVE: A specific target that is one component on the way to achieving a GOAL. Many dictionaries treat Goals and Objectives as being the same, but for our purposes it is important to differentiate between them. An Objective must be measurable (so that I will know, without any doubt, that I have reached it). Often, a time limit or date forms part of an OBJECTIVE. For example, "The roof must be in place before September 15."

PERT: Program Evaluation and Review Technique is an Activity-On-Arrow system applied extensively by the U.S. Government in the early 1960s. It was applied to computer-monitoring/reporting of progress on very large multi-project contracts.

PRECEDENCE: In the context of scheduling, precedence means "coming immediately before in time." Furthermore, it demands that a task must be completed before the subsequent one can start.

PRECEDENCE GRID: A square array of X-marks on squared paper that indicates which tasks must follow other tasks of a project. Symbols for the "follower" tasks (naming the columns) appear across the top of the sheet and an identical column appears down the left side (naming the rows). If task K must follow task G, then an "X" is placed in the cell in row "G" at column "K."

PROBABILITY: Probability is a measure of the chances of something happening, usually quoted as a percent (%). It is based on a person's experience, recorded data, or enlightened guessing. For example, there is a 47% chance of rain on October 31, based on weather records for our city over the last 72 years; or there is a chance of one in fourteen million of winning the lottery this week, when expressed as a fraction (1 in 14 million = 1 ÷ 14,000,000 = 0.0000071%).

PROCURE/PROCUREMENT: According to the dictionary, procure means "to obtain by some effort or means; to acquire." A good synonym is "to get." Resorting to jargon once again, industry has introduced the word "procurement" instead of using the dictionary word "procurance," which is the "process of procuring." Procurement in industry has a broader meaning, covering the whole activity of getting resources (expertise, materials, equipment, etc.): ordering, checking progress and quality, and ensuring the status for delivery (at the right time and place).

PRODUCTIVITY: The unit rate of producing work. If a five-man crew can lay 7500 blocks in 5 days, then its productivity is 1500 blocks *per day* and the productivity *per man* is therefore 300 per day or 40 per hour. The "-ivity" indicates "unit rate."

PROJECT DAYS: See "DAYS."

QUANTITY TAKE-OFF: A term used in estimating the ultimate cost of a construction project. An Engineering Economist or a Quantity Surveyor determines the quantity of each material required for each part of the project.

RESOURCE: Anything that is needed to carry out the work of a task. Most resources can be grouped into materials, equipment, expertise, money and, occasionally, time is thought to be a resource; it is not considered to be one in this context.

RESPONSIBILITY: "Answering legally or morally for the discharge of a duty, trust or debt." In an organization, individuals are assigned responsibility to carry out specific kinds of tasks. Senior personnel assign specific responsibilities to more junior personnel in the hierarchy. For example, a foreman *tells* a carpenter she is responsible for building a wall.

RISK: The chance of encountering harm or LOSS. In business, loss is usually measured in terms of an amount of money; but loss of time, or any of the other resources, could result in an inability to reach an objective or even the GOAL of the project. Different levels of risk must be evaluated and compared in order to select the one having the least chance of causing damage. Thus RELATIVE RISK affects decision making.

SCHEDULE: As a noun: "A written or printed statement specifying the details of some matter." "A detailed and timed plan." Or, used as a verb: "To appoint or plan for a specified time or date." In the framework of this course of study, we will look at "Scheduling" as placing certain tasks into specific time periods to satisfy the pressures required to execute a contract or plan. The performance of these tasks will have to fit together under the pressure of CONSTRAINTS, whether they be forced on us from external sources or whether they have been self-induced.

SLACK TIME (of an EVENT): The difference between the Early and Late Times for an event defines the SLACK TIME for that event. The floats of the task bounded by two events can be found from the slack times of the events and the duration of the task.

SLIPPAGE: The growing disparity between actual and scheduled progress in meeting deadlines (i.e., reaching critical objectives), usually from unclear causes. In contrast, unresolved crises can cause abrupt dislocations in progress, with major effects on the schedule.

SOFTWARE: Computer jargon for a computer program or family of programs. There is DOS software (more than 60 small programs under the name "DOS") and "Super Project Extra," a family of smaller, specific programs for scheduling. There are also general groupings of types of software for faxing, communication, word processing, games, and so forth.

SPREADSHEET: A table is used for repetitive manual calculations but a table becomes a Spreadsheet for computerized tabular calculations. The term is borrowed from accounting.

STANDARD DEVIATION (SD): This is a special type of average used to measure the average "spread" of a frequency distribution. See Chapter 11 for details.

STRATEGY: "A plan or technique for achieving some end." There must be a plan that describes *how* you are going to reach a specific objective; in fact there should be several (alternative) plans for reaching an objective. This is where a creative imagination and/or experience play a real part. The report covering these strategies for a project are often called Strategic Plans.

TASK: An activity that is directed at achieving an objective.

TASK SPLITTING: A technique for reducing the duration of a project by splitting a task into several shorter segments to allow a following task to start earlier.

"TICKLER SHEET": A table of target dates for procuring every resource needed for a project, including the latest date to place the order, several intermediate target dates and, finally, the latest delivery date that will not delay the work.

TIME: See Duration and Time.

EARLY TIME: (of an Event [in PERT]) The latest finishing time of all the *tasks* terminating at this event. (Determined during the Forward-Pass calculation.)

LATE TIME: (of an Event [in PERT]) The earliest starting time of all *tasks* starting at the event. (Determined during the Backward-Pass calculation.)

WEATHER WINDOW: A weather window is a specific period of time set aside in a schedule, during which a weather-sensitive task can occur. Its duration allows for the expected bad weather and the task.

Note: The reader is advised to extend this list as new terms are encountered.

LIST OF ABBREVIATIONS

AOA	Activity-On-Arrow (Network Diagram)
AON	Activity-On-Node (Network Diagram)
avg	average
CP	Critical Path
D	Delay
dur	duration
EFT	Earliest Finish Time (for a task)
EST	Earliest Start Time (for a task)
ET	Earliest Time (for an event)
FF	Free Float
hrs	hours
L.A.	Los Angeles
LFT	Latest Finish Time (for a task)
LST	Latest Start Time (for a task)
LT	Latest Time (for an event)
MIS	Management Information System
p	probability
PERT	Program Evaluation and Review Technique
P-G	Precedence Grid
RMS	Root-Mean-Square
SD	Standard Deviation
SF	San Francisco

TF	Total Float
WBS	Work Breakdown Structure
W-W	Weather Window
YY/MM/DD	Year/Month/Day (using 2 digits each)
+/−	Plus or Minus

INDEX